Carolina Hunting Adventures
Quest For The Limit

by Michael S. Marsh

©Copyright 1995 by
Atlantic Publishing Company
Michael S. Marsh

First Printing 1995

Published by:
Atlantic Publishing Company

Library of Congress Card Number 95-67272

ISBN Number 0-937866-50-4

Printed in the United States of America
by
Atlantic Publishing Company
Tabor City, North Carolina 28463

Cover design by Michael S. Marsh and Victor Forrester

Acknowledgements

The author wishes to express his warmest appreciation to the following persons who helped in so many ways in producing this book—so far, his greatest adventure. The trophy at the end of the quest belongs to them. He only scribbled the words.

Carol Elaine Jobe Marsh, my wife, for unselfishly giving uncountable hours of her time, organizing, editing, typing, and re-typing, and for missing me the times I was out hunting when she couldn't go.

Justin Gregory Marsh, my son, for his patience and understanding on the days I couldn't take him hunting.

Peter and Cathy Meyer, my friends and favorite editors, for setting me an extra plate at dinner.

Bruce Troutman and Emma Crummie for encouraging me through the rough spots.

Gordon Sloan, Wayne Grimes, Miles, Jr. and Deannie Forbes, Eddie and Judy Evans, Ron Haynes, Sholar Powell, and Paul Sasser, for grinning at the camera or snapping the shutter.

All the other hunters who shared their dog chases, blinds, stands, trails, and adventures. I learned something from every one of them.

Fred Bonner, for helping me fulfill my quest in the pages and photographs of *CAROLINA ADVENTURE* magazine.

Curtis Leroy Marsh, Jr., my dad, and Janice Mae Hammer Cardwell, my mom, for giving me a gun and teaching me to shoot, giving me a bird dog and teaching me to love.

Dedication

King Of The Bay

To the members of the Red Door Hunting Club, for teaching me about dogs and deer and trails in the bay.

Li'l Jake

To Ron Haynes, for showing me the view from the top of Suzy's Knob. Also, for Old Tom and New Tom.

A Thousand Sunrises

To Paul Sasser, for the best argument about setting decoys the wrong way in front of a blind.

January Snow

To Miles E. Forbes, Jr., for breaking ice along the trail to blind number 9.

Quest For The Limit

To Joyce, Elizabeth, and Carol.

Disclaimer

The characters in this book are fictional except Duckbuster and Red Rock. Details of their adventures have been fictionalized to protect the privacy of others and to provide continuity. Any similarity of other characters to real people is purely coincidental.

The adventures are fictional, although they are based on factual histories, traditions, game laws, and natural or man-made occurrences as told by the Hunters of Carolina who graciously enriched the author's knowledge by their stories.

Locations of the hunts, accounts of wildlife habits and habitats, and descriptions of hunting techniques are described as accurately as possible based on the author's experience.

About the Author

Mike Marsh was ten years old when his father was transferred from New Jersey by Western Electric Company to work in Winston-Salem, North Carolina.

A country estate south of Greensboro was for sale. The Marsh family was captivated by the "Old J. P. Morgan Place." What formerly was the caretaker's home of a quail hunting lodge built by the wealthy financier seeking sanctuary from the rigors of New York, became the fantasy safari camp of a boy with a BB gun.

At fourteen, Mike was given a half-broke bird dog for his birthday. For Christmas, he received a 20 gauge Remington Model 11 shotgun, inherited from his Great Uncle Dave. Also under the tree was a copy of Robert Ruark's *The Old Man and The Boy*.

The teenager was strongly influenced by Mr. Ruark's writing and was taught Carolina Country ways from farmers in the surrounding community of Climax, who winked and grinned and took pity on the displaced "Little Yankee Kid." They kindled his hunter's fire with tales of Mr. Morgan's adventures and hunts that used to be. Mike worked for them and with them on their farms. In return for his labor, permission was given to hunt the same acreage that a millionaire's dollars once leased.

After graduating from Southeast Guilford High School, Mike earned a degree in Fish and Wildlife Management. A passion for the hunt and knowledge gained by spending his boyhood in the woods and fields helped him graduate as the top student at Wayne Community College in 1973.

A career with the North Carolina Division of Environmental Management allowed him to live near Charlotte on Lake Norman for five years. Migrating to Wilmington to scratch an itch for waterfowling instilled by hunting mallards and bluebills on the lake, the now fully-fledged "Hunter of Carolina" eventually joined a civil engineering and environmental consulting business. He now lives near Masonboro Sound with his family.

Mike's hunting and fishing articles have appeared in several outdoor publications. He is the Southeast Regional Editor of *CAROLINA ADVENTURE* magazine.

Introduction

A non-hunter asks, "Why do you hunt?" The hunter's answer is usually a fumbling attempt to explain an emotional obsession, passed through the genes of uncountable generations to ignite the fire of the chase in the soul of civilized man.

The nearly unexplainable bond between hunter and game is the same feeling that drives the participant in any sport. The desire to possess the trophy in a golf match, for example, was instilled into the one who chases the little white ball by a distant hairy ancestor who needed to possess the trophy of a kill in order to provide food, bone tools, and hide clothing for survival. The success of televised sports serves solid evidence, proving the ancient hunter's instincts thrive in modern man.

Any sportsman worthy of the definition knows the size of the trophy is not measured by golden cup, antler spread, or a limit of game birds in the bag. The size of the trophy is in the chase itself. It is the act of pursuing that gives satisfaction and joy, for the intensity required to be successful in the quest cannot be burdened by the false external pretenses forced onto a hunter to enable him to survive in today's society. In his quest for the limit, the hunter must ultimately find and reveal his real character, his true being.

These hunters' adventures are set in Carolina Country to give the hunters a sense of place. But their quests occur wherever a group of red hats gathers on the porch of a cabin, a lone figure strikes out on a game trail in the glorious solitude of desolate wilderness, anywhere on the planet human beings search for their souls in wild places among wild things.

This book was written for the hunters—for fathers to read and give to their sons, for sons to read and give to their fathers, for fathers and sons to read and give to apprehensive wives and mothers so they will understand and, hopefully, pick up a shotgun and join their quest when they leave the comforts of home in the chilled pre-dawn.

This book was written for the non-hunters—for those who can't or won't hunt, for those who would like to hunt but don't know where to begin. The attitudes and practical field information contained in these pages should be learned by everyone in possession of a hunting license, or anyone who would like to understand those who do.

The next time a non-hunter asks, "Why do you hunt?" hand him this book. Open it to page one, chapter one. Whether he considers himself to be a history or folklore buff, a conservationist, environmentalist, preservationist, or just plain likes a good read, there is something within that will hold his attention and speak to him. All of us are on a quest. We all are hunters trying to fill our limit, deep inside.

Table Of Contents

Gordon Sloan, Justin Marsh, and Old Eli.

Chapter 1

King Of The Bay

October 16, 1989 was just another day for most folks. Oh, they had their appointments to meet and minor celebrations of birthdays, anniversaries, and such.

But to little Davey Johnson this was to be the most important day of his life. For as many years as can be remembered, the third Monday in October has been designated as the opening day of deer season in eastern North Carolina.

In rural Pender County, all boys above the age of nine mark this day on their calendars and look forward to it with as much excitement as to a birthday or Christmas and wonder if their mothers will allow their fathers to sneak them away from the house to participate in the age-old ritual of the deer hunt.

Davey's grandfather, "Old Dave" Johnson, had come for dinner the day before. As usual, the meal had been outstanding. Darlene Johnson was the best cook in all of Carolina and prepared Sunday dinner as the ultimate creation, with a main course of fried chicken piled high on a blue-flowered china platter in the center of the table. The platter was surrounded by steaming bowls of boiled new potatoes, garden grown and home-canned pole beans, corn-on-the-cob and a pot full of collards with streak-o-lean meat added for flavor. A basket containing hot buttermilk biscuits sat off to one side covered by a red and white checkered cloth. Thick, peppery gravy made from the morning's sausage drippings begged to be daubed onto the biscuits and potatoes with an old wooden spoon.

By the time he was done with his dinner, little Davey had trouble finding room in his belly to stow a slice of freshly baked pie. Still, somehow, he managed. Fresh pecan pie was his favorite dessert.

It was the pecan pie that started the debate between his grandfather and his mother. His mother was putting the dirty dishes in the sink with her back to the table where Davey and Old Dave sat, finishing the last few crumbs from their plates.

"The pecans have all fallen and the leaves are comin' off the trees," Old Dave announced. "The woods'll be nice and open for a clear shot at a deer tomorrow."

Davey could see his mother's back stiffen and her hackles begin to rise at the mention of deer hunting.

His grandfather pressed on, "It's time for the boy to join the hunt, Darlene."

Old Dave turned to Davey and said, "Boy! Go fetch me a chew from the truck. It's in a box behind the seat."

Davey was trembling so badly he could scarcely carry his plate to the sink without dropping it. He picked up the fork from his plate as he walked across the kitchen to keep it from rattling from the shaking of his hands.

Nothing else was said until Davey was outside the front door, but he could hear the murmuring of voices as the discussion grew in intensity. He pulled a brand-new pack of leaf chewing tobacco from behind the seat of the truck as instructed and moved back onto the porch. He hesitated before going back inside, not wanting to disrupt the important maneuvers and negotiations taking place in the kitchen.

Turning the knob, he cracked the front door open. He knew that it was wrong to listen, uninvited, to a conversation between grownups. But, after all, his welfare was the topic of discussion. If he happened to accidentally hear a little of what was being said, he figured it would be all right, just this one time.

"He's only ten years old!" his mother argued. "That's way too young to be chasin' around the woods with dogs and guns and grown men."

"Darlene," Davey heard his grandfather say in a firm, even tone, "he will be with me the whole time and I'll see to it that he's safe and sound. You know in your heart that it's about time he learned some responsibility. He needs to learn how to take care of this place and gain some confidence in himself so's he can walk upright in the world. I can't think of a better way to teach him those things than by takin' him huntin' with me."

Davey peered through the crack with one eye. Old Dave's arguments didn't seem to cut no mustard with his mother. It didn't look like she was going to listen to any more of his foolishness.

The strong, sweet, hemp-rope scent of tobacco brought him to his senses. He now realized that Old Dave needed a chew for enhancing his argumentative abilities. Davey had often witnessed his grandfather tucking a wad of tobacco in his cheek while trading at the farmer's market. The resolute act of taking a chew drew out a strategic pause after he had made some particularly shrewd proposal. He always sent a healthy yellowish brown stream of tobacco juice with unerring aim at some spot on the ground for emphasis or when he thought someone was getting the better of him. Davey straightened his shoulders, and opened the door.

3

Making his way through the house, he reentered the kitchen. After handing the tobacco pouch to his grandfather Davey stood at his side, leaning his elbows on the back of a chair. He stared imploringly at his mom and she at him.

She stood in silence. The wooden spoon in her hand drooled a large blob of gravy that smacked loudly onto the floor. Her eyes were dark and her eyebrows sternly wrinkled into an expression of intolerance. For a long minute, she glared her disapproval. Then, gradually, her face began to soften as she remembered her husband, Dave, Jr. and how he had loved the hunt.

Hunting had not been just an autumn and winter pastime to him, but a year-round way of life. During spring planting, he constantly surveyed deer tracks in the freshly tilled soybean and corn fields to see how "his" deer had fared during the winter's scarcity of food. He was always the first to spot the flash of a tail or the flicker of an ear that gave away the presence of a buck timidly lurking in the shadows along the side of the dirt lane leading to the family's home. He tended his hounds in a loving and caring manner, speaking to them in quiet tones generally reserved for newborn babies when he thought no one was around to hear. Taking their large, floppy, soft ears into his hands, he stroked them with his thumbs as he pressed his forehead to theirs and looked into their dark, smiling eyes.

At times, Dave, Jr. had been wound a little too tightly from the strain of tending the family farm and working part time as a logger, cutting pine pulpwood to make ends meet. On those dark days he developed a tendency toward shortness of words with his family. Darlene always knew what was coming when he announced, "Time to go deer huntin'!", and loaded his dogs into the truck to disappear for a few days. When he returned, he was a completely changed man — happy, smiling, joking — his life force rejuvenated just by being out in his woods and fields and bays again, listening to the music of his trailing dogs. As a bonus, he always brought home a fresh venison roast for Sunday dinner.

Yes, deer hunting and hound dogs had been as much a part of Dave, Jr.'s being as his smile, his hair, his hat, his truck, and his wife. She was one-half of him he had always said, and she never loved him so much as at the moment of his return from a hunt, smelling of rich oak leaves and spicy bay twigs, musty dogs and deer hide, gun powder and gun oil.

As he swept her into him with his strong right arm, pressing his wind-cold, whiskery cheek to hers, he would reach out his left arm to gather up what he called his other half, little Davey, crush him to his body and say, "I love you both, more than anything in this whole world."

Those happy times had been brought abruptly to an end. A rain slick road sent a truck out of control on a dark, cold night, taking Dave, Jr. from them. "Hunting over the next hill," the preacher had said during the eulogy at the cemetery behind the old Williams Chapel.

After that mournful night, Darlene's thoughts of hunting had been of the precious moments her husband had not been with her, the days that had been wasted when he was hunting, rather that being at her side for every possible second on his short life's ticking clock.

She could not bear the thought of her son, the last significant portion left to her of her lost husband, not being near her every possible minute of every possible day or, she feared, he too, would not return home, forever.

"No." she said, stomping her foot. "Davey's way too young and doesn't even have a gun. Besides, he has to go to school!"

"Darlene," Old Dave ceremoniously began, stuffing an exceptionally large chew into the side of his mouth, "the boy is ten years old. That's plenty old enough." He paused to situate the cud in his mouth, plucking a course stem from between his teeth.

"As a matter of fact, that is precisely the proper age for a boy to begin." Kicking the back door open, Old Dave spat through it for emphasis. "I've got a gun for Davey to use, if that's your main concern. As for schoolin', there won't be none tomorrow.

You seem to have forgotten that opening day in Pender County is always scheduled to be a teacher's work day, although "work" may not be exactly the proper choice of words. The school system has gotta shut down. Half the kids'll be gone off deer huntin' with their families and, I suspect, so will a good share of the teachers, principals, and bus drivers."

Darlene sensed defeat. She had held her own, arguing with her father-in-law, one on one. But with both young Davey and Old Dave staring at her, the boy with pleading, begging, puppy-dog eyes, the old man with a look of conviction that showed he would not back down, her will began to melt. Blinking hard, she looked down at the lump of gravy splattered on the floor at her feet.

"A-a-a-all right," she stammered, "the boy can go — if he really wants to. I do suppose it would be kinda nice to have a fresh venison roast for next Sunday's dinner."

Davey could hardly contain himself. He leaped across the kitchen and hugged his mom. As she smothered him into her with her arms, she held him close so he could not see the tear in her eye.

Old Dave saw, understood, and turned away to release a final stream of tobacco juice out the screened door. "I'll pick him up about dark tonight," he said grinning. Striding down the steps and around the house, he got into his truck and slammed the door. Cranking the engine to life he drove out of sight down the dirt lane.

Davey had all his things packed an hour early, so he walked out to the empty dog pens behind the house in the edge of the woods to kill some time. The webbed wire fences would have been overgrown in weeds and honeysuckle vines by now, and the dog houses rotted away had they not been cared for by a pair of small boy's hands after the large hands of Dave, Jr. had gone. Dogs and guns were two things not present in the Johnson household since the loss of Dave, Jr. Young Davey realized that these things reminded his mother of his absent father and understood why she had not allowed him to own a gun.

As he plucked at a pokeberry stalk that had woven its way through the dog pen wire, Davey could remember his father cleaning his gun while sitting in a broken-springed easy chair with stuffing coming out of the right arm. Davey had sat on a cracked and creaking wooden stool at his father's feet. Listening intently, he clung to every word his larger-than-life father had spoken to him.

"Son, this here gun is just a tool, like a rake or a saw or a hammer. It only works as well as you do. If you keep it clean, aim it true, and treat it with respect at all times, it will keep meat on your table and help keep your deer herd healthy. If you do your part right, one shot is all you should ever need. Never stretch your gun's range to make a shot that's too far for a clean hit, and always know what is beyond your intended target for safety's sake."

Dave, Jr. hadn't really believed that little Davey could comprehend all these things at the young age of seven, but he felt discussions of this type should take place at a regular pace during the boy's development so the lessons would be forever ingrained into his young mind. Through repetition, the thoughts and, therefore, the actions, would become an integral part of his son when he became a grown man.

Davey never knew what had happened to his father's gun. He scarcely remembered what it looked like and certainly knew nothing of the model, make, or action type. He suspected, though, it was a shotgun because he had found a few empty 12 gauge shotgun shells around the farm from time to time, and reasonably assumed that they had been fired from his father's gun.

His memories of Dave, Jr. were interrupted when the headlight beams of Old Dave's truck played across the yard, silhouetting him against the wire mesh of the dog pens.

This was it! Grandpa had arrived to take him hunting! He felt a twinge of regret that tempered his jittery excitement as he realized how much he missed his father. But the twinge was soon replaced by eager anticipation as he tossed his sleeping bag, a change of clothes and his father's hunting coat into the truck cab and climbed in behind.

His mother waved goodbye from the kitchen window as the truck spun around and headed down the lane. She watched the truck until it turned along the path behind the field. Soon its taillights flickered, then vanished altogether, swallowed up by a plantation of loblolly pines.

The Red Door Hunting Club.

As the truck bounced along the rutted path that lead to the hunting cabin, Davey contemplated the past history of the place. Old Dave claimed to have been born in that cabin and there was no reason to doubt him. The sway-backed, rusty tin roof provided a mute testimonial as to the age of the building. Its clapboard siding was the gray of antiquity. Paint had never touched its weathered wood. Knots in the siding were "fat-lightered," drooling sticky rosin down the cabin sides in the high humidity. A few window panes had been broken out and replaced with jagged pieces of cardboard torn from whatever grocery or cereal box that had happened to be handy at the time they were shattered.

Davey had been smelling the exhilarating aroma of oak burning in the charcoal-blackened, pot-bellied stove since long before the cabin had come into view. As the truck stopped in front of the rickety porch steps he could see that the wooden front door was ajar. Only the screen door was closed to keep out moths that were attracted to the light inside. The heat of the fire inside the stove was matched only by the warmth of the hearty laughter coming from the men within. Davey knew some of them by the sound of their laughter — cousins, uncles, and in-laws of the family. There were a few unfamiliar voices in the crowd, but all were sharing the camaraderie and friendship typical in all deer camps across Pender County the evening before opening day.

As Davey stepped through the cabin door, he felt extremely shy and self conscious. This was a place in which only grown men were allowed. He wasn't sure if he would be welcomed.

He quickly discovered that his fears were unfounded as several men came forward to greet Old Dave with much back slapping, hand shaking, and friendly words of welcome. There were a few minor references to Davey's small stature, as was certainly to be expected to some degree. But it soon became apparent that their joking was all good-natured and that other things of greater importance than the presence of a new, small hunter in their camp required the older hunter's attention. The hammering of a ladle against a double-handled kettle's lid clanged, "supper's ready!"

The hunters served up large portions of their traditional first night's meal of four-alarm chili, a redhot concoction of last-year's ground venison rescued from someone's freezer stewed together with tomatoes, beans, and blazing peppers. Davey scarcely touched it.

"Too hot for me," he said, but he suspected that most of the veterans knew he could hardly eat because he was so excited about being allowed to participate in the hunt the following morning.

Conversation around the table drifted over a few insignificant topics until it congealed and centered on deer and deer hunting. Above and behind the pot bellied stove hung a bedraggled deer mount. Although the original taxidermy work must have been superb, age and neglect had erased its life-like appearance. Formerly sparkling eyes were clouded over with cataracts of grease that had been layered onto them during the preparation of untold numbers of pre-dawn breakfasts of pork sausage, grits, and eggs. The sheen had departed from the long guard hairs covering the neck and shoulders due to acute dehydration from the heat of many decades of bone-warming fires set ablaze in the iron stove to fend off the night's damp chills. Cobwebs hung from broken eyelashes and dusty ears, waving lazily in the thermals rising from the warm stove top. But one look at those magnificent antlers could set any hunter's heart thumping — especially one who was only ten years old! They were wide and high with thick, heavy bases. Eleven long points graced the huge rack. Neither their bleached bone pallor nor the small nibblings made by some irreverent rodent on one of the brow tines could detract from the rack's grandeur.

Davey stared at the age-worn trophy, mesmerized to speechlessness. A man he did not know, apparently from one of the nearby towns, perhaps Wilmington or Wallace, broke the spell when he followed Davey's stare to its source.

"Makes your mouth water, don't it kid?" he asked. "Think you could shoot something that looked like that?"

Davey was embarrassed by the sudden attention and the feeling that all eyes were upon him. One of his neighbors, Mr. Gordon, mercifully came to his rescue.

"Word has it that that there buck was killed by a young hunter a lot of years ago." he said. "Maybe what we need is some fresh, new blood and a hefty portion of beginner's luck to replace that ragged old deer mount ahangin' there."

Davey felt some of the blush ebb from his cheeks. He bumped his chair closer to his grandfather's side for reassurance.

"Old Dave," Mr Gordon respectfully addressed the elder Johnson, "we sure do need us a new camp trophy to retire that worn out thing on the wall, yonder. You know the woods and bays surrounding this camp better than anyone in this bunch. As a matter of fact, I believe you own over half of the land we hunt. So, tell me, how come you don't know where old Eli lays?"

At the mention of old Eli, all peripheral conversation ceased. Anyone who has ever been in a deer camp knows that there is a phantom buck on every tract of deer hunting land. A huge, trophy deer, grown old through wariness and cunning, he is seen only during the off-season or in front of some slack-jawed hunter's headlights on a dark, moonless night. Suddenly materializing from the darkness, then melting away, he leaves the dumbfounded viewer slowly shaking his head from side to side at the massive size of those magnificent antlers illuminated to an eerie, phosphorescent white in the feeble glow of headlight beams and wondering if he has seen a ghost or apparition instead of a flesh-and-blood creature.

Davey looked up at his grandfather to gauge his reaction to Mr. Gordon's question. Old Dave cleared his throat, spat tobacco juice into the fruit can spittoon he held in his hand, and was about to speak when Mr. Gordon's son, Tommy Joe interrupted.

"I think I saw Eli standing in the edge of a bean field last Thursday evenin'. His antlers didn't look quite as big as Old Dave described them the day he missed a shot at him last year. Then again, that slippery ol' buck didn't wait around long enough for me to get a real good look. As soon as he saw me, he whirled around and crashed away through the edge of a bay with them antlers held high like he was ashowin' 'em off. Why, he seemed big as a mule, the way he crunched through them thick bushes with that white flag stuck up two feet in the air abouncin' and awavin'!"

Uncontrolled jabbering filled the cabin. The excited hunters rapid-fired questions at Tommy Joe, never giving him a chance to complete an answer.

11

"Where did you see him?"

"Well, he was beside the dirt road leadin' to . . ."

"How many points did he have?"

"I couldn't tell for certain, maybe eight or maybe . . ."

"What about his tracks? How big were they?"

"I found his tracks where he took off, aleapin' through the beans. They must a been fifteen feet apart! His hoofprints were big as . . ."

Tommy Joe had spread his thumb and trigger finger apart wider than the length of a three-inch magnum load of double-ought buckshot to show the length of the buck's hoofprints. Just then, Old Dave clanked the fruit can spittoon hard to the table, interrupting Tommy Joe and silencing the other hunters' disorganized questioning. Tilting back his chair, Old Dave spoke for all.

"Now, Tommy Joe, tell me exactly which field you saw Eli feedin' in and exactly which corner of the bay he ducked into for cover. Maybe I can figure out where he is layin' up to hide."

"Well, he was standin' in the bean field back of the tobaccer beds and he ran into that finger of brush that leads off into the Big Bay."

"That's Eli's cover all right. How wide did you say his antlers were? Tell me. Honestly!"

"When he turned straight away, I could see about four inches of antler stickin' out each side of his rear end."

"That must have been Eli! It seems to me you may be right about his being grown past his prime 'cause the set of antlers he carried last year was a smidgen wider. Last year, his antlers spread at least six inches beyond his hips when he was runnin' through the bay with his head held low."

The group's disorganized questioning began again, this time directed at Old Dave. He was begged by all to tell the story of missing an easy shot at the dream buck the prior season. Old Dave leaned forward in his chair and paused. Refreshing his chew, he waited for the rumble of voices to quiet before he repeated the tale heard so many times before.

"Jimmy, if I remember right, your dogs were arunnin' him. They were so hot on his heels that his scent must a been burnin' their noses!"

Jimmy nodded, smiling proudly at the compliment Old Dave bestowed on his pack of brown and white Walker hounds.

"Bobby and Sammy, I could hear your voices cracklin' over the radio. I'd have thought he could have heard you boys ahollerin' at me, you were so excited after you seen him turn and run through the Big Bay, acomin' my way. But the sound of his antlers clatterin' against the bushes and the cracklin' of those big feet through the bay leaves must've been even louder! Then, all of a sudden, there he was! He flashed out of the bay and skidded to a stop! I couldn't move or he would have disappeared in an instant. All I could do was stand there 'til he made his move, staring at that rack of his, that crown of antlers that stretched way up over his ears, givin' notice to me that he was king of the bay. He gave me one good look – a real good look! Then he heard Tommy Joe drive up the road and slam his door. That sneaky ol' buck fell right down on his belly and slipped into the bay so fast that all I could see was sunlight gleamin' off his antler tips. I finally got off a shot. But I missed him clean!"

"It looked a lot like a bad case of buck fever to me," teased Tommy Joe. "I saw you starin' at Eli with your gun lowered and Eli starin' back at you with his antlers raised. I was hollerin' at you to shoot, but you acted like you didn't even hear me. Eli did, though! He hauled his boogie outa there quicker'n a wink and just disappeared into the bay. Gone! Like he was never there!"

Then you called for me on the C.B. to come and catch the dogs, 'cause Eli crossed the curve in the logging road and headed for the paved road," added Jimmy. "We had to catch 'em up and put 'em in the box so's they wouldn't follow that buck to the pavement where they could have been hit by a car. That cunning ol' buck knew that! That's why he ran that way! That's how he has

13

given us the slip for all these years. That's how he's lived so long! Ya'll mark my words! That Eli is one smart, slippery, sneaky, buck deer!"

Young Davey blinked unbelievingly at his grandfather, his mouth agape as the story unfolded. He had never seen Old Dave miss anything that he could remember. Old Dave could pick up any of his shotguns, at any time, and drop a high flying dove or speeding wood duck from the air. Hand thrown clay targets and cans were not even deemed by him as appropriate for "wasting shells on."

Old Dave had, however, allowed Davey to shoot at such objects using a battered Stevens single barrel gun. If Darlene Johnson had known about the clandestine activities behind Old Dave's barn, she would surely have put an end to it. But, for two years now, Davey had been practicing.

He knew the range at which he could ventilate a soft drink can with enough number eight shot to cause the fastest dove to fall to earth, stone dead. He also knew, intimately, the distance at which the old gun could be counted on to put four of its nine double ought buckshot pellets through a rusty gallon paint can. His grandfather had looked on approvingly as the young hunter-in-training consistently hit the hand thrown cans at a distance of thirty-five yards or more.

Davey was proud of the compliments and praise he had earned from Old Dave about the ability he had developed at hitting inanimate objects with the old gun, but he was unprepared for the opening of the next hunting camp debate. After all the supper dishes in any deer camp are put away and all the pots and pans are hung on their hooks, the discussion over overly potent bourbons and one-too-many beers always centers around the subject of deer guns. This group of hunters was no exception to the rule.

Old Dave produced the single barrel gun with which Davey had been practicing so many evenings after his chores were done. A couple of the hunters smiled, turning away to chuckle when they learned that this was the only firearm Old Dave had brought. The old scattergun was scratched and scarred. Most of the bluing had vanished from the barrel. The rainbow colors of case-hardening that once graced the receiver had been worn to a rusty brown patina under the grasp of sweaty hands over many miles of hunting and many years of use. Four wraps of black plastic electrician's tape held the forestock to the barrel. The mechanical clip for holding wood to metal had ceased to function long ago and the "temporary" repair had become rather "permanent." The one bit of dignity left the battered gun was the name D. JOHNSON carved neatly into the forestock ahead of the band of tape.

Davey was embarrassed and humiliated at the sight of it. He hoped that his grandfather would have brought one of his shiny autoloading shotguns or a scoped rifle or perhaps one of his sleek double barrel guns. But no, Old Dave had had the lack of sense to bring that beat up old single shot into camp for an opening day hunt!

A lively conversation ensued among the hunters after the single shot was produced from its musty, leather and canvas case. Each man enthusiastically voiced his preference for gauge or caliber, shotgun or rifle. Each hunter extolled the merits of the action type of his personal choice of firearm, whether autoloader, pumpgun, or turnbolt, then defended that choice in give-and-take discussion with all others. The debate was sincere but not serious. With clear winners and no clear losers, the information shared became knowledge learned by one and all.

Davey sat dejectedly in a corner by the stove. Snuggled against his grandfather's knee, he attempted to distance himself from the subject of the conversation. Finally, to his great relief, Mr. Gordon came over and shook Davey gently by the upper arm. In a whisper he said, "That's a fine gun, boy, even if it is only a single shot. I can't remember Old Dave here ever needin' more than one shot to down his game."

Old Dave nodded his thanks to Mr. Gordon and winked down at Davey. That smiling wink of reassurance was the last thing Davey would remember of the night before his first Opening Day. The warmth of the fire and the excitement of the day had his head dropping drowsily onto Old Dave's thigh. A few minutes later the old hunter gathered his grandson up in his arms, carried him to the bunk room beside the kitchen, and laid his sleeping form gently on a musty mattress. Tucking a quilt beneath the young hunter's chin, he patted his head, "Good night."

Davey was awakened all too soon by banging pots and clattering pans accompanied by the boisterous laughter that rang from the kitchen. The smell of coffee hung thick in the air. Rubbing sleep from his eyes he yawned his way to the table and downed a hearty meal of country sausage, scrambled eggs, and snow white grits topped with thick gobs of yellow butter. Old Dave urged him to, "Eat up, boy! It's a long haul 'til dinner time!" Davey heeded his advice. One by one, the hunters finished eating, left the table and added themselves to the group gathered on the rickety front porch to plan the morning's hunt. Dogs pent up in boxes built into the beds of nearby pickup trucks whined and barked their excitement. The closeness of their confinement caused them to growl and nip at each other. Minor skirmishes were broken up by a master's enthusiastic cursing and the loud slapping of his palm on top of a plywood roof.

Twenty hunters gathered in the chilled morning air. Six of them had packs of hounds to "turn out" into the surrounding bays, fields, and woods. These were the "drivers." These were the men with the greatest knowledge of the territory and the most hunting experience. These were the men who had risen before dawn. After wolfing down an early breakfast they had been riding over dirt roads and logging trails. With the aid of headlights, they had been searching for tracks large enough to have been made during the night by buck deer.

There was much discussion as to the best areas to be hunted initially and as to the placement of the fourteen "standers." The standers would be located at strategic points to intercept deer as they were coursed by the baying packs of hounds. After each driver had given his report and made his suggestions, the talk died down to a rumble. The "Huntmaster" was about to make his decisions.

Old Dave was the man to whom all hunters deferred. He had become Huntmaster by default. No one else had gained his knowledge of the deer's habits. All sought to benefit from his many years of experience. When he began to send the standers to their posts, all ears listened.

"Joey, you park under the crooked oak on the Long Road. Look sharp! Watch both directions on that straight stretch! A buck could run by on either side of you! Stop just this side of it. If a deer busts outa the bay, he'll run the path along the creek bottom and bounce out at the curve right in front of you for sure!

Tommy Joe, you go stand at the edge of the soybean field where you saw Eli. He might decide to slip through that finger of bay he ducked into for cover when you spotted him last Thursday. Listen for the dogs to tell you he's acomin'! About the time you hear 'em bark, he'll be atearin' that bay wide open and come aleapin' your way through the beans!"

Old Dave then consulted the drivers as to the best locations to turn out their dogs and take their places among the standers. Once the chases were started, the hunt would become fluid, with the position of the hunters changing as they maneuvered across five thousand acres of varying landscape to assure that the deer would not cross out of their hunting territory without, at least, being seen by someone. The dogs could then be caught and held ready for the next hunt, which would take place during the afternoon, if the weather did not become too hot.

"Gordon. Turn your dogs out on that big track you found along the fire break behind the pine plantation, then come back out on the old loggin' road and have a listen. If they jump that deer from his bed and start a chase, get on the radio and let us know which way they're headed!

17

Bobby. Loose your dogs on that track you saw leading into the bay across from the tobacco beds. Stay right there and wait to see which way they go. A buck could try to sneak away through those bare tobacco stalks, so be alert! If you get a shot, don't miss! If he gets by you, no one will be able to get there in time to back you up, no matter how much you holler on that radio. All we'll be able to do is help you catch your dogs and blow that buck a kiss 'goodbye'!"

After all the hunters had been assigned their positions and all safety rules had been recited, the new-comer, who had caused Davey's discomfort the previous evening, asked where the Huntmaster's stand would be since it had not yet been mentioned.

"I'll be at the dirt pile," he shrugged matter-of-factly. Then he crawled into his pickup and pulled the door closed. Rolling down the window, he nodded the bill of his blaze orange cap at the newcomer and told him to, "Move along to your stand now! This hunt is gettin' ready to start! Follow Gordon down the old logging road and he'll show you where I told you to go. Pay attention to him when he tells you which way to watch and listen."

Of course, everyone else in the crowd who had been present on any opening day hunt for the past several decades had known exactly where the Huntmaster would be at the start of the hunt. The dirt pile was Dave Johnson's favorite spot to stand. From the top of that twelve foot mound, the ebb and flow of the various dog races could be heard quite clearly across thousands of acres if the wind was light, the air clear. From his lofty throne, Old Dave could gauge the progress of the various chases by the sounds of the trailing dogs' voices and scramble down to his truck and direct his hunters to their most beneficial locations with the use of his citizen's band radio. All the hunters in this particular group were tuned to channel seventeen, waiting for his guidance. Even if a chase did not come close enough for an individual hunter to hear its music, he would not feel left out of the events of the day. He could still share in the excitement of the hunt by listening to the chatter of the Huntmaster's voice crackling over the airwaves.

No one objected to the Huntmaster's desire to hunt the same stand, over and over. After all, it was located on property that had been owned by his family for generations, so he had squatter's rights. Then again, very few deer had actually been taken from the dirt pile stand over the years. Oh, there had been the occasional spike or small forkhorn, and Old Dave usually managed to scratch down a ragged-eared doe or two during the brief either sex seasons. But no one could recall a buck of any significance being tagged at the dirt pile during recent memory.

Davey grew apprehensive as the battered pickup bounced to a squeaking halt at the base of the dirt pile. The huge mound of excavated soil marked the end of a trail optimistically called a "logging road" only because of the few marketable slash and loblolly pines that had long since been cut for pulpwood and hauled away over its rutted path. The road ended at the dirt pile because it had to. The dirt pile was the marker that signalled the end of firm, sandy, Coastal Plain soil and the beginning of wet, black humus at the edge of a Carolina Bay.

The greasy organic peat of the bay would never have supported the churning wheels of a truck loaded with tons of sawlogs. It had never been required to. As the Young Hunter crawled his way to the top of the dirt pile with an assist from the Huntmaster's strong hand, he became aware that visibility into the low-growing jungle that stretched before him was extremely limited. The Big Bay covered a perfect ellipse of more than a thousand acres. Not one marketable tree grew within its borders, only scattered, struggling pond pines, deformed blackgums, and the several varieties of dwarfed, magnolia-like trees — the sweet, red, swamp, and loblolly bays from which the boggy depression received its name.

The interlocking limbs of understory shrubs appeared as a solid wall to the Young Hunter in the weak light of predawn. In fact, to a human, they were a wall. The huckleberries, gallberries, canes, myrtles, and pepper bushes were woven together with hooked catbriers and thorny Devil's walking sticks creating a skin-

19

ripping defensive fortress to all but the man who toted a machete or swung a bushaxe.

Whitetail deer found the bay to their liking. They made it their bedroom. Feeding by night in farmfields along its perimeter and in adjoining forests littered with acorns dropped from water and laurel oaks, they sneaked back into the security of the bay before daybreak through a maze of tunnels chopped through its tangled vegetation by the sharp hooves and nibbling teeth of countless generations of deer who had lain in the bay before them.

Deer stuck tighter in the bay than an oyster inside its shell. Hunters could not pursue them into that impossible jungle. Dogs could. Dogs were the knife the hunters used to pry the quarry from the bay. Any pathway a deer could travel, a dog could follow. A dog could find his way by scent through brush so thick that visibility was limited to the distance from his eyelids to the tip of his nose.

"Dogs were the knife the hunters used to pry the quarry from the bay."

The maximum distance the Young Hunter could peer into the bay from his perch atop the dirt pile was about thirty yards. The only clear shot he would have would be back down the logging road along which he had just travelled, or across a deep ditch, the construction of which represented man's sole intrusion into the bay and which had created the mound of dark, organic soil on which he and the Huntmaster now stood, awaiting the first warming rays of the morning sun.

No one was entirely certain how or why the ditch had been dug. Davey had heard speculation that it was created by the hands of slaves during a plantation owner's quest for fertile land with which to increase his tobacco or cotton production. He thought it more likely that the excavation had been undertaken in more recent times by the use of steam shovel or hydraulic dredge as part of a forester's unsuccessful scheme to allow the planting of commercially valuable loblolly pines. The conditions that had created the bay's wet land were not the usual creative forces of water flowing and receding over many centuries to leave an eroded depression with a natural streambed or other water course as its outlet. Theory held that the bay was thrust into being through the violence of destructive forces at exactly the same instant as were all its thousands of sister bays by the release of unimaginable kilotons of potential energy that became kinetic when a comet or other celestial body collided with that portion of Earth that would one day become known as Carolina. Since there was no natural outlet for the waters of the bay, someone had attempted to create one to claim the bay for human needs. But the sphagnum moss that had decomposed over thousands of years to form the bay's soil held its water like a sponge. Big Bay jealously begrudged its water. Although wounded, it would not be drained of its lifeblood. The ditch was long and straight, stretching beyond the point where it was swallowed from sight by interlocked baylimbs a hundred yards distant. Its shin-deep water looked black and cold and uninviting. The four foot high banks on either side had been eroded to a nearly vertical configuration by the violent runoff of innumerable thunderstorms.

The deer were happy the bay had not been drained. The hunters were happy the bay had not been drained.

Davey was beginning to wonder just how he would be able to see a deer running through the bay, let alone shoot at it, when his grandfather spoke.

"He'll run along beside the ditch," the Huntmaster said, as if reading the Young Hunter's thoughts. "He'll be plenty close enough if he comes this way. You stay here while I let the dogs out, back down the road, yonder. It seems like I remember seeing the track of a deer with a big foot in the last sandy stretch we drove over.

The Huntmaster slid down to his truck, stuck a chew in his mouth, then backed down the road in reverse gear.

If the·deer and the hunters were happy the bay had not been drained, the dogs were ecstatic! The Young Hunter listened as restrained whines and whimpers burst into joyous yips and excited barks at the clang of the tailgate being dropped to set them free. He could hear wagging tails thrashing through dried ferns in the bay, stopping occasionally as a hound watered down a bush or tended to other important matters that all dogs must get behind them before getting down to the serious business of vacuuming the ground with their noses for traces of scent left by a buck's passing. All puppy foolishness ended abruptly when the Huntmaster called to his hounds, urging them deeper into the thicket.

"H'yuh, Tiny! Bell! Smokey Moe! Hike in there! Run him out, Sam!"

Dog noises diminished with distance as the hounds searched deeper into the bay. The truck door opened and slammed shut. Davey watched the truck return and skid to a stop below him. After relaying last-minute instructions into the microphone, Old Dave stepped out of the cab. Climbing the face of the dirt pile, he carried the worn Stevens that had been the cause of Davey's embarrassment the evening before. He broke open the action, sliding the lever on the tang to one side with his calloused thumb. The ejector made a loud, metallic ping as he handed the gun, safely empty, to his grandson.

"Time to load up!" he said.

Davey nervously fumbled open the flap on a five-pack of shells, finally managing to plunk one of the stubby rounds into the waiting chamber. Closing the action with a solid click, his apprehension eased. After checking the hammer under his thumb to make sure it wasn't cocked, he hefted the gun's weight. The feel of its balance between his hands gave him confidence. He knew the gun's capability. He had dug many of its double-ought buckshot from a sand bank after practice sessions and knew the power of the nine thirty-three caliber balls of lead contained in each shell.

The blaze orange hunting cap of October dawn had just begun to warm the Young Hunter's face when he heard the first dog strike. The long, drawn out, deep-throated howl drifted to Davey's ears on the damp morning air. An involuntary shiver slithered its way up his spine. The little blond hairs on the back of his neck began to rise. The Huntmaster placed a calming hand on his shoulder to steady him.

"That's Tiny," he said softly. "Listen close and you'll hear the rest."

The entire pack joined in the chase as the deer was jumped from his bed. An incredibly loud and continuous chorus of barks and howls, yips and yaps held together by the melody of the deep, soulful baying by the blue-ticked hound, Smokey Moe, shattered the morning's stillness. The dogs voiced to the world their joy of running fast on a redhot track. The sound of the chase set a racing pace that echoed throughout the bay, passing closely enough to the dirt pile that the Huntmaster and his Young Hunter could see the gallberry bushes shaking. For a few breathless seconds, the dogs lost the scent. Then, suddenly, they wheeled in the opposite direction and ran directly toward the line of standers waiting along the field edges and forest borders that marked the opposite side of Big Bay.

Other dog packs were also active. The varying choruses of hound music shattered the morning mists as they traced the tracks of game along invisible deer trails throughout the tangled maze. A shot was fired, triggering a muffled discussion that was barely audible on the Huntmaster's radio as the hunters tried to determine who had done the shooting and whether to try to catch the dogs or let them continue the chase. Four shots followed, rapid fired from a semi-automatic Remington .30-06 as fast as its sights could be aimed, its trigger pulled.

"Sounded like shooting from the tobacco beds! Did you get him Bobby?" asked Mr. Gordon's excited voice over the C.B.

Bobby's only answer was a kiss against a microphone — a kiss that wished a buck "goodbye."

The Huntmaster chuckled and winked at his Young Hunter. The Young Hunter smiled in return. They revelled in the beautiful autumn morning and the joy of the hunt. This was a special time between them for as long as men and dogs have lived with each other in symbiotic harmony, they have pursued hoofed game together. As long as grandfathers have had grandsons, they have shared with them their knowledge of the hunt.

As Davey stood at the top of the dirt pile with Old Dave's hand resting on his shoulder, he thought of the many things his grandfather had tried to teach him the past few months. He was apprenticed to the Huntmaster, learning to one day take his place. Old Dave spoke of the family land often, of how the fields, forests, bays, wildlife, and human beings were all tied together in the web of life. During one particularly long speech, Old Dave had talked about the necessity of hunting deer to manage the size and quality of the herd as being just as important as the provision of meat for the family table and the opportunity of sporting recreation.

"Davey, do you see those deer tracks in the newly planted beans?" he had asked. "The deer eat some of our beans, but that's okay, because we, in turn, get to eat the deer. We have to shoot a certain number of them each year, does as well as bucks, or there would soon be too many for this land to support. I've seen it that way before. At one time, there were so many deer — poor, puny, and nearly starving — that they ate our bean shoots and young corn plants right down to ground level. They stripped the forest clean of green leaves and twigs. They stripped the bay, too, browsing as high as they could reach standing on their hind legs. Bucks had trouble getting enough food to grow anything on their head but little spike antlers. But now that we have doe seasons those troubles are all in the past. By keeping the number of deer under control, there is enough food for all. The bucks are larger and grow nice racks. It's up to people who are close to the land like you and me to make sure our deer population is kept within healthy limits, for their sake and for the sake of our harvest, whether beans or corn or venison. But we also should remember to leave some of the biggest bucks each year to breed. A man doesn't shoot his prize bull does he? The best time to take a trophy buck is not when he's in his prime, say around age four years or so, but a year or two later when he's past his peak. Then's when a younger, stronger buck will push him out anyway and take his place as the dominant breeder in the herd."

Davey wasn't sure he completely understood all this, but most of it seemed very logical to him. He figured his grandfather knew more about deer, land, and hunting than anyone else in the world. He appreciated the fact that the Huntmaster honored him by trusting him with his wisdom. After discussions of this type, he always felt more adult. Straightening his shoulders, standing tall, he always felt he had grown another inch.

The Huntmaster's grip suddenly tightened on the Young Hunter's shoulder, pulling him back instantly from his daydreaming. His heart started beating faster as he realized the dogs had turned.

For a minute, the hounds seemed to be headed slightly away to his right. Seconds later, it seemed that the chase was veering slightly to his left. The realization gradually struck that they were going neither to his right nor to his left, but that the trailing, howling pack was headed on a beeline course aimed directly at the dirt pile on which he stood. Somewhere between the dogs and the hunter was a deer, slipping, turning, sneaking through the bay, trying to avoid detection! But the hounds were relentless. They would drive the deer from the security of the bay into the open. But where, exactly, would he appear?

The Young Hunter turned his head from side to side, his eyes wide with excitement. His heart hammered so loudly through his open mouth that he thought the deer would surely hear it and dash away. Closing his mouth he tried to swallow, but he found it impossible to do. A gush of adrenaline had dried his saliva. His Adam's apple stuck like a stone in his throat.

What was that? The sound of a breaking twig focused his heightened attention. His wild-eyed gaze followed the pointing of the Huntmaster's leathery finger to a small opening in the bay, twenty-five yards up the side of the ditch. He detected a tiny flicker of movement through the tangled screen of brush, followed by the instantaneous appearance of deer! The doe leapt smack into the middle of the ditch followed closely by her yearling fawn. The splashing they made was horrendously loud as they chugged and huffed their way through the chest deep water toward the hunters. The Young Hunter made an attempt to raise his gun, but the Huntmaster's hand moved to the receiver and firmly kept the barrel pointed down, preventing the boy from inadvertently shooting the deer.

"It's not doe season," he whispered as the pair of deer splashed alongside the dirt pile. At the sound of a human voice, the doe froze in mid-stride. She stood and stared briefly at the two hunters, then jumped from the ditch and streaked across the logging road in a blur of brown motion, her white tail flagging high. Snorting panic she bolted, urging her fawn to follow close behind. Together, they melted into the jungle of greenery on the opposite side of the logging road and disappeared. Only hoof prints and water droplets across the sandy trail marked their passing.

The dogs closed the distance. Their short, chopping barks cut through the bay like a wood cutter's axe felling a sap-soaked oak. The strength of the scent told them they were fast on the heels of their quarry. The Young Hunter assumed that the doe and her fawn were the only objects of the hounds' pursuit. He briefly let down his guard as the dogs narrowed the distance but again he felt the Huntmaster's grip tighten on his shoulder.

A grayish brown streak erupted from the bay as a six- point buck bounded into the middle of the logging road on the far side of the ditch. Before the boy could raise his gun, the deer gathered his legs beneath him and, in a single leap, cleared the bushes on the opposite side of the road to join the doe and her yearling. Quicker than thought, he vanished as if he had never existed, leaving the Young Hunter staring slack-jawed at swishing leaves where a buck deer had once been.

Davey was devastated! He had blown his chance! He turned to look at his grandfather, his lips trembling as he tried to catch enough breath to speak. The Huntmaster whispered, "Moved so fast, I couldn't have gotten a shot off, either. Besides, he was too nice a buck to take for meat and he wasn't quite ready for the taxidermist. It's just as well you let him go." With a wink of his eye he continued, "Pay close attention now. The hunt's not over 'til the dogs are in the box."

Davey's tingling nerves were just starting to think about relaxing when the Huntmaster hissed a single, hoarse word.

"Listen!" he said. His voice was husky with excitement. Cocking his head to one side, his fleshy, sun-leathered ears strained to gather in some subtle sound he had heard coming from the bay over the hammering voices of the approaching pack.

With a sweep of his arm, he removed the gun from the Young Hunter's grasp and slid down the side of the dirt pile to the edge of the ditch. Laying the gun on the ditch bank he plunged to the knees in the murky, black water. Small clods from the dirt pile's shoulder showered in around him. His snapping fingers urgently motioned for the Young Hunter to follow. As Davey slid down the dirt pile, his grandfather was mouthing the words, "Hurry! Hurry!" but in his excitement, he was uttering no sound.

The Young Hunter had scarcely gotten within reach when he felt the strong arms of the Huntmaster around his waist. There was a sensation of flying through the air, propelled by a powerful force and he found himself thumped heavily onto the opposite bank. As he was regaining his feet, he felt the familiar warmth of wood and cold of steel as the Stevens was thrust firmly into his hands. He stared in bewilderment into the Huntmaster's eyes.

"Move over there, down that trail, quickly!" the Huntmaster whispered as he pointed to a barely perceptible opening through the intertwined branches.

Davey took hurried steps, kicking free of the greenbriar vines that tore at his ankles. Finding himself in a tiny clearing, he glanced back at the Huntmaster's torso through the brambles. The Huntmaster's legs were mired in the murkiness of the ditch bottom. His right arm gestured wildly, directing the Young Hunter to watch down a narrow corridor that ran parallel to the ditch, but was separated from its bank by twenty yards of screening bay.

The Young Hunter had just begun to make out the faintest trace of the deer trail tunneling through the bay when movement caught his eye. A shadowy form was ghosting through the opaque screen of vegetation, snapping twigs as it moved rapidly, head lowered to clear sagging branches. Davey's first perception was that of a brown dog with long ears. But, there was something else. Dead, dry tree limbs appeared to be moving in synchronization to the movements of that bobbing head. Antlers! A whole forest of them! The buck jerked his head up with the realization that something was blocking the path of his escape! A shaft of sunlight flashed off the enormous rack as it was snapped upward by the powerful muscles of a rut-swollen neck.

The gun moved swiftly to Davey's shoulder as if guided by some other force than his own young arms. Startled at the sight of the sudden movement, the buck dug his feet into the moist earth and sprang high into the air. With a tremendous leap he cleared the tops of the stunted trees, higher than a man can reach.

The silver bead on the end of the gun barrel sought its mark. Weaving its way through the bay limbs it tracked the buck's flight, dancing and jumping from the panicked pressure of a wildly pumping heart.

At the sound of the shot, all sensation of time and motion ceased. Like the bursting of a white hot flashbulb, the muzzle flash and powder smoke captured the image of a buck deer launching itself free above the bay. That instant was captured forever by the memory of a boy on his first hunt, never to be forgotten or diminished by the passing of the remaining years of his life. The grandest buck of all, whose rack of antlers was suitable to grace the glossy cover of any sporting magazine, hung suspended in midair. Dirt and moss flew from flailing hoofs. Antlers gleamed in blazing sun, their ivory tips raking the clouds, starkly white against the brightness of a Carolina blue sky.

The heavy thump of the gun's recoil shoved the Young Hunter back a step. Losing his balance, he also lost sight of the deer. It all seemed a dream. The shot was taken. The buck was gone. Vanished! Swallowed up by the safety of his home in the impenetrable bay!

Hunter's instinct shouted, "Reload!" Clumsy fingers rattled through pockets for a shell. A thumb found the release lever on the tang and pinged the shotgun open. As the ejector threw the smoking empty high over his shoulder, the futility of his frenzied actions crashed in upon the Young Hunter.

"I missed," he despaired.

"Maybe not," came the unexpected response from the vicinity of the ditch as the Huntmaster heaved himself free. Water dripped from his legs. His boots sloshed as he moved to the Young Hunter's side. He spat a brown stream of tobacco and attempted to soothe his grandson's rattled nerves.

"Try to stay calm and get that gun reloaded," he said softly.

When he saw to it that this had been safely accomplished, he eased Davey in front of him. Together they slipped cautiously along the deer trail to the place the buck had sailed above the overhanging bay. As Davey studied the deep furrows left by the buck's sharp hooves in the wet soil, the Huntmaster reached above his head and plucked a clump of something from the top of a leaf.

"Deer hair! I didn't figure you'd missed him! I knew you were too good a shot!" he exclaimed.

Davey felt the renewed rush of adrenalin. His hands shook and his body tingled with excitement as he examined the tiny tuft of brown fibers held between the Huntmaster's thumb and trigger finger. A small drop of blood beaded the clump of hair together, proving the Huntmaster to be correct.

The pair pushed their way into the bay, looking for the faintest clue that would lead them to the fallen buck. The Huntmaster's experienced eyes were quick to find a broken twig here, or a drop of blood there, or a scratch rasped by an antler in the bark of a sapling that indicated the path of the wounded deer's passing. They had managed to break their way through twenty-five yards of the thick, aromatic vegetation when the Huntmaster suddenly froze. He gave a low whistle. The Young Hunter followed his gaze, trying to peer through a wall of foliage that the taller man could see above.

"You can unload that gun now. I was pretty sure you'd only need one shot." the Huntmaster said, his face breaking into a broad grin.

Old Dave pushed aside a leafy branch with his left arm and reached out with his right hand to collect the gun from Davey's grasp. The Young Hunter stood, speechless. His mouth dropped open until his chin nearly touched his chest. On the soggy ground before him, revealed by the sweep of the Huntmaster's arm, lay the most magnificent creature he had ever seen. For a few moments he stood and stared, unable to move. Then the Huntmaster beckoned him forward and he made his way to the unmoving form. He eased down reverently on one knee and tentatively touched trembling finger tips to antler tips. He attempted over and over to count the number of points, but he was too overwhelmed by the rack's enormous size.

"I make it out to be ten," the Huntmaster said.

Davey nodded but didn't look up. He was experiencing the mixed emotions that all hunters feel at the taking of their first big game — elation that he had not missed the shot, pride in himself that he had killed his buck in a fair chase, success at having made meat for his family's table. But those good feelings of accomplishment were shadowed by clouds of remorse and sorrow at having brought to an end the life of such a beautiful animal. When he sensed the Huntmaster bending a knee to be at his side, he could not speak to acknowledge his presence.

"He's really something, isn't he?" the Huntmaster asked as he gently smoothed the hair on the buck's thick neck with the palm of his hand. "I believe I've seen this deer before."

Davey swallowed hard, mustering courage to look at Old Dave's face. He blinked back tears so the Huntmaster wouldn't see. The instant their eyes met, Davey knew Old Dave had not missed his chance to take this deer the year before, but had fired into the ground to make it appear as a miss to Tommy Joe. Only the Huntmaster could have known how to set up a shot at a fleeing buck as wise to the ways of dogs and men as old Eli. Only the Huntmaster, with his intimate knowledge of the deer, the dogs, and the bay could have known the location of the hidden escape trail that ran through the undergrowth on the opposite side of the ditch. Eli would have escaped, unharmed, had any other hunters besides a certain grandfather and his grandson been stationed at the dirt pile stand. The gap of silence between two generations of Johnsons was closed by the baying of their hounds approaching fast on a scent so hot that it burned their noses.

The Huntmaster stood. Before crunching his way back through the bay, he approvingly squeezed the Young Hunter's shoulder and said, "You just sit tight for a while Davey, and I'll try to get us some help to round up the dogs."

Soon after the Huntmaster disappeared into the brush, the sound of slamming truck doors indicated that other hunters had heard the shot that ended the chase at the dirt pile or had been summoned by the Huntmaster's radio.

"Need some help in there?" asked a voice that greeted Old Dave.

"Sure do. Come help me catch my dogs." Davey heard the Huntmaster reply through the heavy curtain of vegetation.

"Did you have any luck?"

"Oh, a little bit. The boy will need some help dragging out his deer as soon as the dogs are in the box."

"We all figured that that was you or Davey that fired that shot, but we didn't hear you over the radio until now."

"Well, me and Davey was sorta busy," the Huntmaster chuckled.

"Yeah, it looks like you were busy taking a bath!"

The Huntmaster laughed and said, "Yeah. I got so excited, I sort of stumbled and slipped right into the ditch. It's a good thing Davey was paying attention though, or we would never have gotten a shot at that buck."

More hunters arrived as the word of the Young Hunter's success was broadcast to all who were listening on channel seventeen. The dogs were gathered up before they could converge on the fallen buck and rip holes in the slick hide of his hams with their teeth. Two of the arriving hunters joined the Huntmaster, chopping a path around the end of the ditch and into the bay with machetes. Hacking a pathway through the brush to the Young Hunter, they saw what lay on the ground at his feet.

One gave a low whistle of amazement. Removing the cap from his head, he wiped sweat from his forehead with the back of his wrist.

The other hunter exclaimed, "Goodness gracious, Almighty! This little boy has done gone and killed Old Eli!"

There was a stunned instant of incredulous silence among the hunters left standing on the logging road. Then Tommy Joe whooped a Rebel Yell and slung his blaze orange cap high over-head. The assembled hunters joked and jabbered like schoolboys among themselves, slapping one another on the back and taking turns poking fists at each other's shoulders.

Mr. Gordon smiled and stayed calm. Shouting questions to the hunters in the bay, he broadcast their answers to all partici-pants in the hunt through the microphone of the Huntmaster's C.B.

"Is it really old Eli?"

"Davey really shot him?"

"How big is the buck?"

"How many points?"

All doubting and questioning among the hunters present at the end of the logging road ceased as the dead buck was hauled into view and hoisted triumphantly onto the tail gate of the Huntmaster's truck. Eli's head was placed with the care demanded of his status and situated so that all could see the enormous span of those gleaming antlers when Old Dave returned to the cabin.

The hunters were gathered when the Huntmaster arrived. Everyone began talking at once as the truck spun around and backed beneath the pleated tin awning of a tobacco barn that served double duty as the camp's skinning shed. Kidding com-ments flew as the gathered crowd of grown men teased the Young Hunter with references to a little boy who was half the size of his first deer.

"Beginner's luck!" cried Sammy, feigning envy as he mock-punched a fist at Davey's stomach.

"Admit it! Ya'll really ran over him with the truck," chuck-led a voice in the middle of the crowd.

"Naw! That ain't it! That buck died of heart failure at the roar of the cannon you was totin'!" laughed Bobby. But his joke back fired and the group's collective laughter was at his expense when Mr. Gordon pointed out, with exceptional politeness, that a single shot from a twelve bore gun in the thick of a bay was not nearly as hard on the ears as five shots fired from a .30-06 rifle across an open tobacco field.

Laughter quieted to snickering as the men busied themselves with their skinning chores. Every hunter present admired and touched the rack in deference to the lucky hunter. As the buck was being relieved of his hide, Mr. Gordon poked his fingers into holes where double ought buckshot had entered the deer's ribs.

"That was some mighty fine shootin', young fellah," he said to the Young Hunter. "I sorta' figured one shot was all you was gonna need." While Davey beamed at the diversionary compliment, Mr. Gordon motioned behind his back to Old Dave who shadowed himself closer to Mr. Gordon's side.

They mumbled and whispered, discussing some hidden secret. Reaching agreement, they nodded their heads in unison. Both faces showed teeth through broad grins. The Huntmaster straightened his smile, then turned to the Young Hunter.

"Davey, come over here a minute. There's one more thing needs doin' before we start dividin' the meat." Davey looked quizzically at his grandfather, then did as instructed.

All the hunters clustered together. Forming a ragged circle, their conversations and gigglings rumbled to a close. At the center of their circle were an old man, a young boy, and a buck deer. The Huntmaster touched his thumb to a trickle of blood that dripped from one of the wounds in the deer's chest. Tenderly, he touched the thumb to each of the boy's cheeks. Silence reigned under the tin roof as a grandfather's look of pride was reflected in his grandson's eyes. Reaching low, the Huntmaster gently held, then firmly shook the Young Hunter's hand.

Shouting in a voice loud enough for all the world to hear, the Huntmaster exclaimed, "Davey Johnson! Now you're blooded! Welcome to the hunt!"

At the shattering of the silence each hunter in turn clasped Davey's hand. Every orange-capped man joked or gestured or slapped him on the back. Each hunter congratulated him and welcomed him into the ranks as a fellow hunter in his own unique way.

The venison was divided into more or less equal shares to the extent that the configuration of a deer's symmetry allowed. Chance lots were drawn for all who desired to take home a portion of fresh, opening day venison for their table. Davey did not know how he got so lucky with so many others hungry for the taste of fresh meat, but didn't ask too many questions when he saw an entire choice ham go into the ice chest lashed to the top of the dog box in the back of Old Dave's pickup truck.

When they were finished with the deer, the group of hunters drifted to the cabin's kitchen for a hasty lunch of sandwiches, sardines, vienna sausages, potted meat and crackers or whatever else they had packed in their duffel.

The man from town who had made Davey feel uneasy about the old Stevens the evening before, happened to glance up from a spoonful of pork-n-beans. Pushing his chair away from the table, he bumped and dragged it across the floor and situated it behind the pot-bellied stove. Its feet screeched against worn pine flooring that had not seen wax in a lifetime as he shoved it into position underneath the old deer mount.

"Well, I guess we finally have a replacement for this ragged old thing." he said. Standing on the chair he lifted the worn trophy from its place on the wall. A couple of pairs of hands assisted him as he carried the heavy, dust-covered mass of antlers and faded hide through the room and out onto the front porch. Most of the hunters took a break from their lunch to follow the mount outside into the sunlight. All were soon blowing and dusting away with their hands the years of neglect.

"Look, there's some writing on the back of it." said the man from town. "Let's see if we can read it."

Old Dave had been following along at the tail end of the group, supervising with watchful eye to ensure that the mount was treated with the dignity it deserved. It was he who stepped forward to wipe away the remaining dust with a handkerchief and it was he who read the words inscribed on the back of the oak plaque which had supported the mount for many years. It was a wonder, he could read them at all. There was so much dust in the air that it irritated his eyes and made them puff up all red and watery.

Killed by Dave Johnson, Jr.
Age 10 - Dirt Pile.
October 16, 1959.

The quiver in Dave Johnson, Sr.'s voice vibrated in Davey's ears. He moved to embrace his grandfather, whose strong arms enveloped his head and shoulders, pulling his face into the soft comfort of a flannel hunting shirt.

Mr. Gordon caught Old Dave's eye with a wink, then quickly diverted the others' attention to the deer mount to prevent any unnecessary embarrassment to the Young Hunter releasing muffled sobs of emotion in the security of the Huntmaster's arms. Grasping the main beam of an antler in each hand, he tilted the head to one side, then the other, admiring the curvature and graceful symmetry of the rack.

"You know, I believe this old deer head can be salvaged," he said in a decisive voice. "I've heard that a good taxidermist can patch the rat's gnawings, polish the antlers, and fit a fresh cape to make it look as good as new."

The hunters talked over the idea of repairing the mount among themselves. "I know a really fine taxidermist who could do it. He could mount the boy's deer head, too," the man from town suggested.

The men nodded their consensus. A brief discussion followed regarding the cost of refurbishing the mount, accompanied by much scratching of heads and rubbing of stubbly, whiskered chins. It was eventually decided that since the project involved the entire hunting club, everyone should share the expense.

That was the group's only concrete rule - share and share alike. Whether the duties of the hunt or the responsibilities of camp chores, profit or liability, benefit or expense, each man participated equally. Each man received the same degree of reward or the same degree of obligation as all the others. It had always been that way. It would always be that way. And so, a hunting cap was passed from hand to hand, with each man contributing a ten dollar bill or an I.O.U. to the universal cause.

Davey and Old Dave eased away from the crowd to be alone beneath the tin roof of the skinning shed. Davey ran his fingers along the ridges and angles of the rack of antlers on the first deer he had ever taken. In a barely audible, trembling voice, he asked, "Was that my Dad's first deer?"

"It was."

"Why didn't you tell me about it sooner, so I would have known? It was sort of embarrassing to me, all of those men seeing me cry."

"Well, I guess you didn't see more than a few of them turn away so you wouldn't see their eyes all misted up either, did you?"

"You mean some of them knew that was my daddy's first deer, too?"

"Yes, Davey. Those who have been around a few years more than they like to admit knew about your dad and that old deer head. They also knew about your coming along today to join the hunt and have been looking forward to it for a long time. But, you see, if I had told you the story of that old mount in advance, it would have put way too much pressure on a young man such as yourself to live up to other folks expectations, stepping into your father's shoes, or something like that. This way it happened sort of naturally, like it was meant to be, not in the manner of something artificial, like it had to be."

Davey knew instinctively that the Huntmaster was right, as he always was in matters relevant to the hunt.

The weather that afternoon was typical of East Carolina in October, with the temperature climbing to nearly 90 degrees. The heat of the day cut short the afternoon hunt. The dogs had difficulty finding fresh scent in the tinder of dry leaves and the powdery dust of scorched sand. They searched briefly in the steamy bay and crackled along the floor of dehydrated needles in the piney woods, giving out a few frustrated yips before proceeding to flop on their bellies in the first convenient mudhole they happened upon.

Old Dave wondered aloud to Davey as to why they called these "dog days," when it was clearly evident that it was much too hot for the dogs to be enjoying themselves. Some of the hunters, disgusted with the heat and its adverse effect on the hounds, climbed into tree stands at the edges of fields as the shadows lengthened to late afternoon to try their luck at ambushing a buck that might happen to come out of the bay to feed in the cooler evening hours.

Old Dave and Davey spent most of the early afternoon driving along the logging trails and farm roads, rounding up their overheated dogs. All were eventually found and put in the box, except for one — Tiny.

"She's long and lean and can go a ways farther on a hot day," the Huntmaster remarked. "That's one of the bad things about a big, long legged Walker hound, or one of the good things, depending on your point of view, I suppose."

He grinned at his own humor and turned to Davey to share a chuckle, but there was no response forthcoming. The long hours, the excitement of the day, and the steaming heat had taken their toll on the Young Hunter. He was fast asleep, his chin bouncing lightly on his chest to the rhythm of tires humming against the washboard ruts of the road.

The Huntmaster feathered the brake pedal to stop the truck in the sparse shade of a huge willow oak that would lose the last of its browning leaves to the wind and rain of the next thunderstorm. Easing open the door, he lifted the old gun from the rack in the rear window and gently asked, "Mind if I borrow your gun for a bit?" When there was no immediate reply, he softly answered himself on the sleeping boy's behalf. "I didn't think so," he said.

Quietly closing the door, he made his way to the back of the truck. Settling himself comfortably on the tail gate, he smiled peaceful satisfaction as he recollected the events of the day. The gun rested on his lap, waiting to do its work on the odd chance that the howl of a wayward hound named Tiny might startle a buck from the bay.

Listening for the voice of the dog who had lost her master, Old Dave slipped his skinning knife from its sheath on his belt. Rattling through melted ice to the bottom of the cooler on top of the dog box, he retrieved an apple and shook it free of cold water droplets that soaked dark dimples in the sand of the road-bed before being vaporized into oblivion by the heat. The keen steel blade tasted the sweet fruit. Curls of peel fell, landing in a small red heap against the weathered wood and worn metal of the Stevens single barrel.

Darlene Johnson had busied herself about the house all day long, attempting to convince herself that it was actually very pleasant not having a small boy underfoot so she could get some serious cleaning accomplished for a change. She had even found time to bake a country ham with all the trimmings for supper and a coconut cake for dessert.

"That's one thing Old Dave's good for besides huntin', at least," she thought aloud. "He cures as fine a ham as anyone in Pender County."

But it was now nearly dinner time and her doubts gave way to fears at her decision to let Dave, Sr. spirit her son away the previous evening.

"Bunch of foolish old men, cavorting around the woods all day long. I'll bet Davey's had his fill of them today," she muttered.

Inwardly, she hoped that he would not want to go hunting again until he was older so she could keep him close to her and protect him for just a little while longer. She checked the clock every five minutes or so, trying not to become alarmed at the lateness of the hour. It was amazing how loud the hollow ticking of the grandfather clock sounded without the little boy noises of Davey in the house and how slowly the heavy pendulum moved as it swung back and forth in its lazy arc.

Stirring a pot of green beans that simmered on the stove top, she glanced out the window for the fiftieth time to see if, by chance, the hunters were returning down the long driveway. She felt like she had counted off each passing second throughout the day, marking the end of each long hour by the clock's musical chime. The tones were usually very pleasant and reassuring to her. Yet, for some reason, perhaps due to the general emptiness of the house on this particular day, the cheerfulness of the clock's chiming seemed to be diminished, creating a somewhat melancholy sound to the ears of Darlene Johnson.

Hustling to the back of the house, she tried to keep apprehensive thoughts from entering her mind. Busying herself with folding freshly washed linens and tidying up beds did nothing to prevent nagging little doubts concerning the safety of her son from creeping into her mind.

Seven loud tones echoed through the house as the clock's bell rang the arrival of the dinner hour. The windows of the kitchen and the glassware in the oak china hutch vibrated in sympathetic harmony to the resonance of its final note before it faded away into silence. Darlene stood rigidly, clutching a half-folded sheet to her breast. The sheet crinkled as a cold shiver chilled its way up her spine.

She fought the rising surge of panic as a flood of painful memories absorbed her being. The last time Dave, Jr. had been late for dinner was on that terrible night he had been taken from her, never to hold her in his strong arms again, never to reassure her against worrying about his being late for dinner during the hunting season.

"Things happen that's beyond your control when your huntin'," he would say. There always followed some lame excuse for his being late — a truck failing to start or a wounded deer that had to be tracked through the blackness of the bay aided only by the dim beam of a flashlight with failing batteries. Sometimes his or another hunter's dog would be missing. Roads would be ridden far into the night, with Dave, Jr. searching, calling until the lost hound's tired eyes reflected luminous green from the glow of the headlights at the side of some overlooked logging trail. But always, before that night, he had returned home.

The slamming of a truck door and the sound of happy voices rescued Darlene from her dark memories. Her hunters had arrived! She scurried back to the kitchen, stopping abruptly to adjust herself in front of the stove. She smoothed her apron, straightened her hair with her fingers, then turned her attention to the steaming pots and pans as if everything was normal. She put on her most welcoming smile, as if her day had been completely routine and she had not been the least bit concerned for Davey's welfare.

"Well, Davey, we're home at last," Old Dave grinned as he roughly tousled the boy's hair with a strong hand. "We've had quite a day, haven't we, you and I?"

"We sure have," came young Davey's reply. "I guess this must have been the best day of my life."

"You'd better hurry into the house. Your mother is bound to be worried about you after being out so late helpin' me look for Tiny. You go on inside. I'll be right behind you. I've got to get something out from behind the seat and check the dogs in the box to make sure they're all right and don't have any briars in their feet."

Davey ran up the dirt path to the house, then bounced up the porch steps. The wonderful smell of country ham and the heady aroma of cooking vegetables greeted him as he opened the screened door.

"Uh, oh," he thought to himself, "Late for supper. I hope I'm not in trouble." He hesitated for the briefest moment, then turned the knob of the heavy wooden door and stepped inside.

"Mom, we're home!" he hollered as he closed the door behind him.

She jumped in mock surprise at the sound of his voice. "Oh! You startled me! I was so busy I didn't hear you drive up. Did you have any luck today?"

Did he have any luck? What a question! He started talking away, his mouth in high gear as he told the story of the monster buck. His flashing eyes were wide with excitement. His entire body joined in the telling as he gestured with his arms and twitched his legs, describing every detail of the hunt, the shot, and the Huntmaster's outwitting of Old Eli.

Darlene found herself staring in utter amazement as the story of Davey's first hunt unfolded. The sight of the little hunter standing before her brought back a bounty of happy feelings she had suppressed for too long. The excitement of the chase was in him. The scent of the outdoors was on him. The unbridled joy of being alive glowed in his face. He was the image of his father, a perfect miniature of the man she had loved and lost.

A tattered hunting coat hung loosely from his shoulders. The faded, grass-colored canvas had worn through at the elbows. Thorns had clawed numerous small frays in the fabric over many years of use.

"It must have been one of Dave's coats," she thought. Still, in spite of its billowing size, it seemed to her to suit Davey perfectly in the comfortable way he wore it with the sleeves rolled up a couple of turns to keep them from interfering with the use of his small hands.

Her son continued speaking to her, raising his hands in front of his face until the rolled-up sleeves fell back from his wrists. He moved them farther and farther apart, describing in detail the enormous size of the huge buck's crown.

"How big were his antlers?" she asked in astonishment. "King of the bay? I can hardly believe it!"

"Come on, Mom. I'll show you! We've got the rack on the dog box!" Davey grabbed his mother's hand and lead her to the porch. He pushed open the screen door with such enthusiasm that it banged against the clapboard siding of the front of the house.

Davey's mother stepped out on the porch. Her eyes were immediately brought to focus on the massive formation of antlers poking out in all directions from a cardboard box securely fastened on the dog box that covered the back of Old Dave's truck. They seemed possessed of their own inner brightness as their polished surfaces reflected the glow of the outermost circles of light shining from the front porch lamp. Before she could open her mouth to speak, if indeed any words could be formed in her disbelieving mind, Old Dave stepped from the shadows on the passenger's side of the truck.

"I finally found what I was alookin' for Davey," he said. "Oh! Darlene! I didn't see you standin' there. Sorry, we're so late, but we had to find a dog. Come! Have a look at what your young hunter brought home for you."

Davey led his mother down the steps to the side of the pickup. He stood on the very tips of his toes as he tried to reach the antlers to move them closer for her inspection.

"Aren't they somethin' to see?" he asked, as his fingers caught the edge of the box.

"Yes, they certainly are!" she answered. "That's okay, Davey, leave them where they are. I can see them just fine from here."

"The hide and head are still attached so we can have him mounted. Will that be all right with you, Mom?"

Raising her eyebrows she stammered, "Well, I don't know about that. Where in the world would we keep a mounted deer head?"

Old Dave found this an opportune time to interrupt. He cleared his throat and stuffed some tobacco in his cheek. "Don't worry about a thing, Darlene. I'll carry the whole kit and caboodle to my place and put it in the freezer until I can get it to the taxidermist. We'll hang the mount in the cabin, next to the one Dave killed when he was ten."

Pausing to situate a stem in his mouth, he let the last sentence settle in, measuring her reaction with narrowing eyes. Turning he spat into the driveway dust for emphasis. Reaching through the open window of the truck cab he removed the cased shotgun from the rack against the rear glass.

"Davey," the Huntmaster addressed the Young Hunter while re-establishing eye contact with his mother, "judging from the wonderful smells coming through yonder screened door, you'd better get cleaned up for supper. And, while you're about it, you'd best give your gun a good cleaning too."

He handed the gun to Davey, his gaze never unlocking from Darlene's. After making certain the gun was secure in the Young Hunter's trembling hands, he reached into the window again and felt around until his hand found the object he had removed from behind the seat and placed on the dash.

"Here's what I was alookin' for," he said, raising the elongated box into the feeble light. "I reckon you'll be aneedin' this." He handed the metallically clinking box to Davey. It was a gun cleaning kit that Old Dave had taught him to use following practice sessions behind the barn. The chemical scents of nitro powder solvent and gun oil permeated the air.

Davey blinked at his mother, prepared to ask her permission before accepting such gifts. But his mother never glanced in his direction. She stared into Old Dave's eyes, her arms folded tightly above her apron.

Davey opened his mouth to speak, and had actually uttered a couple of stuttering, unintelligible syllables when his mother cut him off short. "Well, I guess you heard your grandfather. You'd better take your gun in the house and get started or we'll all have a cold supper tonight."

Davey let out a whoop and bounded up the porch steps. Snatching the screened door open he yelled, "Thanks, Mom!" before ducking inside. Old Dave moved to Darlene and gently placed his strong arm around her shoulder. He smiled broadly at her. She managed a feeble smile of her own in return. The worry lines tried to smooth themselves from her forehead.

"I figured you'd like to roast us a venison ham for Sunday dinner," Old Dave said, pointing to the ice chest lashed beside the box containing antlers.

Darlene's smile grew when Old Dave dragged the heavy cooler down and showed her what was inside. They walked up the steps and crossed the porch together. Darlene held the door open for Old Dave as he grunted his way inside with his burden. As Darlene gently closed the door behind them, she laughed a little louder than was necessary at some corny and not-really-funny joke from Old Dave. The lines of stress finally vanished completely from her face. Her hunters had come safely home.

Davey hurried to the room in the back of the house. In his excitement he had difficulty remembering what he was supposed to do. He sat in a broken down easy chair and carefully placed the cased gun across its arms in front of him. Stretching out with his right foot he snagged a footstool with his toe and slid it within his reach. Opening the gun cleaning kit carefully, he placed it on the stool and glanced at the illustrated instructions printed across the inside lid.

"Oh yes, how could I have forgotten how to clean a gun?" he asked himself aloud. But, after all, this was his first time to try it without Old Dave's guidance.

The aluminum cleaning rod sections tinkled as he joined them together according to the instructions. He threaded the corner of a flannel patch through the rod's slotted tip and unscrewed the cap from the bottle containing nitro powder solvent. The release of its familiar acid-sweet smell enhanced Davey's memory.

He smiled to himself as he thought through the proper procedures for cleaning the gun and set about his task with confidence.

Unbuckling the butt end of the canvas case, he probed inside until his fingers tightened around the wrist of the gunstock. The gun separated smoothly from its case. He moved his hands apart and let the case drop to the floor. The muscles of his right arm alone were not strong enough to hold the weight of the gun, so he allowed it to return to its place, resting upside down across the arms of the chair. The hammer of the old gun nestled itself into a bed of cotton coming out of a hole worn through the fabric of the right chair arm as though it belonged there.

"This isn't such a sorry-looking gun after all." Davey said to himself as he examined the scratched wood and nicked metal surfaces of the Stevens. "It just needs an extra- specially good cleanin'."

His eyes came to rest on the weathered band of electrical tape wrapped around the gun's forearm. The black strip of plastic was preceded as always by the carved letters of the name "D.JOHNSON." The letters were smooth-edged and filled to darkness with the stain of gun grease and the grime of sweaty palms over many years of use. In sharp contrast were freshly carved letters that exposed the core of light walnut wood. Separated from the original owner's name by the band of tape were the newly carved letters, "III."

The sight of his name carved into the wood brought a smile to Davey's face. He touched his fingers to the letters to convince himself they were really there and not imagined. The tattered wraps of tape fit the former owner's name quite well, but the new owner decided that they should be replaced to match the clean look of freshly exposed wood. Reaching forward, he rattled through the copper bristle brushes and spare gun parts contained in the gun cleaning kit and found a partially used roll of black tape.

"Wow! His gun! Grandpa gave me his gun!" he beamed as his thumbnail lifted the tag end of tape and began to unwrap it.

But that was not exactly true. Old Dave had just been storing this particular gun for safe keeping, holding it in trust, so to speak. He had actually given the Stevens to someone else a long while back as Davey would discover when he completed removing the tape.

The action of the old gun was really as sound as a bank vault and the strip of black tape totally unnecessary to bind metal to wood. It was very necessary, until this moment, to hide the carved letters, "JR."

Boss Gobbler on his way down from Suzy's Knob

Chapter 2

Li'l Jake

The massive brick walls of Freedom High School had been guarding the hillside at 511 Independence Boulevard in the town of Morganton for many years more than the present upper classmen had been alive. To some folks, the distinctive, kidney-shaped layout of the rust-colored structure represented the pinnacle of architectural design. To others, more traditional and conservative of thought, the lines of the building did not conform to their prejudiced notion that outer walls must conveniently end at perfect, ninety degree corners.

To the minds of philosophical adults on the outside, the inner sanctum of classrooms and hallways represented the core of knowledge and learning, where teenaged students were being prepared for fulfilling lives of great works and high achievements. But, to the mind of a certain fifteen-year-old boy trapped on the inside, incarcerated away from the balmy laziness of a warm April day, the school walls seemed no less than a prison.

Jacob Charles Carswell was known to the important people in his life by many names. He signed his school papers, "Jacob C." His mother and father called him "Jake," although he preferred and had asked them to call him "J.C." as did all his closest friends. His older brother, Albert, teased him when he called him, "Li'l Jake."

As he daydreamed out the window on the scraggly form of a fingerling dogwood that was struggling under the weight of its first bloom, he drifted away, escaping to a place he would rather be. He longed to be up high on Suzy's Knob, where the dogwoods were blooming, the grouse were drumming, and prisms of rainbow trout were rising to a hatch in the crystal clear waters of Back Creek. There, the turkey gobblers were a-gobbling, thundering out to the world their dominance of the mountains, their ownership of the warm days following Winter's icy grip that human beings call Spring.

A flatlander must be made to understand that Suzy's Knob is a very real place, although adult humorists may speculate with impropriety over just exactly where upon her anatomy Suzy's knob might be. In the lingo of the Southern Appalachians, a "knob" is a projection or hump of tree-studded rock that rises abruptly above its parent mountain, sticking out prominently like the fighting spur from a turkey gobbler's heel. If a particular knob rises to a great enough height, or possesses some uniquely distinctive feature, it becomes a local landmark. As such, it is given its own name so that mountain folk speaking to one other about a certain prime hunting spot or secret area for gathering ginseng root will mutually recognize its exact location, high up on the side of some roadless ridge.

The name "Suzy's Knob" will not be found on any map, but "Table Rock" can be located by anyone with access to a chart of the North Carolina Appalachian Mountains, specifically the Linville Gorge Wilderness Area. Suzy's Knob grows from the back side of Table Rock, the side facing Shortoff Mountain, but the lowland traveler will need a personal guide with local knowledge to point out which spur peak is named after Suzy.

The three o'clock bell clanged—"School's out!" Daydreams shattered, J.C. refocused his wayward attention back inside to the reality of the classroom. Quickly jotting down his homework assignments, he packed his books and streaked for the door. Jostling and jockeying for position in the middle of a crowded crush of his fellow students, he burst free—free from the confines of schoolhouse walls, free to enjoy the scant remaining hours of glorious afternoon.

The school bus lumbered along much too slowly as it transported him homeward over twisted roads that spiralled up through gaps in the hillsides. J.C. inhaled deeply the scent of fresh cut grass and wild onion tops that wafted in through the open bus windows. The temperature of his spring fever rose to a simmer.

The window-framed view of Suzy's Knob towering above the last leg of road that led to his house, beyond where the pavement gave way to red dirt and peppered granite gravel, was the final ingredient that made J.C.'s kettle boil over. He knew that some way, somehow, by hook or by crook, by gosh or by golly, there would be no school for him tomorrow! The sight of the mountains clothed in spring pulled at him with a magnetism that was too great to be resisted by one who was at that "in-between" age—nearly a man, but at heart, still a boy. Boys do play hooky sometimes, or, in this instance, "turkey."

The bloated yellow school bus backed around into the narrow driveway leading to J.C.'s family home. Its steel doors squeaked open, releasing J.C. from his confinement. J.C. jumped to the ground and raced across the yard. Bouncing up the steps, two at a time, he turned and stood on the whitewashed porch. He watched the bus driver fight the steering wheel to negotiate the sharp turn. Then he and the driver waved goodbye to one another. The bus chugged back down the road, trailing in its wake a cloud of pink dust.

J.C. stared up at the knob for a few minutes, trying to fig-ure out a way to be there come daylight tomorrow, but his mother's voice interrupted, cutting through the haze of his slowly formulating plan.

"Jake! Is that you?" she asked through a window opened to the porch to let in the fresh breath of spring.

Huffing a frustrated sigh, J.C. shot a last longing glance at Suzy's Knob and went inside.

The scheming boy used the remainder of that afternoon and early evening to perform his chores double-duty. He hoed the small garden that sprouted from the only level patch of ground in the back yard, clearing its neat vegetable rows of grass and weeds, chopping the clay clods extra fine. Next, he mowed the narrow strip of bunched orchard grass and dandelions that served as front lawn, taking care where he placed his feet on the dangerous slope that fell abruptly from the front porch to the roadside ditch.

After making certain that his room was tidy, with all his clothes neatly folded and catalogued into their respective places in closet or dresser drawer, he slipped into the dining room— obstensively to set the table. But he moved quietly, stealthily, for he had devious mischief on his mind.

Sneaking to the kitchen door, he assured himself that his mom was completely immersed in the pot-clanging, spoon-rat-tling, cabinet-door-slamming symphony that noisily preceded supper. Quick as a cat, he slipped back across the polished oak floor, tip-toeing over the planks that he knew from experience squeaked the loudest. Positioning himself in front of the ancient, hand-crafted, wormy chestnut buffet, he eased open its bottom drawer. Reaching into the front right corner, he removed the lid from a cheap perfume box, revealing the fragile object he had been forbidden from birth to touch, unless his father was present.

It was waiting there, of course, as it always was, nestled in its protective bed of quilting cotton.

The turkey call was a family heirloom, having been fashioned by a distant ancestor around the time of the First World War. It certainly wasn't much to look at in comparison to the myriad number of slick plastic yelpers or smoothly sanded cedar box callers that could be purchased for a few hard-won dollars across the counter of any local discount store. But looks are not what make a turkey gobbler respond to a turkey call. What attracts a gobbler is the trueness of the sound produced. In the proper hands, this unremarkable-looking call could exactly duplicate the seductive clucks and plaintive yelps of the most alluring turkey hen that ever preened herself before a gobbler on the face of Suzy's Knob.

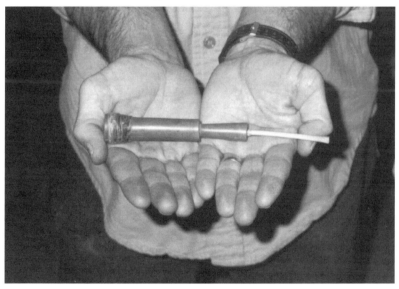

A turkey yelper made from wing bone and wood.

J.C. slipped his fingers around the five inch length of hollow twig that served as the trumpet of the call. With his other hand, he removed the corncob plug from its bell end. The call's tiny mouthpiece was inside, necessarily protected within the wooden tube due to its highly fragile composition. Dumping it into his palm, he visually reassured himself that the eggshell-thin stem of turkey wing bone was completely intact and functional.

He fitted it into its place in a quarter-inch hole in corncob pith that stoppered the opposite end of the twig tube as he had seen his father do many times before. J.C. examined the fully assembled yelper, rolling it slowly between his thumbs and index fingers. His heart beat wildly from the mixture of guilt and exhilaration he felt at holding its magic in his own two hands.

The percussive racket that surrounded his mother's cooking quieted momentarily, tipping off J.C. that she was about to enter the dining room. Deftly slipping the wing-bone mouthpiece back inside the security of the wooden tube, he thrust the disassembled yelper deeply into his jeans pocket, holding it there in his balled up fist to conceal its tell-tale cylindrical bulge through the fabric. Leaning against the buffet drawer, he bumped it shut with his hip just as his mother entered the room.

Myra Carswell clanked into the room carrying a tower of dinner plates topped with silverware. Her body and clothes gave off the steam heat of cooking exertion and the rich aroma of fried, high-country food. Clattering her heavy load to the table, she smiled broadly at J.C.

She announced, "Albert's coming to dinner tonight! Please set an extra place for him at his old chair, will you Jake, Honey?" She abruptly turned and exited back into the kitchen, humming to herself as she put the finishing touches to the evening meal.

Albert Carswell was twenty years-of-age, an age that made him more tolerable to J.C. only because he had matured enough to get a job and leave the family household. He had teased and pestered J.C. unmercifully—as older brothers are predisposed from the time of birth of their siblings to do—during all their years of growing up together under the same roof. But now that Albert had moved out on his own, J.C. almost looked forward to his obligatory weekly visits. Albert was normally so preoccupied with discussions of the various ups and downs of his transition to independent life in Morganton that he would speak to J.C. in a nearly-adult manner. The short duration of an evening's visit usually did not give Albert enough time to indulge himself with the finer points of devilishness that could tie knots in J.C.'s belly. But there always seemed to be the opportunity for him to stick his younger brother with enough needles and pins to make him squirm—just a little bit.

"Hi ya, Mom! Hey, Dad! How ya'll doin?" bellowed Alb as he latched the oak panel door tightly behind him against the creeping chill of evening air. "Where's Li'l Jake? There you are! How's it goin', li'l brother—schoolwork doin' O.K.?"

He rubbed his knuckles through J.C.'s brown hair in an abbreviated version of the "Indian haircut." It was an instinctive display of dominance, even though the younger boy's hormones had kicked in over the past few months and fertilized his thin frame to such height that he could now stand flatfooted and look Albert dead in the eye.

J.C. wanted to punch Albert in his laughing gut, but didn't. He merely ducked his head and twisted free from the burning pain of the knuckles burrowing into his scalp. He tried to say in his deep man's voice, "I'm fine." But his boy's voice cracked and squeaked so that his words were barely audible. Scowling and rubbing his head, he turned away to finish helping his mother set the table. Albert and his father faded into the living room to speak of matters important to men.

Dinner was served on Sunday dishes as it always was for an important guest. J.C. was forced to lay a cloth napkin across his lap and reprimanded by his mother for propping his elbows on the table.

Alb's lack of etiquette went unchallenged. Throughout the meal, he clicked his spoon against his teeth and braced his elbows on both sides of his plate. Stuffing a gluttonous forkful of peach cobbler into his mouth, Alb finished telling a tale, particularly amusing only to him. Laughing out loud, he spewed flaky crumbs of crust. It disgusted J.C. However, it brought forth no comment from Myra Carswell, so happy was she to have a chance to be close to her elder son.

Alb was eventually able to work the wadded mouthful down his throat, lubricating it with great gulps of milk. Sliding his empty dessert saucer across the table, he leaned back in his chair and belched.

Partly closing one eye, he leveled a questioning stare at J.C.. "So, Li'l Jake, have you killed 'ary a turkey yet?" he asked.

J.C. bristled at the degrading appellation, "Li'l Jake," bestowed upon him by his brother. Two springs prior, J.C. had killed his only turkey. A scrawny juvenile, the bird had been called to J.C.'s waiting gun by his father's skills. The young tom had come silently, sneaking in to the hypnotic sound of the yelps and clucks brought forth from the wing-bone caller at his father's lips. J.C. had ambushed the inexperienced bird as it slipped furtively from tree to bush and bush to tree.

John Carswell and his younger son had returned from the successful hunt, proudly showing off J.C.'s first-ever turkey to friends and neighbors. Everyone who saw the turkey politely "ooed" and "ahhed," showing admiration for J.C. and his trophy. Everyone, that is, except for Alb, who had already called and killed two mature tom turkeys on his own. His were genuine, bragging-sized birds, sporting long, thick beards of 7 and 8 inches from the centers of their great breasts.

In turkey-hunting jargon, an immature, young-of-the-year, male turkey is called a "jake." From that day forward, Alb had called his younger brother "Li'l Jake." Only the two of them knew how deeply the nickname sliced through the core of J.C.'s being.

"Alb, you know it poured down rain on opening day, last Saturday. Turkeys stayed on their roosts all morning. They didn't gobble—not nary a time. I've had school today and yesterday. So, how in the world could I have killed me a turkey? As pretty as the weather was this mornin' though, and promises to be again tomorrow, I just know I could call up a big ol' gobbler. But Dad won't let me lay out of school. Even you know that!"

John Carswell spoke up and sided with his fretting younger son, "That's right, Alb. The most important thing in Jake's life right now is gettin' knowledge and learnin' so's he can grow up to think for hisself. Then he'll be able to get a good job and make his own decisions, like you."

Alb's lips curled into a cruel smirk. He leaned across the table toward his flustered sibling. Dryly, he stated, "So, I guess all that explainin' and excusin' just means you still ain't killed a turkey all by your own self."

J.C. narrowed his eyes and looked directly into Alb's taunting face. In a determined, level voice he responded, "That's right, Alb. I haven't killed my turkey yet, but I will!"

John stopped the contest of words between his boys before it could become overheated and spoil the remainder of the evening. "Jake, li'l buddy, how's about helpin' your mom clear the table whilst me an' Alb talk some more. Then, you need to get on up to bed. Tomorrow's a school day."

Alb took one last jab at J.C. as the vulnerable boy left the table balancing armfuls of dishes. "It sure is nice being out on your own. With this new job I have, I get two weeks vacation each year. Why, I could probably even take some time off and hunt turkeys for the rest of the week if'n I wanted. As a matter of fact, I could be up on Suzy's Knob come daylight, if'n I took the notion."

Watching J.C. out of the corner of his eye, Alb gauged his reaction. J.C. ignored his brother's final barb. Pretending not to hear, he answered with turned back and smug silence.

J.C. and his mother had nearly finished washing the dishes when Alb poked his head into the kitchen. "Well, Mom, I've got to get up early in the morning—way before daylight. I guess I'd better be on my way."

Myra looked at the wall clock. Her eyes popped open wide. "Why, it's nigh on to ten o'clock already! My goodness gracious, you can't go down the mountain this time of night! Besides, I've already put fresh sheets on your bed and turned them down. I figured you'd at least spend the night."

Alb smiled at his mother and thanked her for the invitation to stay in his old room. J.C. initially bristled at the thought of sleeping under the same roof with Alb. Although, after a few minutes of contemplation, he grinned to himself as the remaining details of his sneaky plot blossomed in his mind.

Alb hugged his mom, pecked her cheek goodnight, and excused himself. J.C. tossed the dish towel on the counter top and scurried into the dining room after his brother. Catching Alb beside the chestnut buffet, he stammered, "I was wondering, Alb . . ." His tongue stuck against the roof of his mouth as he searched frantically for some quasi-meaningful tidbit of information with which to complete the question.

Alb leaned hard against the antique buffet. With one hand on the crocheted lace that protected the buffet's mirror finish, the other hand firmly planted against his hip, he squared to face J.C. One of Alb's eyebrows was raised in puzzlement. The other was crinkled down, scowling with mild irritation.

". . . do you think there might be a gobbler roosting at the top of Suzy's Knob?"

Alb's expression gradually changed to that of shallow thought, then to that of condescension. Laughing the mean little chuckle of one who knows it all, but grudgingly shares it with no one else, he replied, "Well, maybe there is, Li'l Jake, and maybe there ain't. If there is one though, he'll either be on the side facing away from Table Rock, or down low in the wooded cove. There's water there, for him to roost above. But there ain't no water at the top of Suzy's Knob. So, I doubt there is a gobbler way up there."

J.C. shrugged his shoulders and thanked his brother. Whistling, he bounced back into the kitchen.

Alb took his hand from the top of the old buffet. Scratching his head, he watched J.C. leave, then turned and continued on to bed.

Re-entering the kitchen, J.C. pulled the dining room door closed behind him. "Mom, Alb's goin' to take me to town with him tomorrow and drop me off at school. We're goin' to leave real early so he can open the service station on time." J.C. crossed his fingers behind his back. They trembled as he told the biggest lie of his life.

"That's real brotherly of him," smiled his mother. "I'll get up early with you boys to fix you some breakfast."

"Oh, no, Mom! You needn't get up at five o'clock, just for us!" J.C.'s heart skipped two beats as the fear of being found out seized him. Desperately he searched for a way to keep his mother in bed the next morning so he could slip away undetected. His eyes darted frantically around the kitchen. His gaze chanced upon the bread basket. It was still half filled with homemade biscuits.

"Alb said he sure liked your biscuits tonight. Said he hadn't eaten like that since he left home! Supposin' you just sliced 'em open and slipped in some country ham. I'll bet he would be tickled to have 'em for breakfast. Then you could sleep in, and we could leave real quiet-like so's not wake you and Dad."

Myra smiled at the thought of Alb's enjoyment of her cooking. She nodded in agreement. "I'll leave them in a bag here on the counter. You'd better hurry on up to bed now or you'll be fallin' asleep in school tomorrow."

J.C. bear-hugged his mother and rushed off to bed, taking the stairs two at a time. Reaching the security of his room, he closed the door and fell back hard against it. Sliding down onto his haunches, he let out the first full breath he had taken since walking away from Alb in the living room.

"Phewee!" he said. Wiping sweat from his upper lip with the back of his hand, he thought of how close to a whipping he had come! The cheeks of his bottom were warm with the sudden remembrance of "lessons" and "reminders" that had been taught him at the expense of that tender portion of his body. It had been a long time—a couple of years, in fact—since he had last felt the sting of his father's belt on his backside, or, worse yet, the pain of his scolding words of disappointment.

Stealing! Lying! Laying out of school! J. C. pondered how and why had he gotten himself into such a fix. His shoulders sagged under the weight of guilt.

Undressing, J.C. emptied his pockets, carefully placing their contents onto the nightstand beside his bed. The wing-bone turkey call was gently hidden under his handkerchief against the odd chance that someone might come in and discover it during the night. Winding his alarm clock, he set it for 5 a.m., then placed it under his pillow so that only he would be awakened by its raucous ringing.

As he lay there, listening to the clock's muffled ticking with one ear and Alb's rhythmic snoring through the thin paneling of the wall separating their adjacent rooms with the other, he rolled onto his side and blinked his tired eyes out the window. There, illuminated by the glow of a Half-Easter moon, Suzy's Knob reached up and touched the stars. The risks J.C. had taken were great. The penalty for discovery was severe. But, as his eyelids closed to the first touch of slumber, his lips curved a smile and his toes twitched involuntarily. His feet reacted to the fleeting dream of stalking a long-bearded gobbler at roost near the top. In his dreams, J.C. was certain he was doing the right thing—for J.C. Carswell. Whether in his dreams or in his reality, instinct told him that the greatest goals of a man's life are achieved only through great risk and are paid for at the highest price.

No one saw the faint silhouette of a stripling youth with shouldered gun as it shadowed silently along the whitewashed houseside at the darkest hour preceding dawn. The moon had yawned and set an hour before, leaving only its soft afterglow. J.C.'s escape was easy. No suspicious eye was able to steal an unlucky glance through the dim light to spy his departing form.

The mountain dew was damp and heavy. It clung to all things. It settled thickly onto the dust of the gravel road, muffling the sound of J.C.'s steps. He walked a quarter mile to the point where a hidden trail turned off through a thicket of mountain laurel. From there, the pathway wound its way up to the knob. He had done his best to stick to the tire ruts where the gravel was thin, the walking easy. But the heavy night moisture had turned the dust of the road into a thin layer of greasy mud that clung like tar to his bootsoles. It seemed he had grown two inches in height during the hike. Stooping, he cleaned the clay from between his boot treads with a stick. Rising, he disappeared into the laurel.

Although the rocky path that led to the knob was more gentle to his feet, it was tougher on his legs as they pistoned his wiry body upward, ever higher. Dew-moistened laurel and rhododendron leaves brushed against his jacket sleeves and pants legs, soaking them through to his skin. Never did he shudder with chill. The heat generated by his laboring body burned the dampness into steam. He rested for a moment, panting at the joint of the mountain's toe slope to catch his breath in the thin air before beginning the real climb.

The trail to the top of the knob crept along the spine of a hogback ridge. Its serpentine path twisted and crawled its way through open air cathedrals of immense white oaks and hickory trees. It skirted the edges of dense rosebay thickets and impenetrable tangles of rhododendron hells. An abrasive slide down the sheer, rocky slopes on either side awaited anyone hapless enough to lose his footing.

J.C. moved on through the darkness, unintimidated by the steepness of the ascent. Aided by the weak beam of a pocket light, he negotiated his way over rolling cobbles covered with last fall's dew-slickened oak leaves. He advanced steadily upward. Two steps forward gained one step higher in elevation. The steady cadence of his footsteps at that high altitude and that steep angle would have jellied the legs of a flatlander. But, to a mountain youth with calves of iron, it was merely a stroll through his back yard.

The faintest lightening of the eastern sky from bear-cave black to charcoal gray hinted of approaching dawn. Still a half mile from his destination, J.C. picked up the pace. That mistake cost him dearly! Catching the toe of his boot against the unyielding edge of a leaf-buried boulder, he stumbled hard, pitching down!

Rolling and skidding along the steep slope for some twenty feet, he scrambled and clawed to regain his footing to no avail. His left arm shot out, flailing only dead air, until it snagged the rasping bark of a dogwood trunk, miraculously braking his haphazard slide before bone-breaking momentum could get started.

Hugging the dogwood trunk, he hoisted himself to a sitting position. From a lump in the leaves beneath his rear, he extracted his shotgun and cradled it in the crook of his right arm. Propping his left shoulder against the tree, he realized how quickly and closely disaster could come through carelessness.

"Here I am," he thought as he checked things over for damage control. "No one on earth has the slightest idea of where I am or what I am about. Just think what a mess I would be in if my leg had been broken—or worse!"

J.C.'s finger felt a raw gash in his shin, then fingered its twin in the stock of his gun. He reasoned that he must be all right, since the scratch in the finish of the Remington hurt worse than the one in his leg. The wound in his leg would heal with time, but the scar in the wood would remain forever, as a constant reminder of his foolishness.

Lord only knew where the flashlight had gone. It had flipped away, sailing end over end in a strobing arc. Crashing against granite, it had broken and died.

So J.C. sat there in the darkness, nursing his bruises and berating himself for not doing the proper things taught him by his father—things that meant safety, security, indeed life, in the highlands. He promised himself never again to come into the woods alone without first telling someone where he would be and when to expect his return.

Full daylight approached as the sun tried to peek between cracks in the hills. A few yards below, brown thrashers churred "Good morning" to one another and rustled rhododendron branches as they left their nests to scratch beneath the forest litter for breakfast. A male cardinal lit among the dogwood blooms above J.C. and sang his territorial song. J.C. lingered a few minutes more, watching until the color of the bird began to change from rusty brown to brilliant red in the growing light. Holding onto the tree trunk, the hunter pulled himself shakily erect. He began the final leg of his journey, sending the startled cardinal on its way in a flutter of wings and indignant chirps.

J.C. reached the flat near the top of the knob after a slow, deliberate hike. Stopping every hundred yards or so, he listened for the gobble of an awakening tom or the cluck of a sleepy hen. No turkey sounds came from the surrounding forest. As he approached the hardwood flat that was his intended destination, he knew in his heart that it was too late to catch a gobbler sitting in his roost.

The youthful hunter had found the hardwood flat near the end of turkey season the year before and had explored it thoroughly until he knew it like his own backyard. At one end, the flat adjoined a slope that ran the last hundred yards to the top of Suzy's Knob. From the knob's sidehill flowed a small spring. The water that bubbled from the tiny pocket trickled down along the seams where mountains collided. Growing as it flowed, it was supplemented by the waters of its sister springs until it became wide enough to be called Back Creek.

At the end opposite the spring, the flat sheared away abruptly. From this cliff could be seen a postcard view of the watery mirror that is presently called Lake James. In former times, before construction of the dam, the eyes of a person standing at the edge of the cliff would have been treated to a grand view of the untamed Linville River. It was a scene of such beauty that human eyes could feast upon it for a lifetime, savoring it anew in the light of each day's dawn. Any heart would have been glad to call this place home. This was the first clue that explained to J.C.'s logical mind the flat's past history of human habitation. Rubbled piles of cabin cornerstones and rotted remnants of log walls also gave credence to the legends of Suzy's Knob.

J.C. had heard the stories of days, long ago, when a woman named Suzy had lived a secluded life on the face of the knob. She had lived in a cabin, somewhere near the top, subsisting on the bounty of the forest and a small terraced garden which she nursed to life across a broad flat. She had supposedly captured wild turkeys and made them tame—or was it tame turkeys that she had raised and released them into the wild?

Subconsciously shaking his head, J.C. rejected the latter idea. Well-intentioned individuals who released domesticated stock into the highlands had created havoc with the wild flocks. Domestic birds, having an immunity to many avian diseases, had acted as carriers and transmitted infections that destroyed wild turkey populations.

In certain cases the N. C. Wildlife Commission itself had initiated cycles of disease in their efforts to restock areas of declining turkey numbers. Several of the hundred-acre forest openings that the Commission had cleared and planted with clover and orchard grass to assist the giant birds' reintroduction, had been fertilized with turkey manure from large-scale poultry operations. The effect had been as devastating as the haphazard release of domestic birds. Contact with the contaminated turkey litter had transmitted contagion, killing off fledgling flocks in restocked areas until some wise country boy pointed out the Commission's mistake.

Wildlife managers were quick to correct their error and intensified their efforts. They succeeded creating, in many places, the biologically perfect mix of one-third open area, one-third mature hardwood timber, and one-third regenerating new-growth forest that turkeys needed to reinhabit their former range.

The planted openings gave newly hatched poults massive areas on which to gorge themselves with grasshoppers in spring. New-growth forests gave hens protected nesting habitat and the understory plants and shrubs that provided escape cover for young turkeys. Coves of hardwood trees provided the precious mast of acorns and nuts that sustained turkey populations through the dormant winter.

J.C. studied the site where the cabin once stood. Off to one side, he noticed the stump of a hardwood tree—the remnant of a huge chestnut. From it sprouted feeble saplings that stretched tenaciously upward, attempting to reach the sunlight through the overhanging forest canopy. Riddled with the yellow-brown cankers and orange curling spore masses of chestnut blight, the straining sprouts would probably never mature enough to drop prickly hulled burs of sweet nuts to the ground for a turkey's dinner.

J.C. moved close to the suffering tree. He packed a handful of red earth against one of the bright sores. Mountain lore held that soil microbes would act to kill the fungus. He was determined to help the tree if he could.

The pieces of the puzzle of departed human presence fit together at this tranquil place near the top of the knob. The chestnut blight had been accidentally imported to the United States with infested ornamental chestnut varieties introduced from the Orient around 1900. The disease had decimated native trees by the forestful. Prior to the introduction of blight, one in four trees throughout the Appalachians had been an American Chestnut. Ripe chestnuts were eaten ravenously by man, beast, and bird.

In times before the blight, chestnuts were the staple food that kept folks alive during the ice-covered famine of mountain winters. When the chestnut trees withered and died, so did a way of life. Food, fuel, shelter, fences, furniture, tools, musical instruments, houses, and scores of other items were once made from chestnut wood. It was called the perfect tree. It must have been so, for, even in their death throes, the fallen forest giants had given the mountain dwellers a gift of unsurpassed beauty. Although impervious to rot, the dense wood was vulnerable to tiny borers that cut coils and curlicues under the cover of its bark. The legacy of "wormy chestnut" was left to mountain craftsmen in the hulks of skeleton trees. It was used by them to make some of the finest hand-crafted furniture the world will ever see.

The glory of the chestnut was now past history. Mourning its loss, highland dwellers migrated to lower elevations where food could be cultivated in valleys along fertile flood plains. That was the reason the cabin had been abandoned. Life that depended on chestnuts had withered and died with the trees. Squirrel, bear, grouse, deer, and turkey numbers had all declined; turkeys precipitously so. The remaining few gobblers had been shot on sight by hungry homesteaders, regardless of the season. Turkeys were food and food was needed—even more so, with the chestnut gone.

Passenger pigeons that flew in unimaginably enormous flocks that blocked out the sun for days at a time had disappeared forever from the face of the earth. The last one known, a lonely bird named Martha, died a captive in a zoo in 1914. Some say unregulated overhunting exterminated the vast flocks. J.C. suspected that their loss was inextricably linked to the loss of their primary food source with the chestnut's demise. His country-boy intuition also told him that man's importation of European racing pigeons to the United States had introduced new diseases to which the native passenger pigeon had no immunity, in the same manner that the release of domesticated turkeys had transmitted death among their wild kin.

Hunters and homesteaders alarmed at the diminishing wildlife population joined with government officials to stop the decline. Through their shared efforts, hard work, and plain good luck, the science of wildlife management evolved. The mountain wildlife was slowly nurtured to recovery through wise and careful stewardship. Seasons and bag limits were set. Animals were shuffled about and restocked into burgeoning new forests of hickory and oak that filled the voids left in the wake of the chestnut's passing. Turkeys were captured in gigantic nets propelled by cannon and transplanted across county lines, even into habitats where there had been none before.

Fortunately for the Carswells, restocking had never been necessary on the back side of Table Rock. There had always been a few turkeys up high. Scratching out an existence in spite of the loss of the chestnut, a small flock survived, protected by the remote seclusion of Suzy's Knob.

A ruffed grouse drummed his territorial proclamation directly behind J.C. The sudden explosion of sound startled him and made him jump. The descending sensation of whuffs imitated a soft tennis ball bouncing rhythmically, lower, ever lower, upon the head of a drum. More a disturbance of airwaves than actual sound, the vibrating pulse of wings against feathered breast set up a sympathetic resonance deep within J.C.'s chest. His entire body absorbed the sound, magnifying it to a much greater volume than that which was audible to his ears alone.

J.C. glanced at his wrist watch. It was nearly eight o'clock. He had yet to hear a turkey's gobble. He knew there was a big bird somewhere nearby. There had to be. The location of the spring was the key. He had learned as a boy on his very first hunt, sitting between his father's knees, that turkeys always roost over or near water. Perhaps it was because of the ease of quenching their morning thirst, or for security, or for some other reason that only turkeys know. Perhaps gobblers merely enjoyed listening to the sound of a brook's musical trickling, reassuring them as they slept through the dark hours of night.

Well, here was certainly water and the illusion of safety. Here also was where J.C. had found, in the rain-washed leaves near the spring the Saturday before, the water-swollen, disintegrating, fish-hook-shaped black droppings with cigar-ash tips that told him a mature tom turkey in his sexual prime had staked out his claim. He had also found round, greenish-black dollops of cloacal discharge that told him hens were laying their clutches and setting on nests hidden in the tangled brush close by. Toenail scratchings in the leaves of the flat and on the hillside below gave evidence that turkeys had been feeding, attempting to find tidbits of squirrel-buried acorns left over from the previous autumn.

Reaching into his pocket, J.C. took out the rolled up handkerchief that protected the turkey call. It was time to get on with his work. Fitting the hollow bone mouthpiece into its receiving socket of corncob pith, he paused for a second, looking curiously at one of the chestnut sprouts. Cocking his head inquisitively to one side, he examined the fresh bud scar left where he had inadvertently brushed a newly-formed leaf from a twig while packing the soil poultice against the sore of blight. Holding the yelper beside the twig, like a detective checking fingerprints, he compared a three-quarters-of-a-century-old vascular bundle scar on the barrel of the call against the fresh scar on the side of the living tree. The leaf scars were a perfect match!

The secret of the call was revealed to J.C. The key to its magic was contained in the resonance of chestnut wood. Pleased with himself at having unlocked the turkey call's mystique, he grinned broadly until most of his teeth showed, then licked his lips like a trumpet player warming up for a concert. Pursing his mouth, he sucked gently at the mouthpiece in the fashion of blowing a tiny bugle in reverse.

"Yowp-yowp! Elk-yelk, yelk!" the caller haltingly cleared its throat. Its voice grated and echoed across the vast horseshoe depression of wooded cove that stretched below the cliff.

J.C. winced at the faltering sounds of his first attempt. As the call's imperfect echoes were muffled to silence among the tree tops, he shrugged the false notes off as merely a warm up, hoping in his heart that a lovesick gobbler who had not yet tuned in to their exact source would interpret the series of yelps as the sleepy conversation of a bleary-eyed hen, worn out from sitting on a clutch of eggs all night.

He promised himself that his next attempt would be better. Slipping to the very knife-edge of the cliff where it sliced down abruptly into the head of the cove, he waited for a reply.

He heard nothing. For long minutes he stood, stone-statue still. Listening intently for a response, the hunter absorbed the awesome splendor of the view.

A stratified haze had settled onto the cove, topping out at an elevation a hundred yards below J.C.'s feet. The haze covered all vegetation and rocky features, veiling them to various opacities with descending shades of white, then gray, then violet blue— the blue of the mists that give the mountains of the Blue Ridge their name. The stately peaks that surrounded the cove, rising majestically above the layers of fog, were quilted with a mosaic of flame-red azaleas, brilliant pink rhododendrons, and wine-veined pastel laurel blossoms. These bright splashes of color were tied together in harmonious uniformity by acres upon acres of snowy dogwood blooms that settled upon the mountains' shoulders like a delicately knitted lace shawl.

View from the top of Suzy's Knob.

J.C. stood for a long time, listening for an answer to his call, drinking his fill of the view. Breathing deeply, he inhaled the scent of dwarf purple iris clustered around his feet—or was it a faint vestige of perfume that clung to the turkey call, aromatically oiled onto the chestnut tube from its protective box in the buffet drawer?

Jolted by the scent of perfume from his daydreaming enjoyment of the colors of the mountain spring, he checked his watch to mark the passing of time. Time can stand still and lose all meaning when a man blends his soul with that of a mountain. But, to a turkey hunter, the passage of time is the essence of his success.

"Five minutes and no answer. Nothing!" he hissed to himself. "Time to call again. This time I've gotta do better."

Imagining back to hunts past, when his father had shown him how to imitate his mastery of the notes contained in the wing-bone call, J.C. closed his eyes. Tilting his head back, he cupped his fingers around the yelper's open end to form a living megaphone. Gently, his lips kissed its tip once more. The nasal pitch of each two-toned yelp was batted back and forth between the peaks towering above the fog-shrouded cove.

"Yelp, yelp, yelp, yelp, yelp?" questioned the call in perfect cadence. "Where are you, my love?" she asked.

Response was immediate! The hollow, haunting sound of an answering gobble ghosted up through the translucent mist. The tips of J.C.'s ears perked up against the edge of his hunting cap, nearly raising it from his head as they radar-fixed the direction from which the tom's reply had come.

Needles of adrenaline shot through J.C.'s chest, spurring his pulse to racing speed. The breath he was taking caught halfway as his throat tightened with unconscious effort, attempting to block the noise of respiration from his ears. His entire being became totally involved in the predator's primeval reaction to the closeness of game!

Far below, in the jagged crease scoured through the middle of the valley floor by the timeless flow of Back Creek, the tom gobbled again, then once more, making certain that the hen on the flat above knew his exact location. The booming of his voice bragged to all creatures that he was "Boss Gobbler," unchallenged monarch of Suzy's Knob. The regal bird had left his roost above the spring at dawn's first wink. Flying down to his favorite strutting area along the hardwood floodplain, he had scratched half-heartedly through last fall's leaves and waited impatiently for the call of a lonely hen telling him she was ready.

J.C. fought to control the red-alert condition of his hunter-verses-prey mechanism. Bridling instinctive emotion with controlled thought, he tried to think of a plan for action. The quarry had been "started." The chess game had begun. The next move belonged to the hunter.

Scanning the terrain between himself and the tom, J.C.'s eyes fed raw data to his mental computer. Echoes of John Carswell's voice whispered in the ears of his son.

"The only mating call of the wild turkey is the gobble of the tom. Under normal conditions the hen comes to the tom's call to be serviced each day while she lays in her clutch. You've gotta find a way to make him do the unnatural. You must make him come to the call of the hen."

J.C. looked down, studying the rocky fractures threading up to the cliff from the cove. He tried to imagine which trail a turkey tom would take to come to a female's call. His father's voice continued giving advice to the ears of his memory.

"A turkey will come to you uphill, but almost never down. He won't come at all if the climb is steep. If the angle seems too high for him to make the effort to come up to you, then you gotta go down to him.

A courting pair of turkeys ain't really much different from a human couple in one respect. Compromise is the name of the game! Keep coaxing while you move closer, but never move too fast. Sooner or later, if you're patient enough, and he is willing enough, he will come up to meet you. Tease him a little bit. You know how—just like that pretty girlfriend of yours does to you!"

Swiftly, J.C. laid out a plan of action. The tom would never come uphill to the roost he had left an hour before. He certainly would not walk the final hundred vertical yards back up Suzy's face to the flat on which J.C. now stood. Trotting down a mule-ploughed diversion terrace that had once prevented gravity-propelled water from eroding the homestead's garden, J.C. made his way to a point at which the flat angled less sharply away from the knob.

As he reached down the folded edge where horizontal plane met near-vertical, a thunderous gobble shot up at him, cutting through the haze at the bottom of the cove once more. Its volume made the hair on the nape of J.C.'s neck stand at attention. J.C. steeled his determination against his rising emotions and brought them under control. Opening the action of his semi-auto gun, he checked the chamber and made certain that it was unloaded.

"Never travel in the dark or negotiate dangerous terrain with a loaded gun," his father taught. "If the grade is too steep to stand flat-footed, or you think you might stumble and fall, unload your gun and you might live 'til you're old enough to teach your young-uns to hunt."

Having assured himself his gun was safe, J.C. began his descent. The chute between the edge of the knob and the side of the flat was much too steep to climb down. Sliding was easier—and faster. J.C. knew he had no time to waste. The gobbles blasting from the bottom of the cove might catch the attention of a real hen at any moment! If a real hen were to join the tom, he would never come to the hen in the wing-bone call secured on a string around J.C.'s neck.

Squatting on his haunches, the strong youth used his well-worn bootsoles as skis. Pebble ball bearings rolled under his feet and sleds of oak leaves slipped under the rudder of his hand as he slalomed down the chute at break-neck speed. He thumped against the bottom a hundred yards below in a few seconds. A mini-avalanche of stones and forest litter showered around his ankles as he stood to load his shotgun. From his pocket came three shells: 12 gauge, three-inch magnums loaded with copper-plated lead pellets—number sixes, fours, and twos. He loaded them to fire in that order. The smallest shot, the dense patterning number sixes, went into the chamber in anticipation of a forty-yard shot at the vulnerable target of a turkey's neck and head. Fours were next, for a desperate, follow-up shot at the flopping neck of a poorly hit bird that might bounce up, attempting escape. The shell containing the big number twos was last in the magazine. Tradition placed it there, supposedly to launch its bone and body-penetrating load at the hastily retreating tail fan of a missed "Houdini" gobbler before he vanished like a wraith into the laurel. In reality, though, all turkey hunters know that the last shell, and even the second, are loaded mostly for giving a boost to a hunter's psyche. A hunter seldom gets more than a single shot at a turkey. His calling must be flawless. The turkey must be lured in close to the waiting gun. The hunter must have nerves of steel. His aim must be true.

J.C. studied the more-level topography that spanned the remaining distance between gun and gobbler. Two camel's hump ridges separated him from the bird. Around and between the ridges ran the draw that ended at his feet. Surely, he reasoned, the turkey would walk along the open safety of the draw as he searched for the hen in the call.

Quickly selecting a huge poplar tree that was wider than his shoulders, the youth backed against it to break up the menacing outline of his human form. Removing the cap from his head, he sat on it to prevent the damp sponge humus of decomposed leaves from soaking his backside. Producing a bark-colored, camouflage headnet from his jacket pocket, he stretched it over his head. Matching gloves went over his hands. After adjusting the net's eye holes, he shouldered his gun, sighting along the barrel to make certain his vision would not be obstructed when—if—the opportunity to shoot presented itself. Finally, he kicked up a pile of dead leaves with his heels to cover his bootsoles. No sign of man was left to catch the microscopic scrutiny of a wary gobbler's vision except the lenses of the hunter's eyes. J.C. had become a piece of the mountainside puzzle, an integral part of the forest, another bunch of leaves windblown against a tree.

Sliding the yelper's mouthpiece under the light mesh of the headnet, he licked its hollow tip to moisten it. Updrawn knees hid the movement from the direction he guessed the gobbler would come.

Three long breaths calmed J.C.'s heart, slowing its hammering from hunter's excitement and from the exertion of rapid descent. He sucked the tiny bone tube with pursed lips. The squeeking vibrations were magnified through the chestnut cylinder into the questioning tones of a turkey hen's voice.

"Yelp, yelp, yelp?" asked the call. "Where are you, Your

73

Highness? I've come down the mountainside to join you."

Double gobbles exploded from the belly of the cove. Richocheting back and forth between the rock faces that lined the sides of the draw, their echoes pounded the web of J.C.'s headnet like solid punches.

"I am here! Come this way to me!" commanded the Master Of The Mountain.

From the volume of the sound, the hunter judged the distance to his intended prey at four hundred yards, give or take.

Pulse set again to racing speed by the demanding answer to his call, J.C. pressed the mouthpiece to his lips. However, the sound of John Carswell's voice stalled him, whispering into his mind's ear, "No! Wait! You don't want to call too much. He will think you're excited and are hurryin' to join him. Act aloof! Play hard to get. You gotta make him come to you."

J.C. followed the memory of his father's instruction. Ignoring the hammering of his heart, he slowly lowered the call. Sliding a glovecuff to reveal his watch, he checked the passage of time. It was eight twenty-two.

Once again, then again, the gobbler shook the newly-greening leaves with his booming voice. The hen in the call remained quiet and coy.

Holding his place, the dominant bird refused to venture from his strutting ground. Sooner or later, J.C. hoped he would break. Unmoving, he stared the frozen anticipation of the waiting hunter's hypnotic trance. He peered through the half-dollar-sized openings in the headnet until his eyes watered. Blinking hard to clear them he spied a flickering whiteness that matched the height of an excited gobbler's head.

The initial adrenalin rush of recognition was brief. No sooner did he imagine his first look at an approaching tom than he identified the movement as the bobbing flower cluster atop the plant known throughout the high country as turkey beard.

Relaxing a little, he let out the half-breath that had stuck in his airway at the false alarm. He watched the flowerhead as it nodded to the rhythm of a tiny breeze and smiled at its good omen.

Rare to the sight of human beings is the blossom of the turkey beard. It's numbers are few to begin with. Those that manage to grow to their full height of four feet are greedily nibbled by deer before they can spread their blooms. Normally, their flowers open in May, but the fact that they were maturing in April told J.C. that it had been a spring of exceptional warmth—warmth that would send turkey hens early to their nests.

John Carswell had repeated this secret rhyme to his son whenever they chanced upon the turkey beard's flower in the woods:

> *"When the bloom is on the turkey beard,*
> *and it juts up proud*
> *like the beard on a gobbler's breast*
> *that's when huntin' turkeys*
> *will be at its best."*

Turkey Beard. A Good Omen!

An explanation always followed the rhyme:

"It's always a good sign; one of the odds that tip the balance of success, ever so slightly, in the hunter's favor. Turkey season is timed to open in April when hens begin a-broodin' their clutches. One reason is that hens will set on their nests all day, thereby protectin' themselves from accidental shootin' by an overly excited hunter. The other reason for huntin' in spring is that the turkey gobbler has been callin' as many as six hens to him for mating each day. One mornin' he finds himself alone. After callin' his lady friends to his side for weeks, he gets no response. He shock-gobbles at owl hoots, car doors slammin', crows cawin', and anything else that sounds remotely turkey-like to him. He won't go to those sounds. But, in his urge to reproduce, he becomes less wary and can be coaxed to come to the call of the hen. If you're good and if you're lucky, that call will be made by you."

J.C.'s muscles began to stiffen from immobility. Patience worn, he checked his watch. Twenty minutes had passed.

The bird had not moved. His unanswered demands for companionship were broadcast confidently, methodically-spaced from the same location in the security of the cove.

"You've gotta outthink him, ya' know," came words from his father's imagined shadow at J.C.'s shoulder. "Sometimes you can gobble like a jake to make the old boy jealous. A jake will come more readily to a hen's call. Throwing caution to the wind, he tries to claim his first mate. A full-grown tom is different. He will wait a long time, secure in the cocky knowledge that the depth of his voice projected through his fiery wattles and the brilliance of his displayed plumage will eventually bring his mate to him. So you make the call of the jake, if you can master it. Competition will make an old gobbler madder'n a stuck wild hog. You'd better be ready when he comes streakin' in. He'll be spoilin' for a fight, wantin' to kick the daylights out of that little jake with his long fightin' spurs!"

"Kobba', kobba', kobba'!" The perfect imitation of the abbreviated gobble of a turkey jake issued from J.C.'s cracking adolescent voice.

"K-yelk, yelk, yelk, yelk," he greeted himself with the willing sound of the hen hidden inside the call.

As a finishing touch to his turkey conversation, J.C. mimicked the sound of a contented hen's purr, trilling his tongue against the roof of his mouth.

That did it! The big tom cut loose a broadside—a triple gobble that blasted up the draw through trees in the cove. He told the hen that he was coming. The violence in his voice signalled to the interloper, "Back off—or be prepared to fight me for the prize!"

The steadily increasing volume of the tom's repeated challenge let J.C. know he was advancing. As the fired-up turkey cleared the sound-obscuring boulders of the first hump ridge, his thundering gobbles were magnified two-fold.

J.C. shivered from excitement and from the cold dampness of dew-soaked pants stuck wetly against his unmoving knees. The angry bird demanded an answer, but the hen in the call remained silent, letting the gobbler's jealous ego propel him into range of the waiting gun.

Suddenly, another sound projected across the draw from the opposite side of the mountain cove. It stopped the gobbler instantly, striking him still in his tracks. It stopped J.C.'s heartbeat as well.

The sound was that of a jilted hen's cackle, indignantly protesting the very idea of her lover's moving away from her to join another female.

"Stay," her cackling pleaded. "Please, do not move away from me."

She gave two excited cuts and a low purr that told the tom she was the better choice; he would not have to compromise his dignity by fighting a mere jake for her affections.

Torn between the choice of two hens, the confused gobbler went totally silent. Two hundred yards away, a frustrated J.C. mulled over his next move.

The real hen became more vocal, clucking and cutting frequently as she advanced toward the Master Of The Mountain.

"She's not playing hard to get," thought the disgusted youth. "That blasted hen will walk all the way to my gobbler. Then, off they'll go together. This hunt is done!"

But the hen in the call beseeched him to try once more. He gave three long yelps, followed two minutes later by five more. Trying his best to outdo the real turkey hen, he attempted to inflect his calling with seductiveness and jealousy.

Still, the gobbler remained silent.

J.C. looked at his watch. The minute hand ticked off eight fifty-five. The passing of time perplexed the teen-aged hunter to the point of nearly giving up and heading for home. But the thought flashed in his mind that he had no home to go to. He couldn't go back until at least four o'clock—the time the school bus normally pulled into his driveway in that world far below.

After holding the old gobbler's attention for nearly an hour, J.C. had seemingly run out of tricks. Racking his brain, he tried to remember some detail of turkey hunting lore that would jumpstart the tom into gobbling again so he could pinpoint the bird's whereabouts.

On the opposite side of the gobbler, the real hen continued to call. She slowly drew closer to the longbeard. Soon there would be no more competition for her from the false hen sulking inside the bone-and-chestnut call.

J.C.'s thought processes keyed on the realization that the real hen was moving. One last bit of advice was passed by a master turkey hunter to his son, brought to consciousness from subliminal suggestion.

"Son, when all else fails and an old gobbler won't come to your callin', gain some ground on him. Go to him like a real hen does. Be real quiet—cat quiet—so's you don't spook him. A big gobbler's not much different from a man in this respect, for sure! If the female will go to him, sooner or later, he'll come to meet her halfway. It might be half of a mile, or half of four hundred, or two hundred, or even less than one hundred yards. But, if you're sneaky enough and your callin' is up to snuff, he will come the last half the distance if you'll go the first!"

A lump of leaves rose from a poplar backrest and materialized into human form. Slowly, stealthily, J.C. crept down the sloping draw. Keeping to brushy cover as much as possible, he inched toward the direction from which the last gobble had come. Just one ridge stood between him and the turkey. The gobbler's razor keen vision could easily spot his silhouette if caught in motion. Camouflaged clothes had hidden the hunter as he sat frozen to the tree trunk, but would not disguise the alarming threat of movement if he ventured inside the circle of the tom's defensive vision.

Crawling in snail-like fashion, the mountain youth gained a hundred yards. Scanning the shadows in the woods ahead took its toll on the youth's nerves as he slipped quietly from tree to tree. Sunlight dappled through the canopy of spring leaves onto white-lobed crosses of dogwood blossoms. It made a jigsaw puzzle of the forest, playing tricks of illusion on his eyes. Every clump of dead leaves, every knee-high weathered granite boulder, every rotted stump, became the apparition of a huge gobbler.

Every nerve in his body was tense as J.C. neared the last turn in the draw that hid hunter and prey, one from the other. Afraid to go further at risk of spooking the bird, the hunter paused and stood behind a clump of laurel. The rawness of his alert senses made him jump when he heard the real hen's excited cackle. It was so much closer and louder now than it had been minutes before. Somewhere, he knew, between that hen and where he was standing was a boss gobbler. Somehow, he had to persuade that gobbler to tear himself away from the real hen and come within range.

Crawling on hands and knees into the edge of the laurel tangle, J.C. found a place he could sit with his head barely clearing the lowest leaves. A huge deadfall log hid his lower body. A slope of sixty degrees tilted below and away.

Adjusting his headnet for best vision through the forest of inch-thick laurel stems, he leaned back against a tree. The sound of his collar scraping against the dry curled bark of a Table Mountain Pine was magnified by its closeness to his ears. He flinched at the loudness of its rasping as sticky chips of pine bark trickled inside his shirt and down his spine.

"Now I've done it!" His intuition despaired. "If that old longbeard was anywhere close by, he certainly heard that and ran away—clear off this mountain and into the next county!"

Sitting in the shadows, gun across his knees, J.C. contemplated his next move.

"I wonder if he's joined the other hen," he thought, "or if perhaps he's given up the contest and gone somewhere else."

The real hen sent a series of four plaintive yelps across the cove. She hadn't seemed to move any closer to the gobbler since J.C. had started his stalk.

"Maybe she's hung up on the other side of the creek and won't wade across or maybe she doesn't want to come through a rhododendron hell," he reasoned. The real hen was competing against the hen in the wing-bone caller. Coming no closer, she was trying to lure the wary tom to her, rather than moving closer to join him.

A gentle breeze whispered through the treetops above, causing a large, hollow limb to rub against a hickory trunk. The rhythmic friction of wood rubbing wood sounded strangely out of place in the quietness of the cove. The breeze hushed. The drumming vibrations continued.

J.C.'s face grew owl's eyes! Reflecting glassy amazement through the eyeholes of his headnet, he reinterpreted the sound waves stroking his ears. He had never heard it before, but his father had described it to him many times. The sound was being produced in the throat and chest of a mature turkey gobbler, proudly strutting his stuff. The pulmonic puff of his deep-chested drumming was hollow and eerie. It permeated all voids in the woods. The tom whisked open his wing tips with a rushing, rasping noise, then dragged them, crackling, along the tops of last year's leaves.

This old longbeard was one cunning bird. Patiently, he had waited for one, then both, hens to come to him. Wisely, he had chosen a safe area to show off his plumage, strutting a tight figure eight pattern in the relative safety of the open woods at the center of the cove.

The sound of his drumming did not carry far, at least not to human ears. J.C. now realized that the tom had not gone silent, after all. He had merely done what any proud male would do with two females vying for his attention; he was showing off, preening himself for their review.

Although the gobbler was close, yards away, J.C. could not see him through the dense screen of rosebay laurel. He dared not move to gain a better view. The gobbler's fate was entirely up to the Jezebel hen in the wing-bone call. Perhaps he would come the last few yards. Perhaps he would come halfway to meet her! J.C. carefully slid his glove cuff to check his watch. It was nine thirty-two.

Slipping the wing-bone tip under the mesh fabric that shielded his face from the gobbler's view, he touched it to his lips. Eyes riveted to the sole patch of lighted forest visible through the jungle of rosebay stems, he tried to control the shaking of his hands, the surging of his pulse, the shallow panting of his breath.

Gently, he kissed the hollow bone tip, creating a sound akin to three chirps of a contented pine warbler. "Hello my lover. I am here."

Pulling the call from his lips, J.C. tried to create the purr of a contented hen by rolling his tongue against the roof of his mouth, but the sound wouldn't come. A surge of adrenaline had dried the last drop of saliva from his mouth. His tongue stuck fast against his palate.

Long minutes passed. The hunter waited. There was no sign of the gobbler. His drumming ceased. The other hen spoke no more.

The turkey call's work was done. She dangled mutely, like a pendulum, from the string around J.C.'s neck. Tightly gripped, resting on one knee, the Remington waited to do its job.

The nervous hunter dared not fidget. He scarcely dared to blink his dried, straining eyes. Taking a full breath was a luxury he could not afford lest the movement of his ribcage crinkling the folds of his jacket be identified by the gobbler's telescopic vision. All the woods were under the searching longbeard's scrutiny now, especially the patch of laurel that hid the paralyzed J.C.

A shadow of movement caught the corner of the hunter's eye. Materializing through the maze of branches, J.C. could make out the bobbing gait of a turkey's legs! Echoing three loud answering cutts, like the clucking of an overgrown cock pheasant, the gobbler ghosted in, then out, of view. An intervening dogwood trunk momentarily obscured the tom's head, blocking from his sight the sudden movement of J.C. shouldering his gun. In all his avian grandeur, the regal bird came out from behind the tree in full strut. His head was heated blue-white. Billows of scarlet wattles cascaded down his neck to touch the feathers of his coppery breast. Fan fully spread, brown-barred wingtips furrowing the ground, the gobbler displayed his finery to the false hen hiding inside the thicket.

J.C. acted purely on instinct. He clicked the safety off. Training his gun barrel on the center of the gobbler's neck, he gauged its silver bead sight to be smaller than the gobbler's head. His finger tightened on the trigger. The longbeard was in range!

The gobbler stood erect from his display, held his head high and stopped dead still. A monstrous brush of a beard thrust parallel to the ground from the center of his proud chest. His horn-tipped beak cracked open to proclaim his worthiness to the hen, his lordship of the knob, his mastery of the mountain cove, his dominance of spring.

The thunder of his last gobble was never heard. Instead, the mountains echoed the report of J.C.'s gun!

Faster than a springing panther, the hunter burst from the thicket. In a shower of sticks and leaves, he clawed his way toward the bird. John Carswell had taught his son well.

"Run up to the bird and grab his legs or stand on his neck before he can get up! He might only be stunned!" These were the remembered words that launched J.C. from the thicket.

Thirty yards passed in a blur. But the hunter slowed as he approached the prostrate gobbler. This was one turkey tom that was not going to get up.

The hunter stood, admiring his kill. As the echoes of his shot were dampened to muteness throughout the distant hills, the outspread fan of the gobbler's tail nervously shuddered, then closed.

All the colors of Suzy's Knob were embodied in the giant bird. In the splendor of his tail feathers were all the shades of brown that could be stolen from the carpet of fallen leaves on which he lay. Bands of chestnut rainbowed across his fan. The red of flame azaleas, the scarlet of fall-ripened dogwood berries, the blue-violet of mountain astors and dwarf iris, and the snowy-white of dogwood blossoms were dyed into the folds of skin that graced his royal head. The dusky darkness of his thick body mimicked the solidness of a weathered granite boulder.

A Gobbler that answered the author's voice near Table Rock.

J.C. tenderly rolled the dead turkey onto its back. The sun was reflected in dazzling iridescence from the feathers of the bird's breast. Their jewelled shine hinted the shimmering glow of Back Creek, when it mirrors the colors of laurel blooms in the rippling concentric circles of light created by the feeding rise of a rainbow trout. The sleek surfaces of tan, gray, and russet feather tips were burnished the metallic brilliance of gold, polished silver, and newly smelted copper—like a boulder-strewn slope set afire beneath an April day's dawn.

Set in the middle of the thick shield of breast feathers sprouted the black, elongated bristles that created the gobbler's beard. J.C. stroked and smoothed the coarse hair-like projection, measuring it against the span of his hand. The beard was longer by a solid inch than the nine inches of spread between the tips of his pinky and thumb. The main beard was thick as two fingers. A superfluous strand of feathery hairs the diameter of a knitting needle grew below, creating what is called, in the jargon of those who pursue the wild turkey, a rare double beard.

So completely spellbound was he in his admiration of the fallen gobbler, J.C. was taken completely offguard by a shadow creeping silently over the bird. Blocking out the sunlight, its shade erased the shine from the gobbler's feathers. Their borrowed colors returned to camouflaged blandness, taken back by the leaves of the forest floor.

A startled gasp escaped J.C. as he turned to stare at a pair of hunter's boots standing at eye level on the sloping ground. The outline of a fellow hunter, mere feet away, eclipsed the sky. A gloved hand reached up. It visored away a camouflaged net that hid the hunter's face. J.C. had already recognized the boots that his family had pooled their savings together to buy as a gift, Christmas last. The booted feet and hulking shape towering above belonged to his brother, Alb!

J.C.'s first instinct was to run away, but he wasn't about to leave his trophy. Besides, there was no clear avenue of escape.

He slowly stood and faced Alb, brother to brother, man to man. Caught in the act of laying out of school, the youth knew that the Devil would exact his toll. Payment would be demanded in full!

Alb finished removing the net from his head. Reaching into his mouth with two fingers, he deftly extracted the twin rubber membranes and stitched leather of a double-reed diaphragm call. From a string around his neck, dangled a yelper made from the humerus, radius, and ulna of a turkey gobbler's wing. The bones were cemented together like a telescope with bulbous knuckles of car muffler patching putty. The "real" hen competing for the affection of J.C.'s gobbler had been Alb, all along.

Fidgeting nervously, J.C. waited for Alb to speak. Instead of the expected frowning scowl, his older brother's face cut an ear-to-ear grin.

"Way to go, Li'l Jake!" he bellowed. "That is undoubtedly the very finest turkey gobbler I have ever seen!"

Alb laid his gun on the ground. Reaching out, he clenched J.C.'s right hand in his own and pumped it hard in congratulations. After wildly thumping his younger brother's back in the fashion of testing a mellon for ripeness, he knelt beside the bird for a closer examination.

"Wow! A double beard! A ten-incher, too! And just look at these spurs!"

A ten inch beard

Excitedly, Alb thumbed the black-tipped needle points of inch-long fighting spurs, nearly drawing his own blood in the process. In a single motion he swept the huge gobbler up by the ankles and stood erect once more. Weighing the bird in the scale of his hand, he proclaimed it to be, "Twenty pounds, maybe more!" and presented it to his younger brother.

J.C. relaxed a little, slightly relieved of his anxiety by Alb's bubbling attitude. He smiled at Alb and hefted the trophy's weight himself, raising it up and down.

"Yep, I reckon he'll go about twenty!" J.C. agreed.

Alb smiled back, then his eyes fixed on the wing-bone-and-chestnut-twig call swinging from the string around J.C.'s collar.

"If Dad catches you with his old call, he'll . . . " pausing, stone-faced, he tried to think of appropriate punishment. Shuddering, he continued, ". . . let's not even think about it! Maybe we can slip it back into the drawer without him findin' out!"

J.C. was shocked when Alb said, "We."

"You mean, you'll help me get it back in the house?"

"Of course, I will. As a matter of fact, I'm somethin' of an expert at it. How do you think I've killed my turkeys? I've used that call for years. What did you think I was a-lookin' for when you stopped me beside the buffet last night?"

"You mean, you knew I took the call and you didn't tell?" asked the surprised youth.

"Of course not! Dad would've wanted to know what the heck I was a-rummagin' around in that drawer for and let me know I wasn't too big to whup! I had planned all along to come up to the knob today. I knew—and you did, too—that Mom would make me stay last night. I wasn't certain you was comin' up here until I saw your tracks in the roadruts in front of my headlights this mornin'!"

"So! You knew that I was calling this gobbler and tried to lure him away from me, didn't you?" J.C. asked, anger rising in his voice.

"No sir! Not at all! I thought you was a real hen."

Smoothing the tarnished bronze feathers of the gobbler in J.C.'s hands, Alb lifted his index finger and clicked his nail against the call's wooden barrel.

"If I hadda known you weren't a real hen, I would have let you work this boss-gobbler by yourself. The way it was, I did everything I could to talk him into coming to me, but you got him, fair and square. Besides, I know that nobody alive can compete with the hen bottled up inside Dad's call. Dad taught me how to hunt, same as you. But I didn't get that turkey. You did! I tell you right now, the secret is locked forever in that call."

The satisfied smile of success returned to J.C.'s face.

Alb helped him hang the tom by the neck from the fork of a dogwood limb. He drew the entrails from the bird's body cavity to hasten its cooling during what promised to be a seventy-two degree day. He stripped a bunch of leaves from the end of a twig and dried the blood from his hands. Before he cast them away, he studied them for a moment. A disturbed look crept over his face.

"Look at this, Li'l Jake. It appears to be dogwood blight!" He presented the handful of leaves for his brother's inspection.

In biology class, J.C. had learned to identify the purple-bordered leaf spots and scorched tan blotches of Anthracnose infection. He studied the crumpled leaves in Alb's palm, then examined the rest of the tree. Finding discolored leaves and the orange fungal Discula spores on the dogwood's cankered twigs. J.C. confirmed Alb's diagnosis.

Together they wondered if the frequent rains of this year's spring would increase the rate of defoliating devastation by this, the most recently introduced blight upon the knob. They tried to imagine what the mountains would look like without the lace covering of North Carolina's state flower during the awakening days of spring. They guessed at which species of animals might decline or vanish altogether with the loss of its nutrient-rich berries. Would it be the flying squirrels, or the red, or the gray? Perhaps it would be the innumerable song birds or the chipmunks.

Turkeys would certainly be hungrier in the Autumn with the loss of dogwood seeds. Ruffed grouse, they decided, would be hardest hit, and might disappear from the knob altogether without dogwood seeds to reward their scratching through the drifted snows of winter. Certainly all life would be poorer in the highlands if the day the dogwoods quit blooming should ever come to pass.

Alb set about contriving a plan for getting J.C. safely home without their parents discovering he had skipped school. "Check your watch, Li'l Jake. Let's see how much time we have."

"It's only ten-fifteen," replied his younger brother.

"That gives us plenty of time," said the scheming Alb.

"It sure gives you plenty of time to learn to quit callin' me 'Li'l Jake,' or else there might be a blight of my fist on the end of your nose!" J.C. chuckled uneasily at the half-threat he knew he couldn't carry out against the older, stronger Alb.

Alb stared at him for a long minute, squinting one eye closed. Eventually, a smile crept across his lips. He nodded his head in agreement. "From now on, li'l brother, your name is J.C. Judging from the size of that turkey bird hangin' in yonder dogwood tree, I'll have to admit that the name 'Li'l Jake' just doesn't seem to drape across your shoulders, any more."

The two brothers spent their remaining hours on the knob searching for turkey sign, enjoying the beauty of the mountain spring, and sharing with each other their secret thoughts and life-long goals.

Pausing in their wanderings, the young men dipped their hands into the crystal clear waters of Back Creek. Cupping them to their mouths in unison, they quenched their thirst.

Wiping his face on the back of his sleeve, Alb allowed as how being a mechanic was thirsty work, too, and that he longed to run a garage of his own one day.

J.C. thought long and hard. Standing away from the creek bank, he wiped his hands on his hip pockets, then stared admiringly up at Suzy's Knob.

"Alb, I want to be a biologist or botanist, or something in a related field. I want to go to a college or university so I can learn how to help perpetuate the forests that cover these hills and all the wild things that live within them. I'd like to be the one who brings back the chestnut or saves the dogwood before it disappears from these mountains. Maybe I'll be the one to unlock some mystery of nature that will expand the wild turkey's range beyond what anyone else even dreams of . . ."

A ruffed grouse broadcast the descending tympany of his territorial drumming from a rhododendrun thicket across the creek. A mourning dove in the trees above was startled into giving its soulful cooing in response.

". . . who knows," J.C. continued, shifting his gaze to the dove, "maybe there's even a pair of passenger pigeons left up there, hidden in some secret place, near the top of Suzy's Knob."

☀ ☀ ☀

At four o'clock precisely, Alb burst through the front door. Clenched tightly in his fist was the neck of a huge turkey gobbler. Loudly, he claimed to his mother that the bird had been brought to bag by his own cunning and skill.

The details of the hunt were told to her with Alb's characteristic bravado and high-volume exaggerations. Her attention was focused entirely on him. Meanwhile, the lanky form of a teenaged turkey hunter slipped through the back door. Stealing its way upstairs, it traded fully camouflaged clothing for dress-shirt and jeans, boots for loafers, and shotgun for school books.

After completing the transformation from J.C. Carswell—Master Turkey Hunter to J.C. Carswell—Scholar, the student half of his personna crept back down the stairs, skipping the steps that creaked the loudest. Sneaking out the back door and around to the front of the house, he peeked through a window opened onto the porch at the gesturing silhouettes of Alb and his attentive mother.

Judging her to be sufficiently absorbed by Alb's boasting and by the sight of the magnificent turkey being shaken by the neck in front of her face, J.C. stomped hard on the weathered planks to simulate his scheduled arrival from school. Grabbing the door handle, he shouted, "Mom, I'm home!"

"Goodness gracious, Jake! I didn't even hear the bus when it turned around in the driveway. Come on in to the kitchen and see what your big brother has brought us for dinner, come Easter Weekend!"

J.C. put on his best drama-class face and tried to act both congratulatory and envious in his admiration of Alb's success. His acting worked well enough on Myra. In her mother's adoring eyes, her sons could do no wrong.

The situation was different with John Carswell. It was infinitely more difficult for his boys to spin a false turkey hunting yarn and fool him into believing it. After all, "It takes one to know one," as the old saying goes.

All evening long, Alb told and retold his story of taking the huge gobbler, leaving out no detail. With each retelling, however. the details were ever-so-slightly changed. This was no particular give away, in and of itself. Still, somehow, the description of the actual killing shot did not seem to be remembered and colored by the same gross exaggerations as the calling, the waiting, or the stalk—or, in fact, the entire preceding story of the hunt.

There also seemed to be something different about Jake. The younger boy's attitude toward his older brother had changed. Rather than pouting in envy at Alb's success as he had done in the past, he seemed to share in his good fortune and be genuinely happy at his good luck.

The family sat down to dinner and held hands. Myra said a long grace, with honorable mention of the providence of the turkey gobbler in time for Easter dinner. J.C. uttered the loudest "Amen."

The meal proceeded amicably, without a repetition of the brothers' aggravated bickering of the previous evening. The famished boys ate like they hadn't even smelled food for a week. Climbing mountains in search of an elusive gobbler burns many calories.

"It's small wonder you boys are so hungry." Myra observed. "Jake, you forgot the biscuits I fixed for you. They were still a-sittin' on the counter this mornin'."

Alb spoke through a mouthful of peas, "That right, J.C.? Mom made us biscuits and you forgot 'em? You sorry rascal!" Laughing, he spewed green particles and threw a thumb-sized wad of bread at his younger sibling.

Both boys giggled until their stern-faced father calmed them down. John Carswell had his boys' number now. The good-natured teasing and the mutally shared humor had been merely suspicious. But when Alb respectfully called his teen-aged brother "J.C.", instead of the derisive "Li'l Jake," he knew that they were partners together in some mischievious coverup.

Saying nothing while he cleaned his plate of food, John smiled false little smiles at each joke and innuendo his boys played on and off each other. Waiting patiently, he tried to free spool them enough line before reeling them in like wriggling, undersized trout. But it didn't work. They were joined too tightly together in their mutual pact to slip up and commit the "Big Mistake."

As his wife left the table with an arm load of dishes destined for the kitchen sink, John leaned back in his chair and attempted to set the hook.

"Please Alb, explain to me how you could drive into Morganton, open the service station, drop Jake off at school and still have enough time to climb up to Suzy's Knob and kill a turkey?"

The stunned Alb was struck to the barb. He stared back at his father with lying eyes, searching for a correct answer, squirming for the chance to escape his father's questioning.

"And you, Jake! Since when does a teen-aged young'un leave food—ham biscuits, no less—layin' around uneaten?"

91

The two culprits guiltily looked at each other, attempting communication without speech. Like two turkey poults lost in the woods, separated from their mother and not knowing what to do about it, they swiveled their heads to look at John's stern expression, then blinked back at each other.

"Well? I'm waitin'." John Carswell demanded an explanation.

"W-w-well . . . " Alb stuttered.

"You see, it was like this . . . " J. C. interrupted.

Like good little turkey poults, they acted simultaneously, using unified confusion as a defense.

Alb continued, " . . . when I got to the station, I recognized what a perfect hunting day it was—just like you taught me! I had to go up on the knob because the weather conditions were just right. I had to get up there and try for that big gobbler."

Flattery did nothing to change John's expression of disbelief.

" . . . I was too sleepy to remember to take our breakfast this morning." J. C. weakly finished his lame excuse.

Myra returned from the kitchen with servings of shortcake topped with mounds of fresh strawberries plucked from her terraced garden.

"What's all this talk about events that happened this mornin', John?" she asked pointedly. "That was this mornin' and this is now. Besides, the evidence is layin' in there, fanned across my kitchen floor. A grander bird I ain't never seen! I don't recall you ever havin' brought home a nicer gobbler yourself. You should be very proud of your son!"

She looked lovingly at Alb, then raised her eyebrows at her husband to silence him as he parted his lips in protest. Setting the biggest juice-drooling saucer of shortcake in front of J.C., she placed her right hand on his shoulder. Standing beside him, she balled her apron corner in her left fist and turned to face John.

"You should be proud of both of 'em!"

Stooping, she kissed J.C. on the cheek. She then seated herself and unfolded her napkin across her lap.

"Now then, let's eat before our whipped cream melts. Enough talk! Dig in, boys!"

Alb and J.C. did exactly that. Heaping compliments and praise on their mother's cooking, they ravenously ate their dessert.

John worried his shortcake with his fork. Leaving it half-eaten, he excused himself from the table and sulked into the den to shuffle through the day's mail.

Alb helped his mother clear the table, then wiped it free of crumbs and sticky strawberry juice with a damp cloth. He took the rag into the kitchen and hung it on the dish rack beside the sink. Hugging his mom as she stood in front of the sink with her elbows immersed in dishwater, he offered to help her by rinsing and drying.

"I'll just let them air dry in the rack tonight. You and J.C. need to finish cleaning that bird layin' yonder so's he won't spoil. What a shame that would be! He sure will taste good all roasted golden and stuffed full of hickory nut dressin', won't he? It's shameful there ain't no chestnuts left any more, but hickory nuts should do nicely, don't you think?"

Agreeing whole-heartedly, Alb lifted the turkey by its feet and carried it out to the front porch. Tiptoeing back inside, he eased the door shut and peered into the den to assure himself that his father was sufficiently preoccupied.

"Psst! J.C., all's clear!" he hissed at the bottom of the stairs leading up to the bedroom section of the old house.

J.C. materialized from above and scurried down the stairs, once again avoiding the steps that squeaked the loudest. The pair slipped into the dining room and stood together in front of the wormy chestnut buffet. Quietly, they eased open the bottom drawer. Alb picked up the faded perfume box and slipped off the lid. J.C. gently nestled the wing-bone-and-chestnut call into its bed of quilting cotton. Alb replaced the box with its delicate treasure back into the drawer. Easing the drawer closed with his hip, he whispered to J.C.

"You're the keeper of the call now. Who knows, someday, you might lure in a gobbler even bigger than the one you shot today. Whatever you do, though, be careful not to break it, and don't get caught takin' it out of this drawer. There ain't no tellin' what Dad would do if he ever caught you with the call."

J.C. had already been "caught!" Alerted by the faintest creaking of the dehydrated wooden stairs that his own feet had trodden since childhood, John Carswell had shadowed his scheming sons to the dining room. Listening intently to Alb's every word, he was now standing, unseen, just beyond the doorjamb.

John's first impulse was one of anger. The thought that Jake would lay out of school to go turkey hunting maddened him beyond conscious thought. The idea that their story was a lying conspiracy made him furious.

Lifting his right foot from the oak plank floor, he readied himself to burst into the dining room to confront his sons. But a fleeting, distant, memory held him there, precariously balanced. He hesitated.

Slowly, he lowered his foot to the polished hardwood as he thought back to a time when he, as a teen-aged boy, had laid out of school and played "turkey" using the call secreted in the buffet drawer. Caught red-handed, he had been punished. His tail could still feel the burn of the hickory switch with the sudden remembrance of "lessons" and "reminders" that had been taught him at the expense of that tender portion of his body. Unfortunately, he had not had an older brother, like Alb, to cover for him.

This was the first time John could remember his sons working together to achieve a common purpose. Alb had shown a newfound respect for his younger brother and accepted him as an equal rather than as a bickering rival.

The boys' whispered conversation had secretly informed him that Jake had just taken his first adult turkey gobbler by himself. A grander trophy, there never was! The realization that J.C. had achieved his most-sought-after goal traced a smile on John Carswell's face. Slick as a weasel, he tiptoed over the planks that creaked the loudest and sneaked back into the den.

Maybe tomorrow J.C.'s truancy would be discovered by his teachers at school and he would be punished. That was tomorrow. Today was today—J.C.'s day. School was an important thing in J.C.'s life, so he could gain the learning and knowledge he needed to be able to think for himself and make his own decisions. Obviously, he had made some good decisions today or a certain wily gobbler would never have been brought to bag. Some lessons cannot be learned in any school. They can only be learned at a place like Suzy's Knob—where the dogwoods were blooming, the grouse were drumming, and prisms of rainbow trout were rising to a hatch in the crystal clear waters of Back Creek.

Duckbuster!

Chapter 3

A Thousand Sunrises

When a northwest wind blows, pressing down the cordgrass of Masonboro Sound like a mother's hand smoothing the hair of a towheaded babe asleep in her lap, you know where I will be. I'll be there to greet the dawn.

I've seen a thousand sunrises. No, they are not the sunrises that have caught me unprepared, scurrying frantically about, late for work, attempting to get my act together for meeting some scheduled appointment for one of my life's many occupations that have earned me the reward of mere money. The only sunrises that figure in my count have been viewed from boat or blind as I waited for the new day's light to bring a flight of mallards, pintails, teal, wood ducks or any other of two dozen species of web-footed fowl to my bobbing spread of decoys. Ask anyone who has made my acquaintance for more than thirty seconds and they will tell you beyond all shadow of doubt that they have met the "Duckbuster." Those less fortunate than me have four seasons to their year—Spring, Summer, Autumn, Winter. My yearly seasons are but two. For me there is the "WATERFOWL SEASON," followed and preceded by "the rest of the year."

Phil was beside me, twenty years ago, that first sunrise on the banks of the Neuse River near Goldsboro. He was the one who started me along the watery trail that earned me my hunter's name. We were hungry college students hunting for rabbits, squirrels, or whatever mixed bag could be had for dinner. Our scroungings along the river startled a flock of a hundred mallards to flight. Bursting from cover along the water's edge, they quacked alarm to one another as they took to their wings against sky lit weak pink by a burning red sliver of the sun's early dawn.

"Down!" he commanded. "Don't look up! If they don't see our faces, they might swing over and give me a shot!"

Phil had a duck stamp on his hunting license. I did not. Two and one-half dollars for a lottery ticket chance at having duck dinner was too much to spend for a scholar without a scholarship in 1973. I couldn't have legally taken a shot if the flock had circled back, so I did as instructed and kept my head down.

Phil's eyes stared from beneath the bill of the cap that shaded his face, following jewel-speculumed wings flashing higher and higher above that silver ribbon of river. In his stare I saw a longing that the first primitive man must have felt when he looked up after the passing of a storm, saw a rainbow arcing across the sky, and wanted to reach up to pluck a handful of its color to hold in his hand and possess for his very own. At that precise instant in time, the look of longing was passed from his eyes to mine. I followed Phil's stare, I HAD to look up! The mallards saw the shine of my face and retreated upriver, landing in safety on the opposite side. Phil cursed. I cowered.

"We need some decoys," he said in disgust. "If we were to set out a dozen decoys in this very spot tomorrow morning, those mallards would come back and we would have duck for supper for sure!"

But Phil's decoys were at his parents' home, half the North State away. Brand-new decoys were a dollar each. Textbooks cost even more. So I studied hard, graduated, found a job upstate, propelled forward through life by a fire set in my soul at the memory of wings fanning the embers of a December dawn.

The first paycheck earned bought a ten foot jonboat, a box of short magnum duckloads containing an ounce and a half of number four black lead shot, and, most importantly, a duck stamp to go along with six mallard decoys molded of some sort of self-dissolving wood pulp that felt like paper mache.

From the warmth of a tiny cottage on the shore of Lake Norman, North Carolina's Inland Sea, I set out alone in the cold. Paddling to the head of McCrary Creek Cove warmed me. Sweat turned to steam under too many clothes. I settled my flock on water that glistened under the frosty light of a crescent moon in as much of a wedge formation as six fake ducks allowed.

Too many clothes soon became not enough as steam condensed back to sweat against skin. While waiting for the sun to come up over the trees that lined the surrounding foothills, I shivered in the December cold. The sun was unusually patient in warming the day. Slowly, it inched its way toward the horizon, melting the twinkling stars into the pool of charcoal gray and chasing away the moon. Gray turned to light blue, then glowed pink as I slapped my arms against my body in a belated attempt to keep warm. The only "blind" that shielded me from a chilly breeze that woke up with the sun was the bill of a camouflaged cap and the thinning needles of a stunted red cedar bush cut and moved three yards from where it had grown through a crack in a vein of white quartz. Thinking that the sun would never creep high enough to warm me where I stood, hidden from its touch behind the shadow of the cedar, I blew warmth between my fingers to ward off numbness. The swirl of vapor from my breath temporarily blocked from my vision the six decoys bouncing happily on ripples of water that mirrored the reflections of a cloudless sky. That's when they came. A Susie mallard quacked, "Good morning," to the decoys as she materialized from the sky on cupped wings. Her flock of twenty spilled behind. The steam of my breath cleared from my face on the breeze, allowing me a glimpse of hovering ducks, wings back-pedaling, tails tucking, orange feet stretching for the welcome mat of open water behind the "V" of my decoys. The hen's lazy greeting hails changed to staccato quacks the instant she saw the shine of a hunter's face staring at her from behind the cedar. In a storm of feathers the flock flared at her warning and swung on the wind overhead. Through the thunder of their pounding wings came the asthmatic wheeze of a drake that sounded as though he could not suck enough air through his nostrils to fuel the speed of his escape.

A Fox side-by-side jumped into my hands and tracked the arc of the drake. The front trigger pulled as if by itself. The gun bucked against my shoulder. A chip of a rainbow fell from the sky. I paddled out and plucked it from the water. Holding it in my hand, I possessed it for my very own.

Letting the breeze carry the boat to the bank, I smoothed my fingers into the feathers of the bird. Never had I seen green that was as green as the velvet that covered the head of my first mallard drake, or yellow as bright as the corn-yellow of his bill. The cottony ring of the necklace he wore matched the white of sergeant's stripes that outlined and magnified the colors of the speculum that shone from each of his wings. The sun rose higher and burned the sky to gold. Playing with the speculums' iridescence, its shifting beams tried to decide whether to polish them sapphire blue or emerald green. As the boat bumped against the shore, I poked my trigger finger through the delicate double curlicues that accented the mallard dandy's tail. Mistakenly, I thought that the wonders of the natural world could never again produce such a beautiful creature as the one I held in my hand. But, a second later, the drake in my lap was dumped overboard into orange mud that sparkled with fool's gold flakes of mica dust as I jumped from the boat seat to shoot his twin.

There were plenty of ducks back then. The season was nearly two months long and a unique system of counting "points" for each species in a hunter's bag limited his day's take-home to as many as ten ducks. When the cost of a hunter's last bird pushed his total to one hundred points or more, he was done with his work for the day. Most species were to be had at ten points apiece. Pintails, black ducks, hen mallards, and wood ducks could be bought for the punitive sum of seventy points each because there was not a large enough surplus of those particular species available to all waterfowlers who desired a share of the harvest of the marsh. A canvasback duck could be traded for one hundred points, a bargain in exchange for the total sum of a single sunrise.

The mallard drakes which were the object of my hunt that morning were to be had at the price of only twenty-five points each, so I was half done with filling my bag. Still, on that second sunrise of my apprenticeship, my hunt was all but finished. The velocity of the breeze in my face climbed with the sun. Other ducks decoyed, sailing in high enough to clear the upstretched fingertips of the naked limbs of the white oak trees that grew on a high bluff behind me. Warned of their approach only by the sound of incoming wings ripping wind, I stood to shoot. But the ducks were gone before I could cover them with the barrels of the Fox. Zooming in on my blind side, they never gave me a chance to fire before they were gone like a wish that wouldn't come true.

The breeze blew to gale. Ripples turned to waves, drowning the decoys. They rolled upside down and showed their keels to the sky. Knots that tied lures to fishing lines could not hold decoys against the force of that pounding water. My decoys sailed back to me. One by one, they drifted against the shore at my feet as their anchor lines came unraveled, setting them adrift at the mercy of the wind.

Paddling home against the gale took more time than I had allowed. Upon my return to the warmth of the cinder- block cottage, I found I was already late for work. Changing clothes, I dashed out the door and jumped in the car in such a panic that I forgot to shave.

The needle on the gas gauge read "empty" as I sped around a curve. A row of gas pumps in front of the local marina promised relief. Slamming brakes skidded my car to a stop in front of them. A man under a camouflaged cap with the name "Chuck" embroidered in green thread across a tan oval on the crown came out to "fill 'er up."

Chuck pumped gasoline in my tank while listening with a true hunter's ear to the story of my second sunrise. Each detail told increased the width of his smile. Eventually, his teeth showed through an ear-to-ear grin. At the mention of drifting decoys sending me home, he laughed out loud.

"Fools hunt with the wind in their face," he chuckled. "Waterfowl always land and take off into the wind, so all you'll ever get is a crap shooter's shot at a duck's behind. Never let a duck see the shine of your face or he'll flare away, out of range. Don't set decoys against a high bluff, or incoming ducks will circle high and stay wary. High banks represent danger to waterfowl and indicate a fast drop to deep water. The mallard is a puddle duck. He feels secure in flat terrain and likes to feed in water no more than eighteen inches deep."

After each of Chuck's critical comments, my shoulders drooped another notch, falling along with my deflating pride at what I had considered to be, until that moment, the grand accomplishment of taking home the makings of my first duck dinner. Laying dollars in his outstretched hand to pay for the fuel, I dejectedly turned to go. But he caught me by the shoulder and turned me back to face him. The smile left his face as he looked into my eyes. He saw something there, for his eyes searched mine for an eternity of time. Through the pain of my wounded ego, he saw the glimmer of sunrise on sparkling water and recognized a stare of longing that matched his own.

"Come with me," he said quietly. "Meet me on my dock at four a.m., tomorrow. Bring your decoys and your gun. I'll show you how to tie the knot."

It took less than one second for me to decide to accept Chuck's invitation. Gravel showered from my tires as I waived goodbye and sped off to work.

Puffing and blowing from running to my appointed chair behind a desk, I didn't hear the boss enter my office. "Ahem!" he loudly cleared his throat to gain my undivided attention. Tapping out disapproval on the crystal of his watch with an index fingernail, he frowned over the rim of his glasses at my scruffy face.

"I'll work an hour and a half late this evening to make up for the hour I missed this morning." I meekly offered as compensation.

The slightest twitch of a smile pulled at one corner of his mouth as he considered my offer. Greed for free punchtime eventually worked its magic. He agreed to the deal on the condition that taking time to scrape the stubble off my face was included as part of the contract.

That mutually satisfactory agreement has been kept as a bond between myself and every employer who has hired me from that day to this. Each working day during the waterfowl season, a view of sunset is traded for the opportunity to see the sunrise. A clean, smiling face late above a desk is traded for a tired, drooping face late above a supper plate.

"Good morning," I said to Chuck as I stepped off his dock and into his boat at the appointed hour the following morning. Chuck grunted, then pointed out a place for me to sit somewhere amidship. An enormous black-furred hole in the darkness named "Strong" growled like thunder, then moved over grudgingly at his master's command to share his allocation of seat inches with me. All remaining space in the boat was filled to the gunwales with gear—mostly decoys. Decoys were bagged, stacked, and packed into every available cubic centimeter in the span of a jonboat that was sixteen feet stem to stern and six feet wide in the beam. Adding a burlap grainbag filled with my lowly half-dozen to the top of the heap felt like adding the dot to an exclamation point!

Miles E. Forbes, Jr. and Strong
scan the sunrise on Bodie Island

Pressing the bag down into the pile to keep it from falling overboard forced two plastic teal to squirt from the heap. They filled the space between Strong's forefeet. I felt him giving me a mean look that said, "I'll tolerate your presence only because the boss told me to!" when I bumped against his shoulder while raising my rear to extract an eight ounce pyramid sinker that had embedded itself there. The sinker was attached to one end of a length of three-sixteenths-inch diameter brown nylon rope that trailed off at the other end into the mass of fake ducks. Its weight swung from my hand like a plumb bob while I pondered what to do with it.

The captain switched on the running light and helped me out of my predicament. "Hand that anchor to me," he said.

The hole I had kicked in the pile of plastic birds to make room for my feet collapsed, trapping my legs to the knees. I couldn't actually stand and reach far enough astern to place the weight in Chuck's hand, so I flipped it gently across the expanse of decoys that separated the seat of the mate from the seat of the captain.

The captain caught the lead. A couple of hard jerks on the line extracted a stuck mallard drake from the depths of the pile. Without so much as a glance, he unwound the remaining loops of line from around the decoy's tail and neck in a reverse figure eight, then untied the knot from its keel. His practiced hands whirled a tight coil and placed anchor and line into the pocket of a worn, but functional, marsh camo-patterned flotation jacket. The stripped decoy stayed where it laid.

The captain pulled the starter rope. Three times the outboard engine coughed on cold air before sputtering awake. Leaving behind a cloud of blue smoke that smelled of cylinder oil, the boat backed away from the dock. After carefully negotiating a "No Wake" zone at idle speed, it roared down the lake at full throttle.

Strong shivered. His muscles vibrated our frigid aluminum seat in sympathetic harmony to the rhythm of an artificial thirty knot headwind. Fortunately, the back of my head was turned to the bow, protected from the wind by the hood of an army surplus field jacket. It saved my delicate office-worker's skin from the imagined effects of frostbite. Chuck didn't seem to mind the cold. Steam from his nostrils froze fast to the hairs of his burly black mustache and beard, sealing the bond between his face and the icy kiss of the wind.

By the time the jonboat's aluminum ribs had drummed out the ten miles to marker twelve along the channel of what was formerly the shallow, rocky-bottomed Catawba River and is now the hundred foot depth of the Inland Sea, I was cold to the bone.

"Get a jacket like mine," Chuck hollered as he backed the motor's speed down to an idle. "If we hadda hit a floating log or a tire and flipped the boat you'd've sunk like a rock. Them waders woulda filled with water and dragged you under. A coat like mine will keep water and wind away from your hide and will keep you afloat if need be. Ya wanna hunt ducks? Ya gotta dress like a duck!"

Flicking on at least eight million candle powers of spotlight, Chuck temporarily blinded me as he scanned the shoreline of Goat Island for the dark clump of cedars that bushed his blind.

"Dis am de spot!" he announced triumphantly in the Louisiana Cajun that had migrated up the Mississippi and crossed over the Appalachians with his father's side of the family. He rationed the use of his Bayou-French accent, reverting to its phrases for emphasis, or at times of personal importance and achievement. Without further "adieu," he started unwinding the lines from his decoys, tossing them overboard in a practiced rhythm. He set them in a pattern that was visible only in his mind, for the darkness hid those of their number outside the feeble circle of the running light's reach and to either side of the stab of the spotlight.

"Drive the boat while I put 'em out," he commanded.

He stood, allowing me to sit in his seat. I took control of the tiller and throttle. But after the second decoy line wrapped around the propeller hub and played "ratatat" against the skeg with its lead anchor, after the second time he rolled his eyeballs until only the whites showed and muttered, "Mon Dieu!" he changed his way of thinking. The captain strongly requested me to return to the seat of the black mate, who merely yawned at my clumsiness, pretending that I wasn't there.

"Just sit there and watch! Sit right there and don' do nothin'! O.K.?" the captain begged my cooperation.

Daylight was beginning to glow as the last of a hundred and ninety-nine decoys was settled in place. "What a wad of dekes!" I exclaimed, awed by the size of the spread.

One shy of eight dozen mallard blocks loafed in a semicircle, their bills aiming into a light wind quartering from behind the right shoulder of the blind. Off to the left, a touch downwind, rested a flock of a dozen plastic pintails mixed together at its edge with two dozen teal. Six hand-shaved cork black ducks with movable heads of sanded pine turned into various positions of wariness and rest looked alive as they rode ripples in the opening of the crescent of fake mallards. Five dozen greater scaup decoys formed a phalanx to the right, lead by their generals, a pair of giant Canada geese.

"Divers always toll to the head of the d'coys, skittering their feet on top of the water to break their speed when they land," Chuck said, following my thoughts to the scaup. "That's why they are riding ahead of the puddlers. Geese need a long landing zone, that's why I set 'em upwind of the divers. Puddle ducks just sorta fall outa' the sky to the tail of the spread and jump straight up when they take off. They'll lock up to the rear of the half-moon hole in the center of the mallard decoys, behind those six blackies directly in front of the blind. They don't like to fly across divers like them bluebills."

"Bluebills?" I puzzled.

"Scaup!" he sighed. Mumbling and shaking his head, he rolled the whites of his eyes again.

"Gunner's name! Bluebills! For the color of their bills. Easier to remember and is ever so much more colorful and gracious to the game than 'greater scaup' or 'lesser scaup.' The larger bird has a greenish cast to its head, the smaller, a purplish sheen. But if you ever was to tell me you shot a bluebill, I'd know what flavor of bird you was speakin' of."

Switching off the motor and running lights, the captain let the boat drift free of the raft of decoys. Reaching for my decoy bag, he wrestled one of my hollow cardboard mallards into the feeble light. Giving me a wry, sideways grin of disbelief, he started bouncing on the seat, attempting to stifle a snicker without much success.

"Ya goin' huntin' or fishin'?" he asked.

Shrugging, I dug my hands deeper into my coat pockets and tucked my chin under its zipper.

Removing his gloves, he attempted to untie the sixty pound test braided fishing line I had used so very unsuccessfully to hold the members of the little flock to their anchors. As my eyes adjusted to the light of the first rays of morning I watched his fingers redden in the cold. I heard him cursing under his breath in French when he cracked a thick thumbnail. Giving up the effort, his hand dove under waders and pulled a lockblade knife. With a click and a snip, the decoy was freed. The same hand reached into the pocket of a floatation jacket and found the anchor and line it had so deftly removed from a decoy at dockside. Then and there, in the first light of sunrise, to the hypnotic popping sounds of air bubbles being trapped and released beneath decoy keels, Chuck showed me how to tie the knot.

"Dis am de d'coy bowline!" he announced with a flourish. "It's the only knot you'll ever use if you're gonna hunt with me. A dedicated waterfowler named Babe was eighty years old when he taught me how to hunt ducks. He's the one who taught me how to tie the only knot that holds against the pounding of the waves, the blowing of the wind, the racing of the currents, and the ebbing of the tides. This knot is easy to tie. It holds your d'coys as long as you want it to. It's easy to untie. It releases your d'coys only when you want it to."

He tied the knot to the eye of my decoy's keel, then just as easily untied it. Guiding my numb fingers through the same motions three times, he made certain that I understood. Maneuvering the boat back upwind to a hole he had left in just the perfect place in his decoy spread, he allowed me to drop my fake drake's anchor. The decoy tightened its line against its anchor, then came about like all its kin. Taking its place among them it faced into the wind.

The boat was secreted beneath an overhanging white pine tree on the opposite side of the island from the decoys. Strong was first ashore. Dashing through water, chest deep, he shook himself dry, then hurried to hike his leg and mark as his territory the downwind door of the blind.

"We're late. We need to hurry and get ourselves ready for the first flight," Chuck said. Opening a door that parted the cedars, he shoved me, stumbling, inside. Strong tried to muscle by me to be first into the blind.

"Last one in, first one out!" his captain commanded, holding the flat of his palm in front of Strong's face. The black dog sat instantly. Nervously wagging only the tip of his tail, he drooped his ears in submission. The Labrador watched his master's every move expectantly but ignored the motion of the stranger as the two men loaded their guns and situated their gear inside.

"In! Lay down!" the captain commanded.

Strong did as he was bid. Melting into a lump of tar with a satisfied groan, he rested his shoulder against his boss's lower leg and nestled his chin between his paws. Chuck's arm reached above the dog and pulled the opening in the cedars closed.

From the outside, looking in, the interior of the blind seemed dark. From the inside, looking out, the growing daybreak gave plenty of light to see each detail of the expansive web of decoys through the screen of cedar needles. Settling myself comfortably on the long bench seat, I studied the construction of the first real "piano box" blind I had ever sat in. It was named for the form of its resemblance to one of the player pianos in an old western movie. A three-and-a-half-by-eight-foot rectangular box with a shotgun shell shelf running the front wall full length, it was constructed with only half of a roof. The missing front half allowed me view of the morning sky with cottony clouds lined with shadows of blue where the feeble daylight could not yet reach. The half of a roof gave partial protection to hunters inside from the elements of sun and rain and cast shadows that would hide their movements from the wary eyes of an incoming flock.

An attempt to break from my vision a branch of evergreen-scented needles brought a stern look from the downwind end of the blind.

"You can see fine! You only think you can't! Watch from above the center of those black duck d'coys as far around to the right as you can see through little holes in the branches. I'll watch to the left. Take your shots that way, too. You shoot right, I'll shoot left. That way we won't risk wasting shots shootin' at the same birds. First single comes in will be your shot. Second one will be mine. I'll tell you when to shoot and when not to. Don't do anything at all until I tell you. And watch what you don't do, either!"

I wasn't certain about Chuck's last statement. But I didn't want to argue a case for my ignorance. There was no doubt in my mind who was captain in Chuck's blind.

For thirty minutes we sat, not speaking a word. Nothing with feathers showed up to inspect our trap except a pied-billed grebe that popped up from beneath the surface of the water in the middle of the decoys. The monotonous slapping of the ripples under decoy keels and the drone of a striped bass fisherman's motor a mile distant across the lake were the only sounds to be heard. Strong huffed a bored sigh and poured himself lower onto the floor, pillowing his head on his master's foot. His gentle snoring joined the sounds of a lazy sunrise.

"Blow your call!"

I snapped awake. From daydreams or real dreams of nodding head at lack of sleep, I'm still not sure. My startled heart pounded energy throughout my limp body. My eyelids blinked against the glare of full day.

"Blow your call!" Chuck demanded again as he struck up a tune of his own.

His eyes were locked onto something, high above the former river channel at least two miles away. A walnut mallard with a triple plastic reed pleaded with the sunrise to return an answer.

"Quaack, quaack, quack, quack, quack, quak, quak?" asked Chuck's call in the descending notes of a Susie mallard's laugh.

No reply.

"Blow your call!"

Fumbling fingers finally felt the cheap plastic single-reeder in my pocket. A raucous "Kack! Kack! Kack! Kack!" that sounded more like a fish crow than a mallard Sue was all that I could manage. I spit from my tongue the piece of lint that had jammed the reed.

"Sit on your call!" Chuck glared across the blind. "Don't blow no more!" he rolled his eyes and cursed in duck talk to the flock, forcing them to respond. They heard.

"Ticket-ticket-ticket-ticket-ticket. . ." came a feed call from a dozen birds in the flock interrupting each other in unison.

"Mallards comin' in for sure!" said Chuck. "You musta' got their attention and said something that made 'em mad, loud as that thing was," meaning the call that was bruising my buns.

The mallards' attention had been "got," all right. Moving across the lake faster than thought, they circled out of range above the decoys. Once, twice, three times, four times they circled, flying lower downwind, higher upwind, each time.

"Don't move," Chuck whispered. "Don't move nothin' except to roll your eyes. Look out from under the bill of your cap. Keep your face looking down, toward the decoys."

His call continued speaking to the flock, echoing the same cadence of "quacks" and "tickets" that could be heard above the thunder of their wings. At least three hundred mallards circled warily in that bunch. Each time they swirled behind the blind to break downwind their flutterings shaded the sun from the decoys, making the colors on the fake birds dance, making their inanimate bodies come alive.

Wings rumbled like jet engines landing on the fifth pass. Breaking speed at sixty miles an hour ripped feather tips apart. Ducks parachuted down, facing into the wind on cupped wings. Just as Chuck had predicted, they fell straight down behind the black duck decoys.

Scared to move, or even breathe, with all those mallards right in my face, my reactions were slowed when the command was spit in my ear to, "Shoot! Now!"

What had been coasting bird silhouettes through cedar needles against the dawn became fanning blurs of color as I thrust head, arms, and gun through the brush to shoot. The Fox picked a drake whose orange feet were dripping from the touch of water but he fell before the trigger was pulled. The drake was too far left! A Marlin pump-gun claimed the bird as "Chuck's" before the Fox could fire.

The Fox swung me to the right, capturing the blue gleam of a speculum on a wing. The duck dropped a small clump of feathers and lowered a crippled foot. The second trigger set the bird down hard. Unmoving, it drifted in the ripples of the crescent-shaped opening between the mallard and black duck decoys.

Fetch! Dead!

"Fetch dead!" commanded Chuck to the first one out. Strong ploughed water with a mighty leap. Swimming downwind of the decoys's tails, guided by his captain's slightest gesture, he retrieved first one, then a second drake. Each was delivered with precision to his boss' waiting hand.

My bird was last to shore.

"Hen! You shot a hen?" the captain of the blind asked in bewilderment.

Shrugging off the chance for an explanation, I gladly took my dusky Sue from Chuck who accepted its delivery from Strong and climbed back inside the blind. Chuck followed. Strong was last inside. A pair of plump feathered bodies, his reward for his work, were laid close by so he could lick drops of blood from the down on their breasts and sniffle his nose contentedly at their yellow bills. I laid my first mallard hen on the bench beside me and stroked her feathers with my hand.

"That's a lot of points to spend on just one bird." Chuck sympathized. "You need to be more careful, the next time. The point system forces a hunter to identify birds on the wing and penalizes those that can't. It's a good waterfowl management tool. Hen mallards are in shorter supply than drakes due to raccoons, foxes, and other predators catching and eating them while they set on their nests. Drakes don't stay around to help with the brood so they are relatively safe from predation. Outnumbering hens four-to-one, the drakes are the ducks you want to take home to dinner. Total my two birds at fifty points and your single bird at seventy points and I think you'll see the logic of what I say."

Thinking it over, I searched for a response that would hide my inexperience at judging the species of a duck flying in front of me. There was no refuting Chuck's logic of wise and careful management of birds as grand as waterfowl—the most managed single wildlife resource on the entire planet of Earth.

"Uh-oh. Here we go again. Get ready!" Chuck hissed to me across the blind. His left hand groped for the forearm of the Marlin, his right grabbed the mallard call dangling on the string around his neck.

"Bluebills! Bunch of eight! Low to the water! Your way! Flyin' right to left!"

Chuck's eyes swiveled at the speed of the flock skimming along the water headed downwind. His call changed dialect to bluebill as air was gently released to its vibrating reeds at the roll of his tongue.

"B-r-r-r-r-r! B-r-r-r-r-r!" said the call. The bunch of bluebills sheared off course and made a beeline for the decoys. Watching the apparent size of the birds' bodies grow as the distance decreased, I waited for the word to shoot.

"Get ready! Get ready to shoot!" Chuck whispered. His finger snapped his safety. Mine did the same. Strong found his feet. Scraping his toenails on the plywood floor as he rose to the sound of safeties clicking "off" he bumped the door with his nose, testing it to see if it were securely closed. Fortunately, it was.

"Reeeady - reeeady, ste-e-ady, Strong. E-e-easy, boy. They're gonna do it. They're gonna pile in. Hold it. Hold your fire. Not too soon."

I could hardly stand it! The birds were right there, hovering in my face. They were so close I could have reached out and grabbed one. Eight greater scaup flew over the heads of their plastic look-alikes not ten yards high, well within good gun range at less than twenty yards out. Still, no word to fire!

The flock flared away. I almost took the shot. But Chuck was the boss. I was under his control. The boss is always right.

"Ste-e-eady, partner. Ste-e-eady. We'll take 'em on the next pass when they spread their wings and lower their feet to land. It'll take 'em a second to gather their wits. That's when we'll shoot. O.K! Get ready! This is it! Here they come again! Remember! You shoot right, I'll shoot left . . . Ready! Shoot now! Shoot now!"

Forcing my gun's nose through the cedars I fired it in unison with Chuck's. The report of that pair of shots boomed so closely together that a single echo returned to the blind a few seconds later from across the lake. I'll never forget the sound of that echo or the flare in those outspread wings. I'll never forget those webbed feet stretching for the water, or the sunrise that shined

those bills that cut the wind the glow of the powder blue sky. The sensation I felt was that of the morning sky pouring itself down, literally sprinkling itself among the decoys. Eight bluebills fell at the blended sound of two gunshots, ending our labors for that sunrise and beginning Strong's. With two hundred points as our wage, we packed up the decoys and headed for home. We exchanged our hunting clothes for those of our life's occupations that earned us the reward of mere money that was used to pay for our sport.

The five years of my life spent under Chuck's tutorship were golden as the dawn. Hunting together every possible morning on the lake, we also used all our vacation days migrating with the fowl to the very endings of the Atlantic Flyway along the Carolina Coast. There are many cherished pictures of the pair of us, hidden in a cigar box in my desk drawer, showing two hunters coming fresh from a morning spent in a professional guide's stake blind on Currituck Sound, a blind leased to him by the payment of taxes to Currituck County for its construction, which were in turn paid to him by us for the opportunity to sit on its bench seat and watch the sunrise above a spread of decoys. Ten drake pintails hang by their feet from loops in hanks of decoy line, that drape down our shoulders like the headdress of a Great Plains Sioux Chieftain. Black, spiked sprigtips of tails stand out proudly—the symbols of a successful hunt.

We gunned near Swan Island and Whalehead, or Lighthouse Island as it's sometimes known to Currituck locals. Millionaires from New York, New Jersey, and Massachusetts once gunned those same treasured marshes. I've read the journals from those sporting club's mansion-like lodges and know for a fact that although there were no limits to the number of ducks a man could shoot at the turn of the century, those millionaires take-home pay for a day spent on the marsh could have been no better than ours, for the view of sunrise across the sound always remains the same. But their seasons did run longer than ours, 90 days and more. That is, up until the dark dustbowl days of the "Dirty Thirties" when the dearth of rain on this Continent's plains, along with the destruction of the sod by farmer's plough, turned the once muddy bottoms of glaciated potholes where ducks raised ducklings to ultra fine dust. During the thirties the mansions' journal entries slimmed. Bag limits dropped to nearly nothing. During the Great Depression, there were not many ducks around for shooting at, nor many millionaires to hunt them.

Thanks to the resilience of the natural world, the ducks bounced back with the end of the drought. By the early 1970's, the U. S. Fish and Wildlife Service recorded fall flights of more than 100 million waterfowl coming to, or passing through this nation from Canada to South America and Mexico.

During the "rest of the year" while not pursuing ducks, Chuck and I worked to earn the money to buy boats and decoys, and wood to build blinds. We also used our dollars to join and help organizations formed to enhance waterfowl habitat such as Ducks Unlimited, The National Wildlife Federation, The Nature Conservancy, and a local interest group that created a demand for places near home for ducks to rest and feed in safety like Mountain Island Refuge on the next lake south of Lake Norman on the Catawba Chain.

Through those organizations we met other waterfowlers and included them in our hunts. All were invited to sit at our table for delicious feasts of roast wild duck. It was a fitting way to end each season. To my way of thinking, a human hunter is at least as worthy of a meal of wild duck as a mink, raccoon, alligator, or peregrine falcon. Of the thirty percent natural loss of waterfowl each year, the hunter's take is a mere five percent. That is certainly less than are raised by his efforts for all to enjoy, whether by sight or by sound as they fly overhead, or if only in a photograph taken on a hunter-purchased refuge through the eye of a camera's lens.

The Inland Sea that was my home grew, not in size, but in human population. Duck hunters became ill-perceived, as imported others who had never heard a mallard's hail call, or witnessed the dip of a wing against the sunrise, or bought a Migratory Bird Hunting And Conservation Stamp to help save a wetland from being destroyed to build yet another subdivision for human habitation, claimed to have a greater desire for protection of the waterfowl resource than the love for the game that was forged by the symbiotic relationship between hunter and duck. The only thing waterfowl need more than water is the waterfowl hunter, and the waterfowl hunter needs waterfowl as much as he needs his soul to survive. The hunter is, above all other self-professed conservationists, the one who has stood against the marsh-draining dragline time and again, freely giving his hard-earned dollars to save the wetland from which arc the rainbows of color that are the wingbeat of the wild duck's flight.

Crappie fishermen began to fish in Chuck's decoys, impolitely snagging his anchor lines. Birdwatchers in powerboats warned away flocks of ducks that were warily swimming in to the downwind tail of his decoy spread. Even Duke Power seemed to include itself in the bad luck that plagued the poor duck hunter. Having robbed his waterfowl of the life-giving waters of the free Catawba River by building dams for harnessing its flow to generate power from steam to feed homes starved for energy was not enough. The power company began to fluctuate the lake level as much as twenty feet a year, for flood control or for making cheaper hydroelectric power or for some other reason only stockholders would understand. Emergent and submergent vegetation growing along the shallow shoreline of Lake Norman that are a puddle duck's food supply disappeared. So did the mallards. Only a few diving ducks like the bluebills remained, tenaciously gleaning clams and crustaceans in the forty feet of water that covered the river's former flood plain.

An ignorant birdwatcher, who would have actually been thankful for the successful hard work of the waterfowl hunter had he studied his avocation more thoroughly, burned Chuck's blind to the ground in revenge for his shooting at a duck. For Chuck, that was the final blow that drove him away along with the mallards. With a tear in his eye, he told me the bitter news.

"I'm leavin'! Goin' back to the Louisiana Bayous where ducks and huntin' are appreciated as an honorable way of life. My work with you is done. I've taught you what you need to know. Adieu, Duckbuster. May all your sunrises be filled with d'coyin' ducks."

Squeezing my hand, he shook it hard, then left me alone with the lump in my throat. Trying to kill the pain of his departure, I dabbed fresh paint on my battered decoys and bought some new ones. I built a new blind and brushed it with cedars in anticipation of better days. But, the numbers of the fall migrations continued to decline. The point system was eventually dropped in favor of a system that limited a hunter's take to a maximum of five birds. Only one black duck, one hen mallard, and two woodies could be included in the total of five. A canvasback could no longer be bought for any price. Someone set fire to the stake blind I had built, all by myself, at the end of McCrary Creek's Cove. Only the charred stubs of four cedar corner posts poked nakedly from the water above the sandbar where my blind once stood. Everyone mumbled behind my back. They all thought I would quit.

After a long search, I found a new job and migrated to the edge of the Atlantic, near where the Cape Fear River blends its waters with those of the sea. During former duck safaris with Chuck, I had become captivated of salty marshes whose water levels rose and fell to the natural rhythm of the flood and ebb of the tides. From the porch of my new home, I could smell and taste the brine in the air, hear and feel the thudding of breakers against the beach along the edge of Masonboro Sound. Waterfowlers were welcomed here. After some minor negotiations and adjustments to my work schedule, my new employer shook my hand on the deal that had become my bond.

At first, my flocks of decoys greeted the sunrise with only myself to tend them. With tedious difficulty, I eventually mastered the art of reading the tides after spending many hours stranded on dry sand bars waiting for the return flow of water that would take me home. Soon, there were others who joined me. They taught me, as I learned from them. Together, we advanced our knowledge of the waterfowler's trade.

Paul was one of those hunters. He told me the story of his botched first hunt, with only a lowly merganser to show instead of the pair of widgeon that had escaped while he chased decoys that had been freed from their anchor lines by the unrelenting interaction of pounding waves and whistling wind. His enthusiasm moved me to tell him all the things he had done wrong.

"Baldpates!" I corrected his description of his unshot ducks. "Gunner's name! For the caps of feathers on the tops of their heads that reflect the dawn so whitely they look like bald spots. Easier to remember and is ever so much more colorful and gracious to the game than 'widgeon'."

Grabbing his shoulder as he dejectedly turned to go, I squared him back to face me. Through the pain of his wounded ego, I saw in his eyes the glimmer of sunrise on sparkling water and recognized a stare of longing that matched my own.

"Come with me," I said quietly. "Meet me on my dock at four a.m., tomorrow. Bring your decoys and your gun. I'll show you how to tie the knot."

Stepping into my boat at the appointed hour the next morning, Paul kicked himself a pair of holes in a pile of my decoys to make a place for his feet on the bottom of the boat. A black-furred hole in the darkness named "Smitty" growled like thunder as the stranger jostled against his shoulder. "Friend!" scolded the captain of the sixteen foot aluminum jonboat, "DUCKBUSTER." The storm in the retriever's chest subsided.

Skimming down the Cape Fear River, the ribs of the boat's bottom shook to the rhythm of tops being sliced from frothy waves. Paul faced the stern, toward the captain, and raised the hood of his army surplus field jacket against the cold wind that clawed at the hair on the back of his head.

"You need a flotation jacket!" the captain shouted above the roar of thirty horsepowers. "It'll keep the wind and rain from your hide and prevent you from sinking if we hit a submerged piling or a floating 'dead man' tree trunk, sinking the boat in the dark." The captain spoke through the face of experience. That same advice from someone else had once saved his life so he could pass the same advice to someone else.

A compass needle and a few million candlepowers of spotlight pointed the way to an island of stones in the middle of the Cape Fear where only a strip of sand should have been. The propeller crunched to a stop against a volcanic boulder of banded gneiss imported there from Africa, perhaps, or the Far East, or any of dozens of other ports-o-call that a wooden sailing ship could have been driven there by the wind, a century before.

"Ballast rocks," the captain answered Paul's quizzical expression. "Merchant sailing vessels waited here, on this island, unloading the rocks that leveled their loads to provide as much freeboard as possible before negotiating the shallow channel upriver to Wilmington on the top of a rising tide. Returning downriver on the tide's ebb, they stopped here and took on a few rocks for ballast before sailing across the Atlantic again. We'll build a blind from these rocks to hide us from baldpates' beady little prying eyes as they hover over our decoys at daylight."

At a location selected by the captain, the pair laid out a circular foundation of the multicolored stones that had migrated there on ships from foreign lands. After the foundation had been designed, Paul took over construction of the blind. The captain slid the DUCKBUSTER away from the rocky beach and set baldpate, pintail, and gadwall decoys in a rainbow pattern that followed the curve of what was, on this morning, the downstream and downwind side of the island on the bottom half of a falling tide and the rushing of a northwest wind.

With the practiced ease of long experience, the captain routinely slipped his craft against the tide and the breeze. He flipped out the blocks, half a dozen at a time. Letting the boat drift downcurrent, he unwrapped the line in a reverse figure-eight pattern from around six necks and tails, time and again, then maneuvered the channel between the narrow shoals of ballast rocks to add their number to the spread. The last of six black ducks set precisely at the open end of the horseshoe of decoys made the tally a hundred and ninety-nine.

The boat idled to the shoreline of the island of rocks that should have been sand. Paul huffed as he heaved the last stone in place at the top of the blind. His silhouette was backlit by the glow of imminent dawn. Smitty jumped over the gunnel of the boat. Churning through water chest-deep to Paul's side, he hiked his leg to christen the downwind side of the blind.

Securing the boat among the rocks, the captain stepped cautiously over the side. Carefully stepping over the rolling cobbles in his clumsy waders, he made his way to Paul's side. In one hand he carried one of Paul's luckless widgeon decoys, in the other was coiled exactly thirteen feet of three-sixteenths-inch diameter nylon rope that had been dyed camouflage brown. The rope was tied at one end to an eight ounce pyramid sinker, the other end dangled free.

Paul's plastic widgeon was set on top of the final rock he had set in place on the rim of the waist high blind. A snip from the captain's knife freed the eye in its keel from what was, compared to the three-sixteenths inch rope, a tiny thread of braided fishing line.

"Dis am de d'coy bowline!" the Duckbuster said with a flourish. "It's the only knot you'll ever use if you're gonna' hunt with me. A dedicated waterfowler named Chuck taught me how to hunt ducks. He's the one who taught me how to tie the only knot that holds against the blowing of the wind, the racing of the currents, and the ebbing of the tides. This knot is easy to tie. It holds your decoys as long as you want it to. It's easy to untie. It releases your decoys only when you want it to."

The Duckbuster tied the knot to the eye of the decoy's keel, then just as easily untied it. Paul's numb fingers tied and untied the knot three times under the guidance of the Duckbuster, whose watchful eye made certain that he understood. The pair then picked their way through the ballast rocks to the water's edge. At the Duckbuster's direction, Paul tossed his fake drake baldpate's anchor into a hole left in just the perfect place in the decoy spread. The decoy tightened its line against its anchor, then came about like all its kin. Taking its place among them it faced into the falling tide and the northwest wind.

"We're late! Let's hurry and get ourselves ready for the first flight," the Duckbuster urged as the pair stepped inside the wall of stacked stones. "There should be fresh fowl coming in this morning. See these eight bird bands hangin' from the lanyard holding my calls? The U. S. Fish and Wildlife Service placed these little aluminum bracelets on baldpates' legs so they could discover where ducks migrated from and to. The computer cards the Service sent to me in exchange for the numbers of these bands told me that baldpates wearin' em traveled along the Atlantic flyway to the Cape Fear River from marshes that rim the Great Lakes. Maps, intuition, and experience tell me that the way from Lake Ontario to here is best flown by a duck with a northwest wind at his tail. 'Here' is called by most locals, 'Widgeon Rock.' But you should know, by now, this island's one true name."

"Baldpate Rock," Paul answered.

The Duckbuster nodded and smiled an affirmative reply. His smile quickly vanished, however, replaced by a look of utter seriousness as his ears heard the rustle of wings overhead. His fingers jingled to the end of the chain of bird bands and found an Acme Thunderer police whistle that rattled there. Bringing it to his lips, he blew the life of a baldpate's speech into the cold metal.

"Pe-peep! peeee... Pe-peep! peeee..." Puffs of breath were blown gently to avoid overly disturbing the cork pea inside the whistle's air chamber.

"Pe-peep! peeee. . .Pe-peep! peeee...pee...pee...pee." answered the puffs of breath that powered the wings overhead.

"They sound like rubber duckie bathtub toys," giggled Paul. A stern look from the Duckbuster stopped him in mid-snicker.

"Baldpates! Three! Drakes! Get ready!" the Duckbuster warned.

Paul peeked through a viewing crack he had left between the rocks. His mouth opened in amazement as he watched three ducks coasting above the decoys on cupped wings, their feet lowered to taste tidal saltwater. His finger searched for, found, and clicked off the safety button on a Remington 870 Wingmaster pumpgun. The Duckbuster's finger found and clicked off the safety of its match. The Fox had been retired a season before, the sears of its triggers completely worn out from seeing so many sunrises.

"Now!" shouted the Duckbuster.

Leaping from his seat on a plastic duckbucket, he snapped off a shot, then another before Paul could tear himself from his picture-framed view of decoying ducks through the crack in the rocks. Only a single bird remained in flight as Paul stood, arcing away in a furious storm of wings. Paul's gun tracked, then fired. A chip from a rainbow fell from the sky. Smitty swam with, then against a three-knot current to pluck it from the water. Returning to the blind on Baldpate Rock, he proudly placed the fallen bird in his captain's waiting hand. The captain presented the baldpate drake to Paul, who held it tightly and possessed it for his very own.

Paul smoothed his fingers into the feathers of his first drake baldpate. He had never seen green as green as the racing stripe that cut a swath across the bird's eyes. The whiteness of the feathers on the peak of the drake's head was like the white of the foam capping the waves that chopped in the Cape Fear's current. The rose of his breast was the color of sunrise, the powder blue bill a piece of the dawn. He thought that the wonders of the natural world could never again produce such a beautiful creature. But a few seconds later, Smitty retrieved two identical others that completed the trio to his captain's waiting hand.

"Baldpates come to this place at low tide to feed on sea collards and fingernail clams. They also come to gather grit off the sandbars to grind the food in their gizzards." the Duckbuster explained, holding and admiring the objects of his black mate's retrieve. "From their migration staging areas along the shores of the Great Lakes, they fly to one of the end points of the Atlantic Flyway in marshes surrounding our position on the lower Cape Fear. They'll pile in to our decoys as the ebb of the tide turns their feeding places at Muddy Slough, Buzzard Bay, Snows Marsh, and Masonboro Sound to high ground and waving, dry fields of Spartina grass. With no water left in the marsh grass to paddle around in, they'll fly the Cape Fear's channel. Looking for company, they'll see our decoys. If we're lucky, they'll inspect our bobbing fakes close enough to give us another shot."

Another shot came, and another, and another. The range was long. Baldpates hovered warily, closely eyeing decoys that paddled furiously in the river's current but made no headway. Three-inch loads of a hard, copper-plated, lead shot that was buffered with granulated plastic filler to keep it round and true made clean work of the collection of baldpates at ranges up to sixty yards—unheard of in the former soft lead shot days of the forty-yard Fox.

"I'm done," the Duckbuster announced as Smitty fetched the fifth drake.

"One more for me," Paul smiled.

Stroking his bag of three baldpate drakes and an accidental hen Paul fixed the memory of wings against the sunrise in his mind. His distracted attention prevented him from hearing what hinted to the experienced ears of the Duckbuster the nearness of another type of fowl.

"Blow your call!" the Duckbuster hissed, his fingers fumbling to find his own.

"I don't have one," Paul whispered back.

"Quaaack...quaaack...quaaack...quaaack..." said the lazy triple-reed Sue at the Duckbuster's lips.

"Quaaack...quaaack...quaaack...quaack," circled a response downwind, its maker hidden from Paul's view by the rocks he was ducking his head behind and trying to become.

"Don't move! Don't blink! Don't twitch! Don't move a muscle! They're lookin' over our spread." The Duckbuster whispered. He rotated only his eyeballs to catch a glimpse of the circling ducks beneath the bill of his cap.

"Steady...steady...easy boy," he cautioned the black mate who was so excited and wet with cold that his teeth began to chatter like a flamenco dancer's castanets.

"Ready...ready...ready...OK! Now! Shoot now, Paul! Take the drake! The larger bird on the right!"

Smitty jumped as Paul rose to shoot, caving in the blind and knocking over his master. Somehow Paul held steady and swung smoothly as boulders crashed down on his toe knuckles. Half of a pair of black ducks, a big bull drake, fell from the end of the Atlantic Flyway and drifted in the Cape Fear's current toward the sea. Smitty expertly made the retrieve completing Paul's limit,

*Decoys riding the ripples
in a hunter's eye view of a Pamlico dawn.*
125

unintimidated by his master's cursing between spits that cleared his teeth of bits of oyster shell, rock chips, and river sand.

The vessel, DUCKBUSTER was now complimented with full crew. For years I gunned with Smitty and Paul from south to north, west to east, across the width and depth of North Carolina. We spread our web of decoys on brackish water sounds, named Masonboro, Core, Pamlico, and Albemarle, and on swiftwater rivers named Catawba, Yadkin, Tar, and Roanoke. Stillwater lakes named Tillary, Jordan, Falls, and Catfish were no stranger places to us than our backyards, nor were Islands named Hatteras, Cedar, Bald Head, and Masonboro. No matter where we hunted, the sunrise was our constant, our anchor. It may have varied as much as fifteen minutes, changing with a few degrees of longitude, but the thrill of it bringing the flash of a wing, the sound of a call, the pride of a shot well-taken, always remained the same.

But the specter of drought continued to cast its shadow across the potholes of the prairies of American States and Canadian Provinces. The scant rain that fell in western Canada became laden with pollutants emitted from fossil fuel-fired smokestacks, causing acidification of pristine lakes where the black duck raised its brood.

The numbers of all ducks fell, along with the quantity and quality of their nesting habitat. Their limits allowed to the gunner fell as well. Only four birds paid the hunter for his morning's work. Just two pintails could be included in his daily bag. The taking of black ducks was limited to an open season of just seventeen days. The season length for all other species dropped from sixty sunrises to forty-five.

Paul got disgusted with the lower limits and shorter seasons, changed occupations, and lost his vacation days. He bought a house, married, and took up golf. He forgot how and why the knot is tied. His decoys drifted and were lost at the mercy of life's waves, winds, currents, and tides. A dozen other hunters tried but failed to replace him as permanent second mate on the vessel, DUCKBUSTER.

Life's current also brought me a wife. Everyone thought that lower limits, a shorter season, the loss of Paul, and wedded bliss would surely make me quit. It certainly took an understanding woman to blend the flow of her being with mine. At first, she could not comprehend why a sane man would leave a warm bed and a warm woman's side at four a.m. to go outside in the blowing cold of a northwest wind, even though he politely covered her with his folded halves of the sheets and blankets before leaving to make up the loss of his body's heat. She tried, but could not understand why her warmth was not enough to keep her husband home. She could not comprehend that the warmth returned to her by her husband was a transference of the warming rays of a dawning sunrise above a December marsh.

An icy nose probed under her covers one morning. Seeking out a duckhunter that was hiding there, the nose probed the small of her back. "I can't believe I'm doing this," she groaned, playfully kicking her heel at the dog.

Smitty licked her twitching toes.

"Get away from me, you crazy mutt," she giggled. Pulling on her robe she let the whining Lab outdoors to do his business. Returning, she pulled on layers of cotton and wool insulation, finishing with a pair of her spouse's cavernous rubber waders that were four sizes too large.

"Good morning," the Duckbuster greeted her, setting a plate of steaming buckwheat pancakes on the table in front of her.

"Just coffee please," she yawned. "My stomach isn't awake, yet. At least part of me can get some sleep."

"You'll need to feed your inner fire if you're gonna' stay warm this morning. The weather man says it's thirty degrees. If you drink too much coffee, you'll have to shuck some clothes to get rid of it. Besides risking frostbite to your bottom, the shine might flare away a flock of ducks."

"Ha! Ha! Ha! Very funny," she mocked a laugh. "You care more about your stupid ducks than you do about me. I think you're nuts, but I'll go along—just this one time."

The Duckbuster nodded and smiled. Further conversation was of no importance. He had, after all, convinced her to go along as she said—just this one time.

After a short boat ride in a chill wind, she sat as directed on the lid of a plastic pail surrounded by a reedy patch of marsh. She endured some sort of self-obligatory ritual by her husband about some stupid knot that he used to tie an anchor line to a pintail decoy on the bottom of which he scribbled her name with an indelible laundry marker. She had even mildly surprised herself when she tossed the decoy into a pocket left just for that purpose in a group of a hundred and ninety-nine others.

But now she waited, and waited, and waited, as the cold seeped through seams in her clothes to chill her delicate skin. She tried not to shiver or let her teeth chatter. Most of all she tried not to complain. But, oh! How she had to pee!

The captain sat to her left, the black mate in his turn to the captain's left. She heard the dog's teeth clicking rapidly together like a park duck's bill nibbling crusts of bread. In spite of everything she tried to do to stop them, her teeth began chattering, too. But Smitty's teeth had an excuse. He was wet from a dash through chest-deep water and his excitement was barely bridled, like a thoroughbred racehorse chomping at the bit to get on with his work.

The blackness of night faded. The second mate waited. She prayed through shuddering lips for the warmth of dawn. The sun patiently took its time in warming the day. Slowly, it melted the twinkling stars into a pool of charcoal gray. Gray turned to light blue, then burned the warming promise of hot pink. The only sounds to be heard were the rumbling of breakers against the narrow strip of dunes that separate Masonboro Sound from the sea and the sunrise, the chattering of her teeth, and the slapping of tiny ripples under decoy keels.

Waves on the beach rolled a hypnotic rhythm that lulled her into a trance. A red sliver of the sun began to show. Caressing her cheeks through slits in the reeds, it saved them from the imagined creep of frostbite. Digging her shoulder against that of her husband, she struggled within herself to stay warm and still for his sake.

Laughing gulls began to laugh. Terns peeped in protest as they exchanged toe holds on one sandbar for another as the incoming tide swallowed the islands they had roosted on during the long, cold night. A fish crow indignantly cawed his laryngitic monotone as a shrimper on whose boom he had been sleeping rumbled its diesel awake. Engines of cars taking workers to work stuttered to life along the edge of the sound, behind and to the west. The sun burned to gold from a glowing red ember as a third of its diameter topped the dunes. A flutter of wings hovered above the decoys.

"Another seagull," dismissed her hypnotized mind.

"Now! Shoot now! Don't let him get away!" hissed the Duckbuster's voice in her ear.

Grabbing her by the shoulder, he physically stood her up and pointed above the decoys. A twenty gauge Stevens double jumped at the touch of her hands and bucked hard twice against her frozen cheek. Out there, illuminated to iridescence by the warming touch of sunrise above the sound, a chip from a rainbow fell from its arc across the dawn. Smitty fetched it from the hole in the decoys where it splashed down. At the snapped fingers of his captain's unspoken command, he sat by the second mate's side. He waited for her to take from his mouth the taste of feathers that was his reward for his morning's work. Patiently, he sat for a very long time, until his chin trembled under the strain of holding its weight.

"Take your bird," urged the Duckbuster. "Hold it in your hand and possess it for your very own."

Forcing her eyes from their view of the splendor of sunrise across Masonboro Sound, she blinked hard, twice, to clear them. Taking her bird from Smitty's drooping jaw she turned to her husband, smiling, and said, "Now I know how you can come out here and do this every day of your season."

She smoothed her fingers into the warmth of the bird's feathers. Never had she seen white like the admiral's collar that curved the neck of her first duck, or brown like the smooth, soft velvet that covered his head. The corroded bronze-green of the speculum on each outstretched wing shone like the reflections of the dawn on the ocean that stretched until it was lost from view, beyond the horizon to the east.

Stroking the long grace of a pointed black tail, she dared to whisper through the steam of her breath into the air above the reeds the identity of the first duck she possessed as her own.

"A drake pintail. My first drake pintail."

"Bull sprig," corrected the Duckbuster. "Gunner's name. It's easier to remember and is ever so much more colorful and gracious to the game. 'Bull' for the strength of those thick breast muscles that power the staccato beat of his wings for a migration flight of a thousand miles. 'Sprig' for that sprig of a tail feather you'll stick in your cap at the end of your trip to this marsh on this morning."

The Duckbuster smiled as he searched the soft brown eyes looking down at that bull sprig. In those eyes he saw the glimmer of sunrise on sparkling water and recognized a stare of longing that matched his own.

We hunted together, through most of the nineteen- eighties. But, one morning, my second mate announced she could no longer share my sunrises, for she was soon to bear me a son. Scant clouds continued to withhold precious rain where ducks should have been raising their broods. The duck limit dropped to three per day. A hunter's take-home pay of bull sprig was rationed to only one. I ripped the bottom of the DUCKBUSTER on a floating log with an oyster shell can opener and sunk it in the back of Snow's Marsh. Soft iron shot hunters called steel was mandated for use across the country to prevent ducks from mistaking it for grit. It prevented a few million slow fowl deaths from lead-injected poisoning, but forced the retirement of a 12 gauge Remington 1100 semi-automatic. Hard steel shot could have damaged its barrel, as it was designed only to shoot softer pellets of lead. The inferior ballistics of lighter weight steel shot pellets reduced sure, duck-killing range from sixty back to the range of the forty-yard Fox, making it tough to shoot the wary adults birds that now made up most of the flight. Worst of all, the season was reduced from forty-five to thirty days. Everyone whispered behind my back that with the extra burden of raising a newborn, and the continuing decline of my season and bag limits, surely, now, I would quit.

Traveling from my end of the Atlantic Flyway I hunted for the points of its beginnings. North Dakota and Ontario were places foreign to me. But hunting in those distant places during brief vacations extended my season beyond North Carolina's allotted thirty days. Scanning the sunrises above strange waters, I searched more for answers than I did for limits of web-footed game.

A Dakota farmer named Johnathan spoke with frank honesty when I offered to share with him my day's harvest of a feather bouquet of three greenwing teal. A single pothole gouged in the landscape sixteen thousand years ago by a glacier's retreat was the only damp spot remaining on his land. The teal had come to the decoys I set on that pothole and were fetched by Smitty to my outstretched hand.

"No." said Johnathan. "You take them all back to Carolina with you, for you have traveled so far for such little ducks. Besides," he winked, "I'm not much into fast food and I believe teal are about the fastest food there is on this earth."

Laughing at his own joke, he examined the trio of colorful speedsters dangling by their feet from between my fingers. His humor left him as he turned away and gazed across his irrigated acreage.

"Ya know, there used to be a lot more ducks than there are, these days, on my land. See that low, dark place rowed with stubbles of rat's ear corn. The combine's wheels bogged down and couldn't get in to pick them. It wouldn't have been worth the trouble, anyhow. That used to be what we called a wasteland. Now we call it a wetland. When the rains quit falling, a decade ago, those acres—about twelve by my reckoning - were turned beneath the blades of my plough. The U. S. Government paid me to add the acreage to my farm and plant corn that was stored as surplus that this country didn't much need. I wish they'd pay me again, to put it back like it was. I miss watching ducks raise their broods, especially the canvasbacks. You can't believe how many there used to be, gathering here from miles around, before they left to fly across the country to your home beside the Atlantic Ocean. It seems to me that, these days, we need more ducks than we need more corn. Did you know that it takes 10 pounds of corn to raise a pound of beef and 3 pounds to raise a pound of chicken? I wonder if anyone knows how many pounds of canvasbacks it takes away from all of us to raise that pound of corn? Yessir! I wish I could put it all back, so when the rains returned, so would the canvasbacks."

In Ontario, Canada an Algonquin guide named Dark Goose gave me an obligatory hand shake as we parted company on the shore of a crystalline lake that encompassed three hundred acres. The water looked pristine, untouched, but Dark Goose told me otherwise. Offering me a dipper of cold drink from the lake, he pointed at the water dribbling down my chin.

"Dipper's no good!" he said, touching a fingernail to a rusty red spot in the enamel coated steel. "Lake's acid. Dipper's don't last as long as they once did. Acidity comes with the rain — mostly from your country, but some from mine. People bicker, pointing fingers at one another, trying to fix the blame on each other for the rain that is deadly to this lake and others like it instead of doing something to stop pollutants that are spit into the clouds by coal-burning furnaces. The death that rains onto our lakes does nothing and no one no good. This lake has belonged to my people for as long as they have drawn the breath of life. Black ducks once raised their young ones here, in rafts so thick sometimes they looked like the shadow of a cloud being blown across the lake ahead of a northwest wind. Now they hatch eggs here no more. Lake trout that reached fifty kilos in weight are gone, too. So is almost all other life. The tiny plants and animals that once formed the foundation of life in my peoples' lake can no longer live in its water. That is why the water seems so clear. It is too clear. It is void of life—like a crystal of ice; like a desert. The Canada geese you hold in your hand only rest on the lake. They feed in fields nearby to gather strength for their journey. They could have been black ducks, instead. Maybe you should think about that, a long time. Take my thoughts with you to your country when you fly south with the geese."

Returning to Carolina, I reflected on the words of Jonathan and Dark Goose. I took on an extra job. Working long hours through many spring, summer, and autumn evenings, I still managed to keep "my" season free for the hunt.

Saving my pennies, I scraped enough together in a single pile to purchase a farm that was unproductive of corn, tobacco, and soybeans. Slowly, over several years' time, I reclaimed the land for the ducks with a lot of money, a lot of research, a lot of sweat. Fields reverted to wetlands as ditches were filled with water. Acres formerly planted in row crops were converted back to fertile marshes and swamps. Wetland plants returned. Smartweed, duck-weed, duck potato, arrowhead, and burreed grew back in profusion. Wood duck nest boxes were set on posts above black water that vibrated with miniscule invertebrate life, begging the birds to reclaim their home. They accepted the invitation.

Blending the hard science of exacting mathematics earned at the expense of a civil engineering diploma with the soft approximating theories of an associate wildlife management degree wasn't easy. But I stretched my education to its limits and designed a way to create manmade wetlands that assimilate and treat polluted water that leaches from landfills, sewage treatment plants, scrubbings from coal-fired smokestacks, and most any other source of a duck's dismay that human beings can create. Cattails, irises, pond lillies, and dozens of other plants that waterfowl need in order to thrive grow in abundance on my man-made wastewater treatment lagoons that are just beginning to dot the landscape of Carolina. Imagine that!

Waterfowl can live in our wastes. When I see a greenwing resting himself on one of my ponds after a long migration, I smile at the irony of what a Dakota former once called a "wasteland." It describes my man-made wetlands perfectly. Children enjoy watching waterfowl paddling on the marsh. How I hope they learn to appreciate what they see.

I'm happy to say that my employer broke our bond when he found what my hard work had accomplished. No longer do I have to stay at my desk an hour and a half late for an hour missed early. He now understands that my workday's wages have always begun at 4 a.m. during the short span of a "WATERFOWL SEASON" wedged in between the "rest of the year."

*Smitty anticipates the taste of feathers
in a Masonboro sunrise.*

Smitty died. What chance did a jet-black hole in the darkness have against a gate latch that failed and a car that couldn't stop in time. Too many magnum duckloads shot over his head prevented his grizzled ears from warning him of the car's approach.

It certainly wasn't the driver's fault. Trying to reassure her, I blinked my eyes hard. Turning away with my black mate hanging limply in my arms, tears fell like rain. They did not slow or stop for three days and still return, occasionally, when the glimmer of sunrise shines. Everyone thought the loss of Smitty would make me give up the dawn.

I buried my dog at the exact same place he fetched his last retrieve, under the shadow of an ancient cypress tree from whose gnarled limbs hung great cobwebs of spanish moss. Wood ducks flushed from the pool of water behind the cypress. Squealing as they flew overhead, they cast silhouettes against a gray morning. The place Smitty fetched his last duck was the same place my son received from the Lab his first. At the shoulder of a "greentree" impoundment constructed by my efforts with his tiny assistance, Justin's eight-year-old hand accepted the drake from Smitty. Thanking the dog with a scratch behind the ears, he possessed the duck for his very own.

I knew what was in his mind, read what was in his eyes as he smoothed his fingers through the feathers of the bird. Never had he seen so brilliantly the color red as the red on that woodies' bill. The colors of autumn leaves were on the bird—maroon, purple, and gold. The crest of his head feathers was greener than the evergreen shimmer of surrounding laurel oak leaves. The silver bands that edged them were stolen from the linings of the clouds sailing overhead. No bird that flies, swims, or runs all the elements of Earth is as beautiful as a drake wood duck.

It was difficult for me to believe, at the moment my son held his first, that the southern wood duck had nearly been declared extinct in 1920. The elimination of beavers and the nuisance of their ponds by the unmerciless advance of civilization had also eliminated the rotted hollows in trunks of dead trees that died in beaver water that wood ducks needed to raise their broods. But now, thanks to hunters who cared, the wood duck had become the number one duck in the Carolina waterfowler's bag.

Ten wood duck nest boxes were placed on poles in our ponds of live flooded timber, replacing hollow trees that, for woodies, were in short supply. Water is only allowed to fill our "beaver" ponds when trees are dormant, covering acorns that fall in autumn with oak tree leaves. Water is released before spring buds appear to prevent drowning of the willow, laurel, and water oaks that must have dry summers to survive. Wood ducks love acorns above all else. Flooding the hardwood mast to a depth of eighteen inches set the table for a wood duck's feast. A hundred times more ducks have been raised in our ponds than have ever fallen to a hunter's gun.

"It's a drake wood duck! Look! There's a band on his leg!" Justin exclaimed.

Kneeling beside my son with my hand on his shoulder, I explained, "Most folks call that bird you're holdin' in your hand a wood duck or a woodie. But we call it a Carolina Duck. Gunner's name! Easier to remember and is ever so much more colorful and gracious to the game! Some of them migrate here from other places far away, but the majority of the ones we see are raised right here, in the grace of North Carolina in big bird houses in little ponds like ours."

At home Justin scribbled the band number among the misspelled words of a small boy's first letter sent through the mail to the U. S. Fish and Wildlife Service. The card that returned proved his father to be correct. His first ever taken Carolina Duck was banded by a biologist of N. C. Wildlife Commission near a nest box constructed and maintained by him at Pungo Lake Refuge in the northeastern corner of the state.

While cleaning our guns after the hunt, the eight-year-old Duckbuster-To-Be asked my permission to hold my ten gauge Browning pumpgun that was purchased to replace the retired Remington 1100. With a heavy, hydraulic recoil reducer added in the stock to tame its fierce kick and other modifications by the factory and the local gunsmith to transform the Browning into the perfect fowling piece for shooting steel shot, the gun tipped the scales at more than eleven pounds. Its ponderous mass was much too heavy for a twenty gauge boy to handle on his own.

Shucking the action open to make certain the chamber was safely empty, I balanced the forearm in my palm. Justin sighted along the ventilated rib. Swiveling the gun on the fulcrum of my hand, he coaxed its silver bead sight around the room until it stopped. Pointing motionless for a long minute, it came to rest on my most cherished possession, perched on a mantle of straight grained cypress.

"Will I ever get to shoot one of those?" he asked.

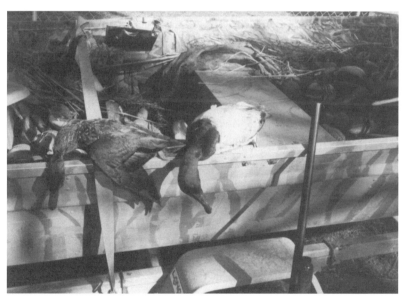

A Canvasback was exchanged for the ultimate price—
100 points and a single sunrise.

Sighting along the side of the barrel at the mounted form of a preening canvasback, I remembered back through twenty years to the morning I had paid the ultimate price of a single sunrise in exchange for the duck on the mantle. I remembered the velvety red that covered his head as being the red of icy waters set afire by a smoldering sliver of the winter's sun. I remembered the gray and white weave of the feathers on his back curving in a silver arc across the sky, as silver as the reflections of the dawn on bleached canvas sails that once powered schooners and merchantmen on the Cape Fear River's waters when his numbers were at their peak. I remembered my taxidermist friend's finest art that preserved the Canvasback's color and grace to rest in perpetuity on my mantle—so I could remember.

"Maybe you will," I began my answer. "The season is closed on canvasbacks now. Not since the drought of the 1930's have their numbers been so low. Less than sixty million ducks remain in the fall flight. Just a third of one million of those are canvasbacks and only a third of those are hens. But when the wonders of nature bring the rains back to places ducks raise their broods, they might just come back with the help of people like you and like me. It's a simple thing to raise a duck. It's as simple as buying a duck stamp. Whether you hunt waterfowl or not doesn't matter. The money you pay goes to purchase or restore wetlands that waterfowl must have in order to survive. It's as simple as turning off a light to allow a power plant to burn one less chunk of coal that may create acid rain to fill and poison a black duck's lake. It's as simple as not putting more food than you can eat on your supper plate. That square inch of marsh needed to raise one mouthful of corn, or beef, or chicken could have provided the morsel needed to raise a tiny puffball of feathers that could have grown up to become a canvasback. If each and every one of us tries to use as little as possible of what we need from Nature's hands, what we don't use can be used by her to raise a duckling. If each and every one of us puts just one tenth of one hundredth of one thousandth of one percent as much effort into restoring the health of the marshes and potholes from which fly the rainbow of feathers that we know as the wild duck's flight as everyone before us had done to destroy them, maybe—just maybe—ducks will return in numbers too many to count. A duck for each person in the U. S. would be a great beginning. Achieving that simple goal would send two hundred and seventy million ducks down the Atlantic, Mississippi, Central, and Pacific Flyways in the fall. Think how many of those millions might be canvasbacks. Then—just maybe—you might be able to take one home after a morning's hunt like the one that you see preening his feathers for you on our mantle."

Justin's face wore a thoughtful expression as I helped him put his Winchester Greenwing twenty gauge in the polished white oak gun cabinet. He carried the same expression upstairs with him to bed. Pulling his covers over his shoulders, I tucked them under his chin. He smiled and closed his eyes. I turned to go and was closing the door to his room when he called to me in his soft child's voice.

"Dad. Would you do one more thing before you go? I'm still a little afraid of the dark, but would you, please, turn out my night light?"

I did.

Back downstairs, reclined in my easy chair, I stared back through time at the canvasback on the mantle, the big Browning anchoring my legs to the cushions. The sight of the canvasback reminded me of a story told by a man I knew only by the name of "Babe." Babe was eighty years old. His eyes were overcast with the clouds of age. But through those milky cataracts I could see, still burning, a remnant of the glimmer of sunrise sparkling on water when he told of the first job he had ever held at the tender age of eight.

"My daddy was a market gunner on Currituck Sound, an honorable profession, back then. He laid me down beside him in a sinkbox that let us float suspended beneath the water's surface in the middle of a spread of a thousand d'coys. Wide, floating wings of wood framing and canvas spread out on all sides to knock the energy from the waves and keep the near-freezing water from pouring down the backs of our necks. My daddy had a pair of Winchester Model 97 pump action shotguns with exposed hammers. Each gun held seven shells. The canvasbacks would come to the d'coys at dawn. They'd come in so thick and my daddy would shoot so fast, my job was to reach 'way out, over the wings, and dip the barrels in the water to cool 'em off before reloadin' 'em. If I hadn't kept the barrels cool that way, the wax water-proofing on the paper hulls woulda' melted and glued the shells stuck in the chambers. The canvasback was best of all the ducks, in speed, in numbers, in body size, most especially in flavor and the price he fetched. There were so many canvasbacks in each flock that they looked like a storm's shadow blowing across the sound. When my daddy would shoot it looked like a huge door openin' up in the sky. For an instant, I could see the colors of the sunrise right through the flock. Then the door would close when the flock reassembled, blocking out my view of the dawn, again. The shadow would boil away, disappearing in the distance above the water...."

As his story had trailed off, the clouds of age returned. The glimmer went out in Babe's eyes.

Stroking the Browning with on oily rag, I marveled that it showed so much wear to be so new. Salt water from the Atlantic that flows into Masonboro Sound through Carolina Inlet had extracted its price from the finish of the gun's metal surfaces. The pock marks where corrosive droplets had scarred the Browning made me think of the worn out Remington semi-auto that it had retired, and the Remington pump that it had retired, and the Fox double that it had retired. All were worn out before their time from seeing so many sunrises.

Thinking of the guns reminded me of the Labrador Retrievers, those black-furred holes in the pre-dawn darkness who fetched the chips of rainbow that fell to the guns. Some had pedigrees and names to match that were much more colorful than mine. The names of "Stronger Than Dirt" and "Baytree's Blacksmith" and "Pinecrest's Neutron Jack" for long had been shortened to Strong and Smitty and Jack in the tight comraderie of a boat or blind. Dogs named only Duke and Ann and Sam had done their work and earned their wages of the taste of feathers with as much enthusiasm as their high-bred kin.

Thinking of the retrievers reminded me of their masters, the captains from whom they gladly received the command to "Fetch." I thought of all the hunters who had been, are, and forever will be my most cherished friends, for nothing binds souls together like sharing the anticipation of sunrise above a spread of decoys bobbing on ripples in the water.

Those hunters are the ones who stand against the effect of the marsh-draining dragline, the dumping of wastes into water and air. Those are the men, the women, the children who unselfishly give their time, their money, their hearts, and their minds to protect our diminishing wetlands, for without waterfowl hunters, there one day would be no waterfowl. Without waterfowl, there one day would be no waterfowl hunters.

Closing my eyes, I remembered all the hunters' faces, each with legs swung beneath that great round table of my mind. A hot-from-the-oven dinner of whole-roasted duck surrounded by chunks of orange carrots, white potatoes, green celery, and purple onions steamed on a platter in front of each one. Their meals of wild duck, whether greenhead, bluebill, bull sprig, Carolina Duck, or any of two dozen other species of web-footed fowl, held better flavor than any domestic duck that has ever been prepared by the greatest gourmet chef in all the world, for their dinner was basted with the sauce of memories of the hunts that brought home the meal and garnished with a story told by each hunter who kept alive in his eyes the glimmer of sunrise on sparkling water.

Phil was there, seated at that table with Chuck, Babe, and Paul. Donnie, too, and Tony, Splinter, Gary, Mike, Peanut, Terry, Ron, Ken, Connelly, Julian, Ralph, Bob, Wayne, Jeff, Harry, George, Deannie, and Lee . . . The names were repetitious after the second Tony, Mike, and Phil, but the faces certainly were not. Rounding the circle to the end of the table I came to Carol and Justin, then to Eddie who was seated directly at my side.

Eddie is currently the mate on the third vessel to wear the brown and tan stripes of salt marsh camouflage with the name DUCKBUSTER spelled out in black block letters across its transom. Eddie is the one hundred and ninety-ninth mate on the boat that bears my hunter's name. He lives just a few doors down the street. Last Saturday we hunted together on the Core Banks. The limit on redheads had risen from an all time low of none to two per hunter per dawn. The raft of decoys we hunted over included a few dozen that belonged to Eddie. A northwest wind whipped foam on the tops of the waves. The pounding of the waves unraveled six of his decoys from their anchor lines. We chased them in the boat across one of Core Sound's many fingers and collected them from against a windward shore, upended and strewn about at the mercy of the water and the breeze. I removed a brown-dyed length of three-sixteenths inch nylon line from my pocket that had been untied from one of my decoys for just this occasion. Picking up one of Eddie's wayward plastic redheads, I taught him how to tie the knot.

"Dis am de d'coy bowline," I announced with a flourish. "It's the only knot you'll ever use if you're gonna' hunt with me. A dedicated waterfowler named Chuck who learned it from a dedicated waterfowler named Babe taught me how to tie the only knot that holds against the pounding of the waves, the blowing of the wind, the racing of the current, and the ebbing of the tides. This knot is easy to tie, it holds your decoys as long as you want it to. It's easy to untie. It releases your decoys only when you want it to."

Untying and retying the knot to the eye of his decoy's keel under my guidance, Eddie smiled at his success when he eventually was certain that he understood. Motoring the boat upwind to the waiting decoy spread I directed Eddie to place his redhead in a void left at its departure. The decoy tightened its line against its anchor, then came about like all its kin. Taking its place among them, it rode the crests of the frothy waves, fought, and held its own against the whistling wind.

Sliding the boat into the edge of rushes, where the waters of the sound lapped at the shore, we covered it with camouflage netting and reeds from deck to waterline. Laying with our backs against the gunwales, we laid in the bottom of the boat, hiding beneath the bills of our caps with only the whites of our eyeballs showing. Eddie had never taken a drake redhead. I had not in over a decade, for in the same year that the surplus of canvasbacks fell so precipitously to the point that they could no longer be included as part of a waterfowler's take-home from the marsh, the shooting of redheads had also been banned. The trip from Wilmington to Core Sound was made by us with one special purpose in mind, for I had studied the stare of longing in Eddie's eyes and had seen in there the flash of a drake redhead's wing against the glimmer of sunrise on sparkling water.

Our anticipation rose with the sun as a flock of baldpates checked over our spread in the feeble light of new day. But the sound of shots never ruffled their wings. Waiting them out, we let them pass by.

A bluebill circled downwind on wings that hissed like a jet plane landing. Joining our spread, he pitched to the head of our decoys.

"Live decoy," I whispered to the mate. "Maybe he'll convince some other ducks to join him."

Eddie said nothing, but nodded in the affirmative. His eyes were wide with excitement and shock at the captain for not having given the command to shoot the bird. Watching the drake bluebill diving happily among his imitations, oblivious to the fact that they did not dip and swim along with him or acknowledge his presence in any way, distracted Eddie's attention. He didn't see the ball of birds dipping low on the water with the wind in their tales until the captain translated a growled diving duck's, "Br-r-r-r-r!" through a puddle duck call.

"There they are! They're turnin' our way!" warned the captain.

"Br-r-r-r-r!" said the call again. The lead ducks swung downwind, pulling the rest of the flock with them. Pale gray lieutenant's stripes showed as their wings reflected the glow of dawn.

"Redheads! Comin' in! Get ready! Don't even twitch your moustache 'til I give the word to shoot!" the captain commanded.

Eddie thought the pumping in his chest would burst the arteries in his neck as he watched the cloud of ducks grow in size. Airspeed gobbled the distance between ducks and duckhunter. He saw brick-red on every other head, and the muted brown that covered every other that instinct cautioned him, "Hen!"

Seventy dark dots grew in size to become ducks. Their wings cupped down to slow their descent. Black feet splayed out from bumblebee bodies. Toes reached down, the webbing between them stretching for holes in the water at the head of the blocks. A swimming bluebill dove in surprise to escape from the shadows about to land on his back.

A pair of black neck collars stood out from the mass, holding red heads high to counterbalance tails that dropped low. Eddie heard the order, "Shoot now!" over the shearing sound of feathers braking air, followed by the thunder of a ten-gauge gun and its snick-snatching action.

Eddie Evans on Core Sound,
after he learned to tie the decoy bowline.

The storm of wings kited the wind and flared away. Four redhead drakes were left behind. The captain poled the boat away from the bank with an oar. Eddie reached into the water and picked up a chip of a rainbow that had fallen from the sky. He held it in his hand and possessed its color for his very own.

The captain knew that Eddie had never seen so beautiful a bird as the one he was smoothing his fingers into the feathers of. The russet velvet that covered his head was accented to perfection by the jet black collar that extended to his shoulders. The gray of his bill was the color of Core Sound reflecting the close-lying vapors that hugged the dawn.

The captain had seen something else, in the sky, at the volley of their shots. A yellow shaft of sunrise smiled through a hole in that wall of wings at the instant those four ducks fell. It wasn't a large enough hole to be called a door. Perhaps it was a window— a window through which shone a ray of hope.

Eddie can't go with me tomorrow. He has to work to earn the wage of mere money—money that he will use to buy state and federal duck stamps, decoys and line, boat and fuel, shotgun and shells, also, he tells me, to buy back a piece stolen from Carolina that was once a wetland and is now the farmer's and forester's domain. He wants to try to return it to its former status as a year 'round home for the Carolina Duck, and a winter's retreat for mallards, black ducks, and teal.

The mate's seat on the vessel, DUCKBUSTER will be empty when it leaves my dock at 4 a.m. Come with me. I'll show you how to tie the knot. Will you be the two-hundredth mate to place your decoy in my spread? Or, will you be one of those I hear, stuttering your car's engine to life as you scurry frantically about, late for some scheduled appointment that will earn as your reward mere money? If so, turn to the east. Face the sunrise. If you happen to catch the sound of a walnut mallard hen's hail call, the dip of a wing, the sound of a shot, think of me, out on the sound.

A hundred million ducks were in the fall flight in 1973. There are less than sixty million in 1993. Then, there were two million duckbusters. Now, there are less than a million. Over half of this nation's wetlands have been destroyed by drainage, fill, or pollution—over five million acres in North Carolina alone. But I'll never quit the dawn. It is up to those of us who have unlocked the secrets and mysteries of the waterfowlers' trade to pass them on. It's up to us to train the retrievers to retrieve and hunters to hunt during seasons that are short and limits that are low. The knowledge must be kept alive, waiting patiently for the day that water returns to shallow, sheetwater pools so hens can raise their ducklings in the vast number of former times. I've seen the number of bull sprig in a hunter's daily bag drop from ten to one. But with your help, I won't be out there, some sunrise in the future, hunting only a memory.

When a northwest wind blows, pressing down the cordgrass of Masonboro Sound like a mother's hand smoothing the hair of a towheaded "Babe" asleep in her lap, you know where I will be. I'll be there to greet the dawn. I've seen a thousand sunrises. I hope to see a thousand more.

Snow Geese at their winter home on
Pea Island National Wildlife Refuge.

Chapter 4

January Snow

  South of the village of Nags Head on North Carolina's Outer Banks rises a structure of concrete and steel which allows the gray ribbon of Highway N. C. 12 to arch upward and over Oregon Inlet. It provides the only terrestrial link between the landbound residents of Hatteras Island and the rest of the world. A monumental marvel of construction by man's standards, the Herbert C. Bonner Bridge has held its own against ripping tides, hurricane winds, and pounding surf since 1963.

  On the day the bridge was opened to traffic, no one could have foreseen that the inlet would move its channel southward at what is considered, according to Nature's time table, a rapid pace for the next three decades. Today, the bridge rests its head on marshland created in the wake of the inlet's retreat at the southern tip of Bodie Island. Its concrete footings are in dire danger of being nibbled away by the surging of the tides at its south end where its toes kiss the sand of the north point of Pea Island National Wildlife Refuge.

All those whose fortunes rose and may fall with the bridge know of only two choices that exist for its salvation. Either the bridge will have to be moved and re-erected above the new channel, or the inlet will have to be stabilized with stone jetties to prevent its incessant migration. Each option represents an enormous undertaking, requiring great expenditure of workmen's time and taxpayers' money. While engineers, scientists, and politicians argue the fate of the bridge, Nature's assault continues unabated.

As if to add an exclamation point to the precariousness of the bridge's situation, Nature's hand reached up from the salty depths on a night recently past to deal their efforts a slap in the face. October 26, 1990, was a scowling, moonless night of wind-driven rain. Storm waves churned to foam, ripping a heavy anchor from its tenuous hold on the violently shifting sands of the inlet's bottom. A massive dredge boat which had been working to keep the channel open was set adrift to be tossed and slammed by an angry sea into the bridge's support pilings. The relentless hammering of steel hull against concrete pillar sent a 369 foot section of bridge crashing down—down to be swallowed by the heaving brine below.

Some faulted the vessel's captain for causing the damage. But those who were familiar in the ways of the water knew that he was fortunate, indeed, to have saved his own life and those of his crewmen from the storm's fury. The security of his men is of paramount importance to a skipper, much more so than that of a bridge whose doom at the hands of the elements has already been foretold.

"The Bridge be damned! She was a goner anyway!" These were the thoughts of William R. Styron as he waited impatiently in line for his turn to ride the makeshift ferry south from Bodie

Island to his home in Rodanthe. The inefficient transport had been rigged to serve as a temporary replacement while the bridge was being repaired. Like 6,000 other residents of Hatteras Island, Bill had waited weeks for the opportunity to cross Oregon Inlet north to the mainland. Now, he was being detained again, waiting impatiently for his chance to return.

He fidgeted and fussed irritably in the cab of his salt-air rusted Chevy truck. The lengthy delay was preventing him from keeping his most important appointment of the day.

Bill, more than most others waiting in the long line of traffic, knew that changes in human schedules due to uncontrollable natural events was a continuous occurrence on these islands of shifting sand. In fact, change was perhaps the only constant of existence here.

Bill's family history was the story of the settlement of the Outer Banks. His roots ran as deeply as those of the sea oats which anchored the fragile dunes against the onslaught of pounding surf and raging wind. For three centuries, his ancestors had wrestled a living from the sea and vast marshes surrounding Hatteras.

The original Stryon had come, seeking change, from England in the early 1700's. Fitzhugh Styron was a tough man. He had been among the very first inhabitants to live a complete life and raise a family in this harsh New World environment. A fisherman and a sailor, he also claimed to be a maritime merchant. Others whispered his occupation as "pirate." Whatever he had to be, he became, to ensure the survival of himself and his family.

And, oh, what hardy men his progeny would be—Whalers! Fishermen! Oystermen! Sailors! Merchants! Shipwrights! Tradesmen! Craftsmen! A succession of Stryons kept beacons of light aglow in the Cape Hatteras and Bodie Island lighthouses. Their powerful beams warned passing ships off the treacherous shallows of Diamond Shoals. If, by chance, the piercing signals went unheeded by some careless captain out at sea, the rasping impact of eggshell keel on course sand bottom would grind his ship's hull to matchsticks in seconds. In the frantic space of a few panicked heartbeats, a feeble distress signal would flicker shoreward from his stricken vessel through the dead darkness of a lonely night. If the smallest shred of luck was left to him and his unfortunate crew, the flashes of their final plea for help would reach the Bodie Island or Chicamacomico Life Saving Service Station. Other descendants of Fitzhugh Styron would respond to the call, forcing their tiny, walnutshell life boats through unyielding walls of towering surf in their attempt to steal back the shipwrecked victims from the jealous arms of a raging sea.

Bill could remember his father's eyes flashing the same fierce pride as those lighthouse beacons when he told the stories of daring rescues he had piloted as a member of the U. S. Life Saving Service. His were stories of snapped oars and frantic men, shouting desperately to make their voices heard above the roar of thundering waves. His were tales of disaster and duty, of compassion for mourning families, their loved ones lost, clenched forever in the sea's last embrace.

Now the old ways of life were also dead or dying. The completion of the very bridge on which everyone's welfare seemed so desperately to depend had signalled the next generation of change for the Hatteras area, for better or for worse, as only the passing of time would judge. Modern communications and electronic navigation equipment had rendered the lighthouses conveniences rather than necessities. Their brick and masonry spires served primarily as historical markers, tombstones at the head of the "Graveyard of the Atlantic."

Bill, himself, had been a fisherman, an occupation that had endured as long as there had been Styrons and sea. A lapstrake-sided vessel of white juniper planks, the "Miss Becky," had shuttled Bill and his crew through the sole ingress and egress to the rich fisheries of the Atlantic Ocean for two-thirds of a lifetime. In recent years, anti-fouling paint had been scraped from her bottom numerous times. Her seasoned skipper had done his best, coaxing her carefully through Oregon Inlet. But the restless, temperamental nature of the currents inevitably altered the lay of the channel. With each passing day, the inlet shallowed and shifted until, even Bill, with his vast navigational experience, could not tell trough from crest of the unseen sandbars. Safe navigation had become possible on only the highest of tides.

"Well now, ain't this a proper fix to be in?" Bill asked himself. "You can't get through the inlet by boat and you can't cross over by bridge!"

He rubbed a calloused palm across his perplexed brow, pushing back coiled locks of salt and pepper gray hair. Laughing out loud at the irony of his situation, he glanced to the west, toward the setting sun. It was time! He could wait no longer!

Bill eased his truck out of the stalled traffic and spun 180 degrees to the north. There was another vantage point from which he could view the spectacle he longed to see.

To find the soul of a Styron, you must peel off more than the crusty outer shell. You see, each and every one, from Fitzhugh on down the line, whether by necessity or choice, by vocation or avocation, had been a waterfowler. Hunters, every one, they were masters in the art of obtaining goose flesh for the table.

In the earliest years, waterfowl were killed out of necessity. Their protein-rich flesh provided a dependable source of red meat in a diet of mollusks, fish, and hardscrabble vegetables.

By the 1800's uncountable numbers of ducks and geese were being slaughtered. Their carcasses were salted a hundred to the barrel and shipped to markets north and west. More than a few of the bills of laden were marked with the name "Styron." The succulent flavor of waterfowl flesh was in ravenous demand to feed the growing population of a prosperous and hungry young nation.

The supply of ducks and geese seemed inexhaustable to the market gunners. Then came the shock of the early 1900's. Almost imperceptibly at first, the valve that unleashed the mighty torrent of waterfowl down the flyways was beginning to close. Slowly, so agonizingly slowly, the feathered flood was being turned off.

Bill was a boy in 1934, during the "Great Depression." In many parts of the country this meant no money, no jobs, almost no hope. But, to the people of the marshes in and around Hatteras, it was "Duck Depression" that touched most hearts and households. Drought had turned the potholes of the northern prairies to dust. Hens returning to traditional brood ponds in spring from their winter vacations at Bodie Island found only dry, cracked clay bottoms where life-giving water had glimmered for a thousand years. No cool waters greeted the fowl with their own sparkling reflections. They huddled together in bewilderment, contemplating their shadows on the dry ground instead of raising ducklings as eternal instinct drove them northward to do.

The spigot was turned nearly closed and the days of relentless market hunting were officially over when Bill was learning to hunt. But, on Hatteras and Bodie Island, "High Tide Pheasant" could still be bought if you had the right connection and handed over an appropriate amount of cold, hard cash. For the price of two one-dollar bills, a brace of plucked birds remarkably similar in form and flavor to canvasback ducks could grace a host's holiday table.

Bill had learned to hunt at his father's side. Canada Geese were the big game "Down East" on the Carolina Coast. As duck numbers had dwindled the numbers of Canadas had increased. The season on Canadas was nearly twice the length of the season on ducks. A hunter could legally take home four gray geese per day compared to only two ducks.

The season on white geese was closed. Prized for the brilliantly white, incredibly warm down feathers against their skin as well as for their flesh, greater snow geese had been hunted ruthlessly, nearly to extinction. By the early 1900's, only a tattered, remnant flock of 3,000 remained in all the world.

"Snow geese! Don't shoot!" Bill would hear his father's voice hissing in his ear whenever he spied the wavering line of a distant, passing flock through tiny gaps in the dried foliage camouflaging a duck blind. His father's eyes would follow the flock until they became a tiny row of specks, indistinguishable between the edges of the clouds except to a man whose gaze had been upon them from the point of nearby passing. If Bill blinked or looked away for an instant, the flock would be lost from his sight.

Bill would steal a glance at his father's face and sense his father's mood, as only a son can. The intensity of the stare would be keen. The steel blue eyes would be sharply focused into the infinite distance. As the geese disappeared, the brow would soften, the set jaws relax, the eyes would cloud with mist. Often, his father would blink away accumulated moisture as he turned his attention back to the decoys. "Dryness of the wind" or "piece of grass" would be the explanation as he rubbed away the glistening globule of a single tear with the collar of his coat. Young Bill knew that, in reality, it was a tear of emotion. Guilt cannot be hidden by a father from his son.

James Styron had been the very best gunner of snow geese in the history of the Hatteras area. His prowess at hunting the great white birds was legendary. His techniques and intensity were etched into local lore. Ears would bend attentively to the sound of his voice or the mention of his name as the snow goose migration reached its peak numbers. Any citizen of Hatteras or Bodie Island who felt the touch of the hunter upon his heart would try to glean some tiny tidbit of information, some secret shred of knowledge, some fragment of wisdom that would bring him one step closer to being as skilled at taking snow geese as James Styron. The evidence was always starkly visible for all to see.

"That's no snow drift! That there's a pile of Styron's geese going to the markets," was a phrase of envy and admiration commonly heard on the docks when James was a young man.

Only young Bill had been given the answer to the riddle of his father's hunting success. It wasn't anything that anyone else could learn or be taught to do. No deep, dark secret was kept selfishly hidden from the rest of the world, for James loved to tell his hunting tales. He told them with the same enthusiasm as his thrilling, first-hand account of the heroic rescue of 42 men from the ill-fated "Mirlo" —the day a broken tanker's lost cargo of oil burst water to flame. Sinking ships, decoying geese—both stories were told with the same adrenaline-kindled fire flashing from his eyes, his arms gesturing wildly like two fighting cottonmouth moccasins. His entire body became animated as he transported himself back to the time and scene at which the actual event had taken place.

Although he certainly knew every intricate detail of setting out the proper decoy spread for luring the great white birds into range of his gun and could coax the most cautious flock in close enough to take a hunter's breath away using only the sound of his own voice as a "call," there really was just one other thing that set James Styron apart as the very best hunter of Hatteras and Bodie. Only Bill knew that his father's true and only secret could be summed up in the single word, "obsession."

Obsession was the key that made James the successful hunter he was. Obsession cannot be learned or taught. It cannot be passed on by word of mouth. That overpowering urge, that narrowly focused, single purpose ambition, that burning, driving desire to pull snow geese from the very tops of the clouds and possess them for your very own cannot be transferred from friend to friend. The triumphant feeling of the thick, heavy weight of snow goose as you clench your left fist tightly around a muscular neck and feel the lingering warmth of the last of life ebbing away is a feeling that cannot be gained by reading great writings. Obsession is something that is inside you from the very beginning, an intensely burning spark that is part of you from the very instant of your conception. Yes, Bill Styron knew the weight of this fact fully well, and anyone who knew him and his father even casually could tell you beyond any shred of doubt, obsession can only be inherited.

"Well, I didn't make it to Pea Island, but I got here in time," thought Bill as he pulled off the pavement. He feathered the brake pedal to slow the progress of his pickup and stopped in front of a row of creosote bumper posts. Through the windshield he read the letters and numbers burned into a weathered wooden plaque announcing, "PARKING AREA BLINDS 15, 16, 17, 18."

He sat for a while, staring into the western sky. A few pillows of clouds reflected the pastel pinks and golds of imminent sunset. No lines of geese were yet visible against the back-glow of fading light.

Bill raised the door handle. Shoving the door open with a muscular shoulder, he snaked his left foot down the pavement. He shot a quick glance across the cab to the passenger side and thought briefly about making a grab for the walking cane at rest against the dash.

"Not today! I'll make it on my own," he said aloud, shaking his head slowly from side to side. He swung his right leg around to join his left in its descent to the hard asphalt. The left was strong and sound and whole as a pillar from many years of effort, holding a burley body above a swaying deck. The right would have been the same but for a twist of fate. A churning sea had caused the "Miss Becky" to lurch and roll at the instant of greatest pressure on a haul line being power-wound around a massive steel winch drum. The line was as thick as a man's wrist, but was not strong enough to handle the great stress of that precise moment.

A few thousand pounds of flashing silvery fish—money!— was being lifted onto the aft deck. At that same moment the ship's bow came crashing down off the back of an eight foot wave to be slammed by a concrete-hard wall of water. The force of the impact shook "Miss Becky" to her very keel, causing every board in the sturdy vessel to creak and groan. But she held intact as she had so many times before. That is, except for the cable holding the great net full of fish.

With a report as loud as that of a shot fired from a high-powered rifle, the line snapped. The skipper, who normally would have been at the wheel, was aft admiring his catch as all fishermen are prone to do. The snarling coils became entangled around his right leg as the net with its weighty contents started slipping back into the sea. A cursing Bill was cut free, maddened beyond all comprehension that his crew had sacrificed the catch to save him from further injury—or death.

The hospital stay had been long and painful. The months of rehabilitation had been even longer and more painful. The pain now was mostly inside. To cover his medical costs and loss of income, the idled skipper had sold "Miss Becky."

Bill stood and steadied himself against the rust-scaled fender. He squinted across the vast marsh towards Pamlico Sound. Any moment now, they would come.

He drew himself up and straightened his back. Tensing every muscle against the ache in his right leg, he began crossing the few feet that separated him from the wooden observation platform. Reaching the bottom step, he rested for a minute. Although there were only eight risers in the set of stairs leading up to the deck of the platform, Bill thought long and hard about remaining at the bottom.

"No!" he finally concluded. "No more cane! No more crutches! No more waiting!" Up the stairs he went, one step at a time. The cracking, weathered paint covering the wooden hand rail gave him good purchase with his left hand. He ascended by placing his left foot on each step, then lifting its injured mate beside it. In this limping manner, like a toddler just learning to walk, he eventually achieved the top.

Bill settled his slightly protruding belly comfortably between his hands against the guard rail and began his vigil in earnest. Eyes swiveling north, he gazed into the clouds a couple of miles away.

"Ah, I hear 'em now," he thought as a nearly inaudible sound pricked his ears. What, to an average man, would have been an insignificant sound, not unlike the barking of a distant dog, had alerted Bill to a flock voicing its arrival.

He watched a tiny bead chain of geese grow larger and longer. Each bead in the chain slowly became an individual, easy to see now, but still well beyond anything like good gun range. The great white birds, twenty-four to be exact, were headed south down the entire length of Bodie Island on their way to the safe haven of Pea Island Refuge. There, they would spend the night, secure in the safety that great numbers provide. 40,000 snow geese strong, an immense blanket of white feathers would greet them. Those already there would appear as a covering of new snow that had settled upon the marshes, providing a luminous landing zone in the fading twilight.

Bill was absorbed in watching the flock as it passed by, 300 yards up, 500 yards out. Instinct told him without the prodding of conscious thought that the geese were directly over blind 16 as he studied their seemingly effortless motion. The steady beat of each black-tipped wing was clearly visible as it stroked the air with its velvet touch. The five-foot wing span made up most of the surface area exposed to the friction of the air. Snow white feathers covering seven pound bodies were smooth and slick to cut down drag. It takes a lot of sail to propel the heavy mass of a snow goose a couple of thousand airmiles each year.

"From the Canadian Arctic to Pea Island is quite a long way, isn't it?"

Surprised by the sound of a human voice behind him, Bill twisted his head around and looked over his left shoulder to assess the intruder. He was more than a little upset by this rude interruption in his private moment that was the highlight of his day.

"I can't see them, but I surely can hear them," said the voice. Bill winced at the accent, sharp and staccato in stark contrast to the melodius tones of goose conversations he had been listening to so intently.

"A Yankee, no doubt," thought Bill. His mind had already categorized the man from the gritty way he enunciated his words and the manner in which he had barged his presence into another man's private thoughts. Bill grunted some unintelligible syllable, more akin to a curse than a greeting, and nodded his head toward the flock of snow geese disappearing rapidly to the south.

Of course, the man took the sound of Bill's answer and the sight of his gesture to be an invitation to join him on the observation platform. Without further hesitation he switched an open power window closed, turned off the ignition of his car, and opened the door. Slamming it loudly, he ascended the steps.

Bill began muttering under his breath, "Tourists! Yankees! To heck with them all!" They had no respect for the rhythm of the ways of life in these marshes. Most of them came from the heart of some great, noisy, bustling city—a sterile environment of concrete and steel where the only living creatures they had contact with were rats in the alleys, squirrels in the parks, and pigeons that bombarded poop from the ledges of buildings onto their heads and into their outstretched morning cups of coffee as they scurried about on the sidewalks below.

They came to gawk at the marvels of Bill's ancestral world and the fascinating plants and animals which shared his world with him. There was no respect born in these foreigners for the fact that life creates life, that it is all part of the circle of sun, sea, and sand. They were not taught from their first breath that in order for something to live, something else must die. Yes, most of all, they seemed to deplore and despise that which Bill loved most—hunting. The killing part, the most insignificant portion of the total concept of the hunt, was all they could see, or wanted to see. They seemed hell-bent on stopping it, destroying it with their pollution, their attitude, their very presence.

After "The Bridge" was built, the "Big Change" had come. At one point in his life, Bill had been a waterfowl guide. To supplement his fishing income, he had always been glad to accept money from sportsmen visiting from "Up North." He had been just as glad to see them go.

Like the geese, hunters, fishermen, and other tourists had migrated south in winter and during the hot summer months for two week vacations. Like the geese, they had always returned to their homes.

That was before the bridge. Now there was easy access to the mainland—well, most of the time, anyway! There were also chemical insect repellents and window screens to ward off the hot ice pick bites of swarming hoards of sand gnats and the itchy stings of salt marsh mosquitoes. Electricity had also come to Hatteras with the bridge and along with it came the amenities which make life easy, but not necessarily better. Air conditioning against the scorch of the summer sun and heat against winter cold without a burning blaze gave comfort to outsiders who were not born and raised to cope with the harsh conditions of the barrier islands.

Insulating oneself from the pulse of the natural world in a hermetically sealed environment of constant 72 degree temperature was no way to live to Bill's way of thinking. The searing heat of the sun's rays magnified through air-suspended water droplets onto a man's shoulders as he went about his days work with the heavy sounds and thick smells of the sea in his ears and nostrils proved to a man his right to exist. An ice-covered morning on the marsh with clouds of steam from every breath hovering about his face obscuring ninety snow-white decoys from unblinking view through the bushes of a blind—these things were the facts of existence that made a man like Bill feel alive.

Bill could feel heat from the presence of the Yankee's body close behind, but said nothing. Apparently, the intruder could not read body language, or didn't care to. As the two men stood silently, another flight of snow geese approached from the north end of the island.

"I think I hear more geese coming from the north," said the voice of the intruder.

"Definitely a Yankee," thought Bill.

He was certain of it by the way the percussive sounds of the man's speech grated on his nerves. Northern folk always did seem to be a little short on manners, pushing their presence on others, uninvited.

"Oh, well, I'd just as well say something," Bill decided to himself. "This guy ain't gonna go away."

Bill turned to his right and faced the approaching flock. Extending his arm, he pointed to a faint line two miles away in the darkening sky.

"There they are," he said.

The Yankee moved to his side and peered along his out-stretched arm.

"I don't quite see them," he said.

"Keep lookin' hard, they're right over there, under that puff-ball cloud."

The Yankee turned and studied the profile of Bill's face. "You must be a local, a 'High Tider.' Isn't that what they call you? I can tell by the way you talk and the way you can see snow geese coming from so far away."

Now, to a dweller along North Carolina's Outer Banks, the term "High Tider" can be taken two ways. Properly pronounced "Hoy Toyder," or something "loyke thot," it mocks the vocal inflections of the local dialect which has descended through the years from the Old English language spoken by the first arrivals there, Fitzhugh Styron for instance. Cut off from outside influence for centuries by the surrounding moat of Oregon Inlet and Pamlico Sound, parts of the old way of speaking remain intact.

Bill's ego did not allow him to take the term "High Tider" as critical or condescending from the Yankee since the term was spoken in the same breath with a compliment about his ability to spy approaching snow geese.

Without thinking, he blurted, "And you must be a Yankee, judging by the way you talk and the trouble you have spotting them when they're so near!"

With a sarcastic chuckle he turned to the intruder. He instantly perceived a pained look on the Yankee's face and momentarily felt ashamed for calling him a Yankee in a cutting way. The thought flashed through his mind that maybe he shouldn't try to run this man off the observation deck. After all, anyone interested in snow geese couldn't be all bad. As a way of apology, or perhaps from ingrained reflex as the gentlemanly thing to do, Bill offered his right hand to the stranger.

"Styron's the name, and them geese are my game!"

The Yankee hesitated for a second with some apprehension, then caught the sound of genuine laughter covering the initial sarcasm in Bill's voice. He smiled a little, then began to laugh in unison with Bill. Reaching out, he firmly grasped the offered hand of friendship and introduced himself as, "Grainger, Bill Grainger."

"Well, what do you know about that? My name's Bill, too," smiled the High Tider.

The strength of the Yankee's grip as he clasped the High Tider's hand took the injured man by complete surprise, pulling him off balance. He nearly fell as he was pryed away from the railing, but the Yankee caught him by the right shoulder with a powerful left hand and steadied him until he stood erect and stable.

"I got hurt a little while back, but I'm on the mend now," the High Tider explained.

The Yankee glanced at the right leg of the man before him, then hastily averted his attention back to the sky. "I don't understand how you can spot the geese coming from so far away. But, then again, you did say those geese are your game, didn't you?"

Bill Styron took this to be an invitation to speak on his favorite subject, snow goose hunting, but was unsure whether the Yankee was one of those anti-hunting, bird watching, Bambi-hugging types, or whether he was truly interested in knowing the secrets of the great flocks.

"Well," he hesitantly began, "when I said those geese are my 'game,' I meant it in every sense of the word. I've hunted them my entire life and I come by it honest, having been taught to hunt from birth by my dad. He may have been the best snow goose shooter this part of the world has ever seen."

Suddenly, he stopped, cocking his head to one side.

"Listen!" he hissed, "There's two more flocks coming from the upper end." His arm once more projected a calloused finger, pointing it at two precise places in the sky above the northern marshes. Again, the Yankee's eyes tried to focus into the great distance, to lock his stare onto the invisible makers of the music.

The High Tider continued, "It always helps if you can hear them before you see them. It sort of gives you a clue as to where to watch for them in the sky. You could see them right now if it wasn't so nearly dark. Just you keep watchin' those two spots with your ears and you'll soon be seein' geese with your eyes."

The Yankee stared into the graying dusk that smothered itself across the sunset's reflected afterglow to no avail. Once again, the flock flew onward, never to be fixed in his gaze.

Bill Styron, of course, had seen the geese as they ghosted by, silhouetted against darkened clouds in the nearly night sky.

"You know, it is getting a little too dark to see them any more and the moon won't rise until the short hours in the morning. That makes it doubtful that more snows will be drifting down this evening. These are, more than likely, local birds feeding in corn stubble and winter wheat fields on the mainland to the north and returning home to roost on Pea Island."

The Yankee was grateful for the comment about it being too dark to see the geese, even though he sensed that the High Tider had actually eyeballed them with some sort of infrared, telescopic, night vision.

"Bill," the Yankee broke in, "I've read that these geese migrate from their nesting grounds in the Canadian Arctic and that they are 'greater' snow geese, whatever that means. They have always wintered here in the Hatteras area. I have been seeing them on Pea Island by the thousands, yet only an occasional flock here on Bodie. How come they don't like these marshes as well? They all look the same to me."

The High Tider studied the Yankee's question and thought long and carefully before answering. So far, the Yankee hadn't seemed to be offended like the typical tourist at the mention of hunting on the refuge areas.

So he began to explain, "At one time, the geese were as plentiful here as they are now on Pea Island. But if you noticed when you parked that high-dollar car over there, there is a sign that tells you which hunting blinds are accessible from this parking area.

Snow geese aren't particularly smart, but they are wary birds that know how to survive. Landing in the vicinity of a wooden box full of red-eyed hunters buried in the marsh who want to shoot them full of little round holes is not particularly good for prolonging a snow goose's happy life. There was a time, though, back when we first got the season reopened in 1976, that they would lock in and decoy to anything white. You couldn't even wear white underwear in the marshes! If you did and had to hunker down behind a myrtle bush to heed a call of nature, you might get 'goosed' with your pants down and it's a little difficult to shoot in that particular position!"

The Yankee nodded his head in agreement and laughed at the humor, but had a look of disbelief about him. The High Tider set about further explanation to assure the Yankee that his tale had credibility.

"No foolin'. I've worked up a hard sweat walkin' out to those blinds and taken off my white long handles, hung 'em on a bush, and had snow geese decoy to 'em. We used cloth diapers as decoys back then, but they got wise to that trick after a few years. There wasn't no store bought snow goose decoys so we did the best we could. I also happened to have a few of my dad's old canvas and wire hoop decoys that I fixed up and used a while, until most of them sort of just rotted away. I still have a couple left that I set out, but only on special occasions."

The Yankee's forehead wrinkled in thought. "Bill, your father hunted snow geese, but when you say the season reopened, I assume that snow geese were protected at some point in time. Did something happen to decrease their numbers? Right now, on Pea Island, they form what looks like a white wall-to-wall carpet spread across the marshes. They even feed in the roadside ditches. At times you have to be careful you don't run over them when your car startles them into flight!"

The High Tider turned to the marsh. Contemplating the depths of its shadows, he searched for the proper way to put his explanation of the ups and downs of the snow goose population into just the right perspective. It was a tall order to be asked to give a stranger insight into the ways of these islands without knowing if he understood and shared the bond between hunter and bird.

Bill Styron stared into the solitude of the darkened marsh. It was illuminated only by the faint light of stars reflected from the mirrored surface of cordgrass-edged waters. One loud, lonely goose "honk" echoed through the stillness, reaching his ears and those of the stranger's above the lowering background gabble of the enormous flocks bidding each other "good night" in the security of the refuge's borders far to the south. The High Tider turned to the Yankee to gauge his reaction to the call of the wild goose. He heard only the Yankee's thoughtful silence, saw only twin eyes matching his own staring across the marsh, and knew instinctively that this man could, or already did, understand.

Clearing his voice, the High Tider began to speak in his quietly rolling tone. "When my dad was teaching me to hunt, snow geese were strictly off-limits. There were lots of things I could do and get away with only a scolding or other light punishment, like stealing pies and such. But, if I hadda shot a snow goose and my dad hadda found out, he'd have tanned my hide with a switch cane stick and nailed it to the side of the oyster shucking shed. He felt personally responsible for shooting snow geese to the brink of extinction. When he began to notice that fewer and fewer snows were wintering here and that the survivors were becoming warier with each passing season, he was the first to voluntarily stop shootin' 'em for the markets. With Canada goose numbers on the increase, there were plenty of tastier targets around. But the demand for snow goose feathers remained high for insulating coats and quilts and the like. The federal government finally closed the season on snows and started buying up marsh land for the refuge. Initially, the opposition against the condemnation and purchase of these marshes was fierce. Compensating the families of local folks that had owned the land for generations with money from the very duck stamps they were forced to buy for the privilege of hunting really went against their grain. Some even set the marshes on fire in retaliation, though that's kind of ironic. Now the refuge personnel set fire to the marshes periodically to make them produce new growth to feed the geese and ducks. Fire keeps woody shrub and tree growth down and lets the grass grow back nice and green. As a way of appeasing the local folks who thought their hunting rights were being taken from them unjustly, the U. S. Fish and Wildlife Service created a system of hunting blinds on this part of the refuge, Bodie Island, as part of the purchase agreement. My dad was dedicated to seeing that the hunting of ducks and Canada geese would continue, especially since the marshes you are enjoying right now once belonged to him."

The High Tider paused to let the weight of his words sink in. The Yankee digested that last sentence for what he supposed was a sufficient length of time. When it appeared that the High Tider might not continue without further prompting, he coaxed him to tell more.

"You mean to tell me that your family once owned all this?" he asked. He swept his arms in a semi-circular gesture, seeking to encompass some great area out there in the blackness.

"Well, not quite all of it. Only a few hundred acres. But every square inch of it was prime hunting territory and it went a long way to provide us with fresh fowl. It also provided a good income for these parts with market gunning and, later on, guide fees from hunters coming from New York, Maryland, and other foreign places so far away my young mind could not comprehend the distance. It hurts me sometimes, to know that this marsh could have been mine, my sons, and his after him, though I guess it's all been for the best. At least I know that these marshes will never look like that!"

The High Tider turned and pointed an accusing finger at the speckling of rectangular lights shining through the windows of the numerous retirement houses and vacation cottages across Highway N. C. 12 on the Atlantic Ocean side of the island. To him, the very sight of the boxy roofpeaks silhouetted against the evening skyline was an abomination, in sharp contrast to the smoothly rounded domes of the dunes, the wavering tops of the sea oats, and the rolling breakers of the surf.

The Yankee was obviously shaken by the angered tone in the High Tider's voice. He tried to muster the courage to defend the fact that he now owned and lived in one of those cedar-shake covered houses, so new that the smell of fresh latex paint still permeated its rooms.

He searched for words of regret, for it has always been etched in the nature of the human heart that a newcomer moving into any previously occupied area of Earth must somehow justify his presence to those who were there before him. Bill Grainger stared up at the night sky and tried to think of a way to make peace with this offended man, to apologize for his intrusion into Bill Styron's ancestral home.

Apologetic words would not come to mind for he had no apologies to make. Perhaps as an explanation or, more likely, to enable the interesting conversation he had been having with the crusty personality beside him to continue, he took a deep breath, partially exhaled, then, folding his hands behind his back with eyes still affixed to the dense ceiling of night sky, he began to speak. His first words came almost involuntarily in a breathless voice that was almost indistinguishable from the hushed whisper of the wind rustling through the rushes.

"You know Bill, I worked and lived for most of my life in a city. For thirty years, I couldn't walk out the door, look up, and see the stars at night. The height of the buildings and the glare of the lights mingling with the haze of car exhausts and factory fumes obscured their twinkling from the view of a man standing at pavement level. I broke my back working in a factory to make spare parts that allow trucks like that old Chevy of yours parked over there run forever."

He glanced at the High Tider's face but could not make out his expression in the failed light. When no argumentative words returned through the chilled air, he took it as a sign to continue.

"My greatest joys in life when I was young were hunting and fishing. These were my escape from the stifling walls of the city. My grandfather was a lobsterman who sold his catch in Boston and New York and he used to take me with him when he checked his pots. To reward me for being his mate, he would take me waterfowl hunting in the fall and winter. We would drive all night, sleep in his truck, and get up early to hunt some fabled spot he knew of on Long Island Sound or some secret place no one else ever heard of. He would plop a flotilla of decoys on the water in front of me in the darkness. Then we would wait for the sun to rise enough for shooting light, though sometimes I felt saddened when the daylight came because it would chase away the stars I had been gazing at through windows in the clouds. On a moonless night, the light from the stars alone was so bright that I could see well enough to untangle knots in the decoy lines while my grandfather busied himself about adjusting the stool until everything was just perfect. My consolation for the sunrise burning out the stars was usually pretty good, though. The sky would fill with black ducks and Canada Geese searching for a safe place to land. They were safe enough from me, all right, but my grandfather was a dead-shot and I don't remember him missing very often."

The smooth roll of the High Tider's accent interrupted. "What about your dad? Didn't he ever fish or hunt?"

The Yankee's defensive posturing eased. At least he had received a positive response indicating he should continue speaking. He sensed he had reached some middle ground that could be safely trod upon by two men drawn together from different niches in the world.

"Well, I think when he was a young man, my grandfather wanted him to follow in his footsteps and take over his lobster boat when he came of age. But, the lobstering waters were already full of pots and the competition was keen. Then came the pollution from factory wastes that progressively lowered the catch. Also, more and more people wanted to live near the water who thought the sights and smells of commercial fishing were unappealing to the eyes and nose. They forced the lobstermen from their dockage. It became hard to make enough money to raise a family, so, my dad decided he would be better off in another line of work. He started working in a factory, making automotive parts for a good wage. Then, when I was old enough, he helped me get a job in the same plant so we could work together. I continued to hunt at every opportunity, usually weekends and vacations. Dad went with me sometimes, but he never had the opportunity to go as often as I did. He was promoted progressively higher in the company each passing year and his dedication to his work consumed him."

Bill Styron found this man beside him to be interesting. Hours of toil at factory work explained the strong grip of his handshake. Curiousity aroused, he put to the stranger his most important question.

"So, what makes a city man such as yourself move to a mosquito and sandspur infested stretch of gritty sand beach like this, leaving your family and work behind. I know there're places up there where you can see the stars, so that can't be the only reason you moved here."

"The place where I worked was under a union labor contract, as is the situation with most large industries up there. They had a 'thirty-and-out' policy, which means that you work thirty years and are forced to retire. A younger worker can then take your place. The only drawback is that you can't work anywhere and still draw your retirement pension, not even at a fast food hamburger joint as a fry cook! I sat around for a couple of years and got thoroughly disgusted and bored. That got on my wife's nerves after a time so she decided to come down here and visit her family. Marge's last name was Midgette before she married me and I found out she was related to about half the people in Dare County. She was happy down here and I wasn't particularly happy up there. We discussed moving for a long time, then came the northern winter—January cold—and with it, snow deep enough to cover a giraffe's eyeballs. That did it for me. I was convinced that moving down here was a good thing. I won't have to shovel snow any longer like I did for most of my life. Can you imagine that! No more snow!"

The High Tider's mind couldn't instantly grasp the concept of a worker being paid only if he did not work, though he considered it for a few seconds before shrugging the idea off as yet another crazy Yankee invention that only they could understand. To his thoughts, a man worked until he died, or physically could no longer function in his life's occupation. Commercial fishing being essentially a cash-on-the-barrel-head, self-employed type of business, the only pension a man could have was what he managed to salt away over the years and the loving support of his wife and children to sustain him in his old age.

With a touch of irony he chuckled, "Well, I guess I made 'thirty-and-out' too! Worked a trawler for thirty, actually nigh-on-to forty years, before she got mad at me and broke me down. She threw me off her deck forever for workin' her so hard!"

A late flock gave noticed of its arrival, temporarily diverting the attention of the two men. It was the Yankee's voice that first disturbed the stillness as the goose music faded away.

"You say you hunt those geese. Is the season finished for this year? It seems to me that you should have been hunting today, rather than just bird-watching."

"It's Sunday! Everybody knows it ain't proper to hunt on the Sabbath!" He frowned in incredulous thought. That was another fault he had found in many of the northern folks. They came up a little short on religion, at least in the traditional, southern way of observance.

"Besides," he added almost as an afterthought, "this bum leg has stopped me from goin' out at all this season. I haven't even been able to tend to my blinds in Pamlico Sound. They may have blown away by now, except for the pilings. So, as you can see, I do the best I can. Just for the time being, I try to get out to see how they're flyin' on the odd chance I might be able to hunt again soon. I try to get to the refuge on Pea Island most evenings. That's where I would have been now if the traffic jam at the bridge hadn't stopped me. That's why I came to this place. I don't usually stop here to watch, or to hunt—because of the sight of all the houses and condos and such. But, if I turn my back to the buildings and highway, the marsh still looks pretty much like it always has—all quiet, serene, and peaceful. I guess it's no wonder that ducks and geese, maybe even people, come south to spend their winters here."

The Yankee began nodding in agreement, then suddenly jerked his left wrist up to eye level to gauge the luminous dial of his watch. "Oh my gosh, look at the time! Bill, I'm pleased to have made your acquaintance, but I've really got to run. Marge'll be worried about me!"

He hurriedly pumped Bill's hand and rushed down the steps. Beating a fast retreat, he looked over his shoulder and shouted, "Bill, if you ever need anybody to tag along as a hunting partner, I'd like to go with you sometime. I've never shot a greater snow goose."

The High Tider threw some offhand, non-committal comment at the departing Yankee and stroked his chin, "That's another thing about folks from up north," he thought. "Always in a hurry, always short on time. Yep, this one fell hot from the mold allright—short on manners, short on religion, short on time. All things considered, though, he's not such a bad guy—for a Yankee."

The High Tider watched as the Yankee hurriedly backed around in a complete "U," giving him an unobstructed view of the rear end of an older model Lincoln. He saw the distinctive hump of the truck lid surrounding the spare tire inside under the red glow of vanishing tail lights and knew, without being able to actually read, that the hump was branded with the word "Continental" in silver, stamped-on block letters. The car was overly fancy and pretentious for a man like Bill Styron. Wrapped around a man like Bill Grainger, it fit very well.

The High Tider hobbled down the steps in the same fashion as he had climbed them, one at a time. The tap-tap, tap-tap, sound of shoe leather slapping against pine steps was strangely hollow and melancholy now that human voices had fallen silent. The old fisherman had nearly forgotten his pained leg while talking to the Yankee, focused as his mind was upon the things he cherished above all else, especially his beloved snow geese.

The tail lights of the Chevy soon followed those of the Lincoln onto the southbound lane of N. C. 12. Worn tires hummed a high pitched whine against the blacktop as the Chevy gained speed. Bill was hoping that the long line of traffic had grown shorter by now as people reached their evening destinations and settled in for the night.

This was not the case, he soon discovered. He gave a muffled curse under his breath as he approached a double row of tail lights that spanned the distance between himself and the whale's hump arch of the broken bridge. Approaching cars in the left lane, bound north for the mainland, signalled that the temporary ferry had docked and off-loaded its passengers. Soon the process of loading those bound for Pea Island and Hatteras Island would begin. Hopefully, the wait would not be so long as to be intolerable to a man who was tired of waiting.

As the Chevy eased to its place at the end of the line, Bill was surprised to see the distinguishing trunk lid of a Lincoln Continental mirroring the glow of his headlamps. He wondered if this was the same automobile that had left him abruptly at the observation platform a few minutes before. Gold! That was the apparent color reflected back to him by the brightness of high beams. That was definitely a suitable color. Yet, how could he be certain this was the Yankee's car. He looked casually at the license plate and saw, not the usual numbers, but a series of letters. Obviously, it was one of those "vanity" personalized plates which can be purchased in North Carolina with the extra proceeds going to beautify road shoulders with plantings of wild flowers.

It didn't take long for Bill to decipher the message, "NOMOSNO." When the meaning became clear to him, he was certain that, indeed, the Yankee was seated behind the wheel of the car ahead. The High Tider remembered the Yankee's parting offer of joining him for a hunt. He hadn't really given the idea serious consideration at the time. Now, however, the tiniest twinge of doubt about letting the offer pass into oblivion, unaccepted, pricked at his conscience.

"After all, the big Yankee has been a working man all his life, just like me," he reasoned with himself, "and you've got to believe that any man who appreciates the sight of stars shining against the backdrop of a moonless sky must have some good qualities. He seems to want the opportunity to hunt and is sort of interesting to keep company with. On the other hand, though, he is still a Yankee."

The arguments, pro and con, fought inside the High Tider's head with neither side gaining an upper hand. What should he do? Let the opportunity pass or invite the Yankee along to see if he was up to the test of the marsh, the goose, and the gun.

As he stared at the shining reflection of the license plate before him, a nagging thought burned itself into his brain. The chopped syllables that were tied together in seven of the maximum allowable eight spaces on the license tag to form a single word began to take on new meaning. The acronym seemed to taunt him, almost as a dare. He decided to take the perceived challenge.

"No more snow, eh? Well I guess I'll just have to show that Yankee it may not necessarily be true!"

The High Tider got out of the pickup cab and left the engine running. He made his way to the driver's side window of the gold Continental and tapped against the glass with his thick fingernail, startling the man inside. With an electric buzz, the window powered down exposing the Yankee's surprised face. His expression changed quickly to one of recognition.

"What's the matter, Bill? Everything all right?"

The line of traffic was beginning to inch ahead. "Your number, Yank. You forgot to give me your telephone number," shouted the High Tider.

The number was hastily scribbled on a corner torn from a brown paper bag and thrust through the window into the High Tider's hand. Amid the curses and blaring horns of frustrated drivers that were being held back as the line of traffic inched ahead, Bill Styron stiff-leggedly hopped back into his truck, slammed the door, and ground the transmission into gear.

The gold Continental preceded the Chevy south a short distance before turning left and disappearing into the maze of streets that curled along the ocean front. Bill Styron's turn to board the ferry eventually came. As the slow-moving boat carried him

The Herbert C. Bonner bridge after repair.
Erosion control stones were place on the Pea Island side.

beside the damaged bridge Bill could see the point where the row of warning lights ended abruptly, identifying the point of the bridge's collapse. These last red pinpoints of light also marked the severed end of electrical power lines that served Hatteras Island.

To the south lay nothing but unspoiled night—blackness and stars. Bill didn't really mind the inconvenience of being without electricity. His wife did.

"Well, it's about time you got home!" came a feminine voice from somewhere in the darkened recesses of the house. The sound of footsteps on the porch and the creaking of door hinges had told Becky Styron her husband was home. "There ain't no supper on the table — won't be any either, unless you brought somethin' to cook and somethin' to cook it with."

Bill produced the lantern fuel and groceries which had been his reason for venturing off the island. He fueled and fired the hurricane lamp, then the camp stove, and soon had a pot of oyster stew bubbling away.

"How's that for service?" he asked his wife.

"I suppose it will have to do for now, but I sure will be glad when we have electricity again. It is kind of romantic though, sitting here with the lantern hissing and no TV to bother you." She sat close to her husband and snuggled against his shoulder while they sipped their stew from steaming mugs.

Bill described to her the events of his day—the ferry ride with its interminable waiting both going and coming, and the trip to Manteo to buy groceries and fuel. He paused when he was done, staring at the lantern, then began to tell the story of his chance meeting with the Yankee. He finished his tale on a negative note.

"I don't know why I got his number, him being a Yankee and all. Besides, how will I be able to wade out through that sucking marsh mud with this bad leg."

Becky Styron had listened to her husband's whining long enough. She had seen his sullen moods and knew that it was time for him to be healed. It wasn't his body she worried about. The leg would heal with time. But she had seen a progressive worsening of his attitude brought on by the loss of his boat and with it the dignity of performing an honest day's work. Months of inactivity had made him cranky and short tempered.

176

Uncharacteristic sarcasm and belittling comments had crept into his conversation with greater frequency until they had become part of his everyday speech. She decided her husband had been feeling sorry for himself long enough. He was really beginning to grate on her nerves, especially now that there was no electricity with all its little diversionary conveniences. Somehow the walls of their already-too-small house seemed to shrink tightly in around them, forcing them together until the friction of their close confinement was bound to ignite sparks of discontent.

"Bill Styron! You oughta be ashamed o' yourself! That has got to be the lamest excuse for not taking a man huntin' I've ever heard!" Becky slammed her mug down on the coffee table where her feet had been resting comfortably a moment before. Hot froth geysered onto her hand, scalding her index finger. The finger went instantly into her mouth as she sucked it to stop the pain. Jumping erect she squared to face her husband.

Bill feared he was in for a real tongue-lashing. He knew his wife's temper. She would vent her anger at him until she could get it all out. All he could do was sit and take what she dished until whatever was eating a hole in her belly was purged from her system. Only problem was, he never could tell what had her pants twisted in a knot until her tantrum was over. It might take minutes, hours, or even days for her to come to the point.

"Oh well," he thought, "she's gotta be better entertainment than watchin' TV."

Bill sunk down into the couch cushions as low as a man can go and retracted his head into the folds of his threadbare wool sweater in his best imitation of a loggerhead turtle. He tried his utmost to tuck his ears below the level of his shoulders in a conscious attempt to deflect the sharpness of her words from his sensitive eardrums.

Becky Styron snatched her finger from her mouth with a loud pop and levelled it at her husband's nose like the barrel of a loaded pistol.

177

"You've laid around this house doing nothing for months, ever since you cracked that leg. The only thing you ever get off your lazy butt to do is to drive up to Pea Island and watch your silly geese sail in every evening. I've seen you stand there long enough, like some sad-eyed puppy with his mouth watering for a bone. You get out there with that Yankee fellah and hunt! I don't care if you fall down head first into that stinkin', suckin' mud you care so much about and stay there 'til the bubbles quit coming up. Maybe, if I'm lucky, he won't even pull you out and he'll just leave you there until your attitude gets better."

Bill tried to open his mouth to defend himself but was immediately interrupted.

"I'm not through with you, yet! You just listen to what I have to say! You haven't had anybody to hunt with since Jamie left last year. If you don't find a new partner soon, you're gonna' get too old and decrepit and spiteful and hateful and there ain't nobody ever gonna want to hunt with you ever again! Besides, you said this Yankee fellah, this Bill whats-his-name's wife is a Midgette. You know I've Midgette kin on my mother's side and that makes them family! So, the least you could do is show some common courtesy and call him up and take him hunting, you ill-natured, ill-mannered, poor old worn-out excuse for a goose hunter. If he's got any sense at all, he'll turn you down flat. But since you took his telephone number you implied that you would take him. Have some manners! Call him! Now!"

With that, she pointed her reddened finger at the telephone on the coffee table. She stood like a statue, staring at Bill with the countenance of a marsh hawk whose eyes were locked onto potential prey.

He looked into those fiery eyes reflecting the flickering flame of the lantern's light and knew that she would not allow him to get to his feet until he made the call.

She was right, after all. If his son, Jamie, had been here, he would have kept their stake blinds out on the sound in good repair and had them bushed with aromatic boughs of white-cedar and wax myrtle. Jamie would have taken his father hunting even if he had to carry him on his own back like a sack of water-logged decoys. But Jamie Styron, like so many others, had to leave Hatteras Island in search of a better living, or, more accurately stated, a way to make enough money to pay his way through life. With hard times for commercial fishing, too much competition, too few fish, and, finally, the near closure of Oregon Inlet, Jamie had ventured inland. He managed to find a new life on a flyway far to the west. He called often and wrote from time to time about the wonderful hunting there, with five different species of geese to hunt in the cornfields near his new home. Bill was happy for him, although he was not fond of the fact that with all the new people immigrating to Hatteras from other areas, there seemed to be less and less room remaining for the island's original inhabitants.

"Oh well," he thought, reaching for the phone, "A bridge does move two ways. People can come. People can go." He looked at his wife. She was immobile except for an angry tremble in the scalded finger she aimed at the phone.

Bill imagined he had discovered what was eating her, now that she had vented the poison from her system. She must have missed Jamie terribly. Surely she couldn't be that angry with an old goose hunter.

"You're right as usual, Becky," the High Tider said humbly as he held the hand-set to his ear and began to dial. "That Yankee is family and I should call him. I don't know where my manners were. Oh, no! I still can't do it."

She nearly worked herself into a rage again but before she could get really wound up, he playfully handed her the phone. Laughing, he said, "The bridge is out, the electricity's off, and the telephone lines are dead. I'm not the only thing around here that doesn't work any more."

In her anger, Becky had forgotten that the communication cables had been cut along with the electrical lines when the bridge collapsed.

"Well, Becky, I guess all I really wanted was your opinion. You sure gave it to me! I'll ride back across on the ferry and extend him a personal invitation the next chance I get."

Tension relieved, they began to laugh together at the window-rattling fuss Becky had raised over a telephone call that couldn't be made.

The High Tider procrastinated for a few days, putting off the contact he knew was inevitable. He acted as though he was having difficulty in reconciling himself to the fact that he must take an outsider hunting. In reality, it was the inability of his mending leg to support him during the inevitable slogging through the marsh which caused him to shy away from what he knew he must do.

Becky made certain her husband knew what his duty was. Her incessant nagging drove him out-of-doors on extended walks to give his ringing ears a rest from the sharpness of her tongue. It was on these walks that he found he could travel long distances if he proceeded slowly and paid close attention to keeping his balance, adjusting his gait to offset the differences in muscle strength between his legs. He hobbled the painful miles along the shoulder of N. C. 12 to Pea Island and back. He would have crawled on hands and knees through dunefuls of sandspurs, spiney cactus, and black thorn-tipped Spanish bayonets to catch a glimpse of his homecoming snows.

The hunting season was rapidly drawing to a close. He grappled with the fact that his days of hesitation could be put off no longer. Making the necessary arrangements, to the great relief of his scorched ears and his wife's strained voice, he arranged to meet his new acquaintance at the Whalebone Junction Hunter Check-in Station on the very last day of snow goose hunting permitted by law, January 31.

"Good morning, High Tider!" The tightly clipped syllables of Bill Grainger's greeting cut the icy crispness of morning air.

Bill Styron reached forward to shake the bear-paw hand offered him, echoing the reply, "Good mornin', Yankee!" His smoothly rounded speech mimicked the rise and fall of the breakers that could be heard rolling against the sea shore, to the near east.

They stood among twelve other pairs of bleary-eyed hunters outside the check-in station, waiting for the arrival of the ranger, referee for the day's hunt.

The two Bills signed the standby sheet since they did not have advance reservations. The High Tider explained to his partner that reservations could be obtained by a mail-in drawing held in October of each year. Any slots which remained open for each of twenty blinds in the marshes of Bodie Island could be filled by walk-in hunters such as themselves. With only thirteen parties of hunters participating on this particular day, that meant that all would have the opportunity to make their way through the marshes in the darkness, spread their decoys, and await the dawn flight of snow geese that would be channeling northward along the flyways from Pea Island Refuge.

A cold front had come to the Outer Banks, preceded for two days by a howling northeaster with winds gusting upwards of forty knots. It left a legacy of relative calm, with frigid air that penetrated to the very marrow of men's bones. The hunters muttered and complained among themselves about having to stand outside, unshielded from the elements, while waiting their turns to draw lots for one of the blinds.

The High Tider reached into his truck to retrieve his coat and suggested the Yankee should do the same.

"It sure is different than it was a few years back," breathed the High Tider through puffs of condensed steam. He nestled into his ragged, goose-down coat and leaned back against the door of the old Chevy.

The Yankee stretched on a coat made of modern miracle fibers, so new that it crinkled as it was zipped closed. He settled his backside against the window of the gold Continental and nodded his head toward the High Tider, signalling him to continue.

"The drawing for blinds and the hunter check-in used to be conducted at the former lighthouse keeper's house. A man could keep warm inside or go out on the porch to sit on the railing, if need be, to kinda' adjust his temperature. But now they make us wait outside, with precious little protection from rain or cold."

"I understand that they are going to renovate the lighthouse keeper's house next year and make it into some sort of historic site or visitor's center," interrupted the Yankee. "It should be good for that."

"Yeah, good for tourists, but not for hunters. A long time back, my boy and I worked hard and managed to shoot our limit of snow geese at first light. The limit was two birds per hunter back then, so we had a total of four geese. We returned to the lighthouse keeper's house. It was used as a centralized tourist's orientation site, ranger's office, and hunter check-in station, all rolled into one building. I had gone inside to report our kill and was talking with the ranger. My son was young then, I guess about fourteen. Without thinkin' about it, he reached into the truck bed and grabbed those strung-together snow geese. He dragged 'em out and held 'em up proud to admire them, turning them this way and that, strokin' and smoothin' their ruffled feathers. All of a sudden, this little old woman from some foreign part of the world pulled up alongside him in a big, new shiny car—I think the license plate said 'New Jersey.' Jamie stood there and held them geese up for her to see, smiling real big because he was so proud. Well, let me tell you, that woman flew out of that car and into his face so fast she looked like a turpentined cat! Acted like one too! She lit into him with a sassy tongue and shook her finger right under his nose, shouting and screaming about how he ought to be ashamed of himself for killin' those 'pretty white ducks' that were probably 'somebody's pets.' He was just a lad and not at all used to dealing with the scoldin' ways of a woman's waggin' tongue. So, he just stood there, dazed and shocked, with eyes and mouth opened wide, not havin' the slightest idea of what he had done to offend this stranger. When I saw what was happenin', I flew across that wooden porch and leapt down the steps, touchin' nary a one. I got myself between Jamie and that woman and gave her a lecture of my own. I tried to explain to her about the way that hunting increases a man's enjoyment of the marsh and that it was an honorable and important part of life to us. Instead of listenin' to what I had to say, that she-cat grabbed her pocketbook and began flailin' away at me and Jamie. The ranger rushed over to try to calm the woman down, explainin' that this portion of the refuge was open for controlled huntin'. Then he looked at me accusingly, and said, 'I do believe though, that sometimes we spend too much of our time, on a one-on-one basis, with hunters and hunting related activity.'"

The High Tider paused as he noticed the arrival of the ranger. The ranger unlocked the glass doors at the front of the tiny building. The pairs of sportsmen clustered around. The few that would fit followed the ranger inside seeking refuge from the cold air. The remaining hunters waited outside, listening as the morning ritual began.

The High Tider continued his story as he climbed the steps toward the groups of hunters crowded around the doorway.

"That's when I finally lost my temper! I began shoutin' at him about how there wouldn't be a refuge at all if we hunters collectively hadn't bought up all our own land with revenues from the sale of duck stamps. Then I told him that those same hunters gave the money that paid his salary and threw in some emphatic comments about how we were nice enough to let people like that woman onto OUR refuge for free when we had to pay for the privilege of huntin'. By 'emphatic' I mean I cussed him—more than a little bit! The ranger said nothing more but simply stared at me like he didn't believe me or that what I had to say didn't matter. He put his arm around the woman's shoulder to console her. They turned away and walked toward the old lightkeeper's house. As they went inside, Jamie tossed our geese back in the truck bed. We left and never went back. It really hurts me, because years ago, I had kin—hunters, by the way—who lived in that house. Now you know why the lighthouse keeper's house is for tourists and why this little shanty is for hunters. It keeps us separated and out of each other's way."

The two Bills waited their turn. Then each presented his hunting license and driver's license to the ranger. The ranger checked each license for the appropriate information; expiration date, Federal Migratory Bird and Conservation Stamp, and North Carolina Waterfowl Stamp. In all, the fees for the privilege of hunting totalled sixty dollars as identified by the amounts shown on the face of each stamp.

The ranger copied the name and address of each hunter from the face of his hunting license, then checked that information against his driver's license. He noted that the address on Bill Grainger's driver's license didn't concur with that which was shown on his resident hunting license.

"New Jersey, eh? How did you manage to buy a resident hunting license?"

Bill Grainger explained that he had just moved to Bodie Island recently and had not yet had the opportunity to obtain his N. C. Driver's license.

The ranger peered suspiciously at the Yankee from beneath the brim of his Smokey-The-Bear hat to study his features. He glanced around at the group of men impatiently awaiting their turn to draw for the morning's blinds. Quickly, he decided that the mismatched non-resident driver's license and resident hunting license were perfectly legal. Handing them back to the Yankee, he smiled and said simply, "Enjoy your hunt."

The ranger took twenty tarnished brass discs from pegs on a board and placed them inside a container. He shook the container vigorously to mix the discs, then placed them into a dispenser which stacked them like a roll of coins, leaving a lone disc accessible through an opening in the bottom. He called the first hunter's name on the list. The designated hunter stepped forward through the group and drew the bottom disc.

"Blind 18," he said as he read the number stamped into the metal.

As the ranger made note of the two hunters which would occupy blind 18 for the day, the two Bills drifted out the open door to the rear of the group to gain relief from the closeness of the crowded ten by twelve foot room.

Outside the entryway, they listened to the sound of each blind being drawn and assigned in its turn. The Yankee asked the High Tider which blinds were the best for hunting snow geese. The High Tider explained that blinds 19 and 20 were good because they were at the south end, nearest Pea Island. The snow geese would likely pass over them on their way to feed in farm fields to the north at dawn's first light. Blinds 15 and 18 were also good since they were directly beneath the flyway used by the snow geese on a cold, clear morning such as this one following a two-day northeaster. Blinds 1, 2, 3, and 4 would be favored in the afternoon, but were a long walk out through thick muck. The closest walk would be to blind 16. That would be the easiest on his stiffened leg. It seemed that every blind had its good and bad points.

Bill Styron heard his name called by the ranger. He and the Yankee made their way through the gathering and stood before him. The ranger impatiently shook the dispenser with a metallic jingling and said, "Hurry up and draw a number." He extended the dispenser toward the two men. The High Tider licked his fingers for luck and drew. "Blind number 9," he read aloud. He blinked and held the disc close to his eyes to make certain that a number 1 had not preceded the number 9 and perhaps been worn away from years of constant handling by weather-reddened hands. "Maybe it was a 7," he thought as he checked one more time. But, no, it definitely was a number 9.

He smacked the disc into the ranger's outstretched palm and grumbled to his partner, "Let's get moving. We have a long way to go and not much time to get there."

The High Tider rushed to his truck as quickly as his limping gait would allow with the Yankee close behind. He nearly lost his balance as he opened the door to climb in. Bill Grainger caught his elbow and steadied him into the cab.

"What's your hurry?" asked the big man as he closed the door behind his guide.

The reply came as the door slammed, "It's the longest walk on the island! Most difficult, too! We have only an hour to get there. Instead of standing there, you'd better get in that fancy car of yours and follow me—quick as you can!"

The ranger looked up as he heard two engines grumble to life. He watched the battered Chevy lead the shiny Lincoln through the parking lot, shaking his head from side to side. He pondered what circumstances would compel two men from such obviously different backgrounds to share a hunt, then turned his attention back to the remaining hunters who were impatiently awaiting their turns to draw for the remaining blinds.

"Of all the luck!" The High Tider complained through the chilled darkness to his hunting partner as they prepared their gear for the long trek through the marsh.

The long, soggy trail to blind number 9.

The Yankee shined the beam of a krypton-bulbed flashlight against the weathered sign that showed this to be the parking area for those drawn to hunt from blinds 8, 9, 10, and 11. In the fringe of light at the edge of the beam, he could make out a worried look on the High Tider's face. A tassel of graying hair swished across the old Fisherman's eyebrows as he gazed across marsh, surveying the depths of its blackness.

"What's wrong, Bill? Isn't number 9 blind a good one?" asked the Yankee with a touch of concern in his voice.

When he spoke, he noticed the condensed vapor of his breath forming a cloud about his head, partly obscuring his view of the High Tider's face. It was definitely a cold morning. The thermometer had risen to 20 degrees, at most. He shivered, causing the flashlight beam to wriggle and bounce.

The High Tider was preparing two antique canvas snow goose decoys for the long walk ahead, tying their necks together with a length of tarred nylon fishing hand line. The dancing of the beam irritated him as he tried to secure the knot.

"Yes, it's a good blind, a great blind, the best blind if you want to know the truth about it! It's way out yonder, beyond that line of pond pines and myrtle bushes. You can just make them out if you look hard enough. There's just enough light to allow you to see the edge of the trees if you turn off your light and let your eyes adjust to the dark. There's only this one problem and it's a big 'un. It's this bum leg. There's a mile and a quarter of marsh between us and the blind and it's the coldest morning of the season. When your eyes get used to the lack of light, just you keep lookin' out there and tell me what you see." The High Tider busied himself while the Yankee attempted to make shapes from far shadows.

The Yankee squinted to see the edge of a tree line. He thought he saw something in the general direction indicated by the High Tider. At least there was a transition where absolute blackness met dim light. The only faint light on this moonless morning came from the shining of stars.

187

Stars! As his eyes became attuned to the limited amount of available light, the Yankee pivoted his head in an arc. Upward, skyward, swept the Yankee's gaze until the vista of a million sparkling points of light stretched before his eyes. From horizon to horizon spanned tiny single pinpricks, larger undulating beacons, and clustered constellations. Together in their entirety, they formed the vastness of the Milky Way. The Milky Way! He understand fully why it was named that now. The closely-packed trail of stars looked as though an infinite pathway of powdered white diamond dust had been smoothed across the heavens by some enormous hand and been backlit by some miraculous phosphorescence. There was no end to the length and depth of the stars. He stood there, transfixed, mesmerized, until brought back down to earth by the impatient other half of the hunting team.

"You're lookin' the wrong direction, Yankee. If you look down here at the marsh, you'll notice there's no reflection from those stars you're staring up at so hard. Don't you wonder about that? Never mind. You're gonna find out soon enough."

The High Tider slung the pair of antique decoys over one shoulder. Over the other, he looped a coarse length of tarred line that was attached at one end to the silver-worn barrel of a Winchester Model 12 shotgun. The other end of the line was attached to a stock which had, years before, lost the last flake of varnish to the sandpapery grit of a calloused palm. He thrust a bundle of switch canes, machete cut to a length of two-and-a-half feet into the Yankee's arms. They were wrapped around with two gray bands of duct tape and shoulder-strapped similarly to the Model 12 with a hank of tarred line.

The single explanation word, "Decoys!" accompanied the bundle of canes in response to the question the High Tider knew was forming on the Yankee's lips.

The Yankee swung the nylon detachable sling of his current issue, 100% factory camouflage-painted, 12 gauge 3'" magnum chambered, Mossberg slide action repeater over his shoulder to join the cane bundle. He hurried to join a departing High Tider and caught him, standing and waiting, at the edge of the band of needle rushes that marked the beginning of water and the end of land.

"Ice!" The sickening crunch of the High Tider's first step into the frozen marsh crackled its name. Now the Yankee knew why the twinkling of stars had not been mirrored by the water. As the northeasterly winds had died with the passing of the cold front, a cloak of refrigerated calm crept over the marsh, crystallizing its top half-inch into a solid sheet.

The High Tider proceeded a few steps, struggling against the ice cutting into his shins through the black rubber of his commercial fisherman's waders. The Yankee watched nervously as the injured fisherman forced his way through the ice. Following closely, he could hear the High Tider's panting and see the steampuffs of great exhalations coming from beneath the edges of his coat hood. Their whiteness swirled in the near-blackness, suspended in dead cold air, as he labored against the ice to make headway.

Left leg sliding forward, breaking ice, kicking. Right leg sliding forward beside left, planting itself in soft marsh bottom, pivoting. Left leg breaking ice, kicking once more. The process repeated itself methodically, over and over again. In this manner, the High Tider led the Yankee at a snails' pace through the marsh, advancing slowly, but ever so certainly, in the direction of blind number 9.

The Yankee heard and observed the fight of man against marsh, marsh against man for two hundred yards. He hurt inside for the proud man breaking the pathway, crippled in body, but obviously not in soul or spirit. Every fiber in the Yankee's being cried out for him to take the lead, to break the ice. But he was not invited to. He sensed that this was a struggle the High Tider must win for himself. Besides, of the two men, only the struggling man in the lead knew the location of the invisible trail that threaded its way through the frozen marsh pools and rush spikes that would eventually take them to a wooden box hidden somewhere ahead.

A pair of young hunters, recently graduated to manhood from the semi-mature status of their teenaged years, caught up with the two creeping men.

They whispered to each other, making snide comments about old men being too slow. A sneering remark escaped them, audible above a pause in methodical crunching, "It sure would be nice if those old buzzards would move a little faster. We might be able to make it to blind 11 by daybreak."

They had no appreciation for the enormous physical effort being expended by the High Tider. Novices they were. They did not realize that the reason they had gained easy access through the marsh to this point was due to the effort of a broken man, who, using his one good leg, had churned frozen solidness into thin floating icebergs left chattering and clinking together in his wake.

The brashness of their remarks had its intended impact on Bill Styron. He speeded his efforts ever so slightly, imperceptibly so to the newcomers at his heels. But to Bill Grainger, who had been part of the agonizingly slow-paced process of wild goose chase follow-the-leader from its very beginning noticed the subtle change in the High Tider's rhythm.

He watched the High Tider press harder and faster, breaking the coordination of his movements. His left leg kicked ever harder, taking bigger bites from the ice. His right leg pivoted faster when planting itself in the muck. His movements became unbalanced as his cadence increased. What had been a smooth and naturally flowing process a few moments before had become a melée of frantic actions on the old fisherman's part.

"I'll show those young'uns how a grown man can beat the ice!" was the maddened thought that drove him on.

Their remarks stabbed his ego to its core. The violence of his effort increased with each step. His smoldering anger melted the frigid marsh, shattering it into decreasingly smaller slivers, making a generous path for those behind to walk through.

The Yankee watched the High Tider's erratic silhouette against the pre-dawn luminescence reflecting from the frosty marsh surface. He was just before asking the proud man to let the late comers pass, to let them take the lead, to let them match their strength against the board-like mass. The words were forming inside his mouth. His right hand was reaching forward to tap the shoulder of the tired man to slow and calm him when he asked the question that must be asked.

At that precise instant all semblance of balance in the High Tider's frame dissolved. His right foot thrust too deeply into a hole filled with sucking mud, stuck fast, and failed in its pivot. His left leg attempted to kick its way upward to freedom through the ice, but could not muster the necessary energy. Bouncing back with shin-bruising momentum, it upset an already unsteady body.

Down it went, not all at once, but a piece at a time, like a child's tower of building blocks, or a barge-struck bridge that sways from side-to-side before it disintegrates into a pile of rubble.

Two fragile canvas decoys went first. Spiralling away they thudded hard to the ice. A canvas hood slipped from falling shoulders, releasing a cloud of vapor from a gasp of surprise. Arms flailed the air wildly, seeking something secure to cling to in their effort to save a sweating body from immersion in freezing water.

The realization struck the High Tider that falling would be the end of his hunting this year. It was his last day, his last chance. No man could hunt, saturated to the skin on a twenty degree morning, without being frozen into a blue-lipped block of ice himself. He balled his fists defiantly, punching toward the ice in a futile effort to lessen the impact. But his knuckles had barely brushed the ice's surface when his descent was suddenly slowed, then stopped altogether.

An astonished and thankful Styron was held dangling, an inch from disaster, suspended above the icy water which would have ended his luck for the day.

Chaos! Mayhem in the making! That's what the Yankee had seen. Just as he had been reaching forward to tap the High Tider's shoulder it began to shudder violently, like a tower in an earthquake. He grabbed instinctively at the only thing available to save his partner from falling.

Firmly clenched in the steel vice grip of his powerful hand was the barrel of a model 12 Winchester. A tightened loop of tarred line secured its stock to the shoulder of a crippled man.

Groaning ice complained as the seismic shock waves of sudden commotion radiated in all directions. The Yankee gripped the gun barrel tightly, pointing it skyward to steady the High Tider while he worked his foot from side to side to release it from the suction of black muck. The sulfide stench of marsh gas bubbled to the surface as the stuck foot came free.

Bill Styron was amazed at the strength of the arm which had saved him from a heart-freezing dunk. He was pulled free from the mud, hoisted erect like a helpless kitten being dragged to safety by its mother. Slipping his arm free of the loop of tarred line, he nodded speechless thanks to the Yankee. The Yankee, who never once lessened his grip on the barrel, slung the gun over his shoulder, clattering it into position beside his own.

The two late arrivals mumbled something intelligible only to each other and began to break a path around the older hunters. One of them paused beside the canvas decoys and started to make a reach, attempting to retrieve them for their owner in some lame gesture of goodwill.

"Leave them where they are!" commanded the Yankee. "You boys are in such a hurry, we would hate to detain you any longer."

He turned to the High Tider. In a voice loud enough for the others to hear he said, "Let them fight the ice for us for awhile. It's only fair since you broke it this far for them."

The High Tider caught his breath while the sound of crunching ice died away in the distance. "You sure saved me from a cold bath this mornin', Yank," said a very thankful Styron. "I'd worked up quite a sweat, but I'd much rather be under a nice warm shower at home than washing it off in chilled marsh brine on such a bitter mornin' as this!"

The Yankee retrieved the fallen decoys and swung them into place on the bundle of switch canes slung over his left shoulder. As he started along the trail of broken ice left by the departed hunters, he turned and chuckled, "Well, I didn't know if it was you or that stinking marsh mud I had been smelling. I thought for a minute about letting you go! But, since I don't know the way to blind number 9, I figured I had better learn to put up with the smell."

As the High Tider followed the white beacons of a pair of antique decoys bobbing above the Yankee's shoulder, he noticed in the gathering light that one of them was lumpy. The fall had bent one of its wire hoops.

"You know, Yank, this old muck does kinda stink," he said to the form ahead of him. There was no reply. The Yankee couldn't hear him over the sound of water splashing against his waders and the tinkling of fractured ice.

A small white stake with an arrow made of scrap pine marked the path the younger hunters had taken to blind 11. The High Tider straightened the Yankee's course westward. Even though the big man had to break his way through the ice on his own, loaded with both men's gear, he was still able to move at a much faster pace than the High Tider. He stopped frequently, slowing his speed so the High Tider would not be left struggling behind, alone.

Together, they reached an isthmus of land that was high enough in elevation to grow the row of scraggly, wind-twisted trees that separated them from blind number 9. The trail through the tree line was well marked, having been worn through the cattails and cedars by the passing of thousands of human feet over many years time, feet that had churned the marsh bottom to a collidal mush that was not wet enough to be called water and not dry enough to be called land. The vacuum of sucking black mud threatened to pull wader boots from feet at every step, slackening their progress as much or more so than had the floating ice sheet.

Sky glowed the pink sleepy smile of imminent sunrise as the hunters passed through the tree line and stood at the edge of the pond. The awakening gabble of great flocks of snow geese could be heard far to the south as the hunters paused to rest before completing the last leg of their arduous journey.

The High Tider pointed to the center of the pond at a tiny dark speck that looked remarkably similar to a muskrat house. "That little man-made island is the blind and we're about as late as we dare to be," he explained, gulping air to supply his oxygen-starved lungs. "You go on ahead and flip those snow goose decoys about thirty yards on the upwind side. Start bailing the water out of the blind and I'll join you as soon as I catch my breath. Be sure to load your gun and keep it ready because the geese are gonna fly at any time now."

The Yankee adjusted his load, hiking the guns higher on his right shoulder. The barrels kissed with a metallic ping. He looked toward the sound of awakening geese, then across the pond to gauge the distance remaining to blind number 9. "No, Bill, I think I'll wait here with you. If I got to the blind without my guide, I wouldn't know what to do. Besides, I have the entire day to just enjoy being here, and I'm not going to rush through it."

"Well, that's fine with me if that's what you want to do, but those snow geese ain't gonna wait. Look!" The High Tider poked his chin to the south as the wavering line of the first flock moved into view of his experienced eyes.

The Yankee strained and squinted, but could not see the wavering "V" until it cleared the edge of the tree line a few hundred yards away. Sixteen geese in all, they passed over the pond between hunters and blind, conversing contentedly among themselves as they headed for breakfast in wheatfields to the north.

Onyx-tipped wings were boldly visible against plump white bodies brilliantly reflecting the first rays of the dawning sun. The men could not yet see the sunrise. The geese could, advantaged as they were from their high altitude view. The flock had wisely left the refuge early, knowing that by becoming airborne, they could bask away the chill of the night, catching the sun's warmth high in the air before it inched its way above the shading curvature of the earth.

Another flock passed over the hunters before they completed the last hundred yards to the blind. A blazing sliver of the sun's yellow disc was edging its way above the tree line as they readied their trap for the morning's hunt.

The High Tider stood at the edge of a foul-smelling pit and directed the Yankee's placement of the two canvas decoys in a ragged hole broken into the ice, upwind. He untied the bundle of hollow quarter-inch diameter switch canes and dumped them in a jumbled pile on the ground.

The Yankee looked at him inquisitively, like a heron eyeing a tiny movement beneath the surface of the water. Cocking his head to one side, he asked, "How are you going to turn that pile of pick-up sticks into decoys? Are you going to show me a magic trick?"

The Magician unbuttoned his coat and produced a couple of 90-count boxes of white kitchen garbage bags. He held the

The author sets a spread of plastic bag geese.

boxes out for the Yankee to examine. "And now, for my next trick I'm a-gonna turn these plastic bags into a flock of happily contented snow geese," he announced with a bow and a flourish.

He zipped open the boxes and began tying the plastic bags to the canes, one by one. The Yankee, an intelligent man, was a quick study, and was soon helping to create the decoy spread, shaking each bag open, filling it with air, and knotting its open end closed around the knuckles of a bamboo-like cane to simulate the shape of a snow goose head and neck. Each time ten "decoys" were assembled, the Yankee gathered them up, like the man who sells balloons-on-sticks at the county fair, and churned a pathway to some particular point in the marsh grass at the edge of the pond or to a hole broken in the ice at a location directed by the High Tider. He thrust the ends of the canes into the marsh bottom, securing the balloon decoys against the morning breeze.

The scattered, sporadic sounds of gunshots could be heard as more snow geese left Pea Island and flew over blinds to the east. At times, the noise of geese departing the refuge seemed to be a solid, unbroken wall approaching from the south. It reached a crescendo as flocks several hundred strong passed overhead a half mile high, then gradually decreased in volume as the flights continued on their way.

"We'd better hurry!" the High Tider shouted to his partner across the pond, who was hidden from the waist down by waving saw grass. "The big flocks are lifting off and we need to get ready. Jab them sticks in the ground to your left. Now adjust that one so's the corner points up like a tail and push his head down like he's feedin'. That's it! Just right! Over there now. That one is kinda squashed lookin'. Grab stick-and-all and throw it in among that bunch in the grass to thicken up the spread. Don't worry about the wind carrying it away. There ain't enough breeze stirrin' today to hurt anything, just enough to move 'em about and turn 'em a bit so they look real life-like. Now come and get another load!"

The High Tider was pulling a plastic neck knot tight around a switch cane knuckle with his eye teeth and watching the Yankee wading through the water when a nearly imperceivable shadow of movement caught his attention. Was it the bottom of a cloud or a wisp of marsh vapor? In an instant, his practiced senses knew that, no, this was not a shadow or imagined movement, but the distinctively steady rising and falling of a flock of snow geese as it caught a spiralling thermal, then accelerated as it fell, gathering speed. He threw the goose balloon onto a pile of nine identical others, grabbed his gun, and thumbed in three shells.

All the while he was hollering at the Yankee, "Run if you can, but don't fall! Here come our geese! Don't turn around and look! Just come on!"

He urged the Yankee on, windmilling his arm to draw him to the blind with greater speed. The Yankee's legs churned molasses-thick water to white froth and sent creaking shock waves through the ice-covered pond, animating the air-filled garbage bags and the pair of canvas look-alikes with the life-like rocking and waddling motions of feeding birds.

The High Tider splashed to the bottom of the three by five plywood box that served as blind number 9, releasing a powerful odor of putrefying vegetation. The Yankee grabbed his gun from where it rested against one of the wax myrtle bushes that rimmed the top edge of the blind and dove to join the High Tider. Losing his balance, he fell in a helter-skelter, headlong crash, almost pitching face first into the stinking, nearly frozen liquid. He would have taken a cold dunking and drenched his gun, too, had not the High Tider grabbed him by the collar, hanging him precariously with one heal stuck on the blind edge and the other slipping off the partly submerged plank that served as a seat.

The High Tider dragged the Yankee into position. The Yankee frantically fumbled in his pocket. His numb fingers found shells and stabbed them into the magazine. Two were lost, plunking into the knee-deep water.

197

"Get down!" hissed the voice in The Yankee's ear as a prickling bewhiskered chin ground into the side of his neck.

"Don't look up!" ordered the chin as it pressed the Yankee ever lower into the murky shadows.

Look up indeed! He couldn't have if he wanted to, not with a hundred and eighty pounds of Styron resting its weight upon his shoulders, digging its right elbow into the small of his back!

He thought he heard a noise, the tiniest nasal shred of a flying goose's dual-note greeting call—the call that was only used when formally addressing members of another flock.

A reproduction of the call, "Au-ungh," echoed in his ear a fraction of an inch away, imitated perfectly by the vocal cords of the High Tider. The Yankee's eyes widened. He shuddered with excitement as the lips at his ear hoarsely rasped, "Don't look up! They're lookin' us over! At the slightest movement, they'll be gone!"

The Yankee swiveled his eyeballs sideways till they bulged from their sockets, attempting to see geese materialize through the cracked fingers of twigs that lined the top of the blind's plywood walls. He knew he dared not turn his head or twist his body in order to gain a better view, pinned into position as he was by the mass of the High Tider.

After scant seconds that seemed like hours, he detected the slightest movement of a hovering wing beneath a dangling wax myrtle leaf as a goose dropped low, sliding downwind for a second pass.

There, the bird held, along with two dozen other bleached-down bodies. Five in front hung motionless as the others wadded together and piled in from behind, breaking the perfection of their "V" formation. The leaders began calling suspiciously among themselves, unsure of the safety of landing among the feeding strangers below. The sound of their voices blended together in what, to most human ears, sounded like mass confusion, each goose tootling or honking at the same time. But above the riot of wild, high-pitched voices could be heard by the trained ear, that singular, deeper call—that of a wise old female who had lead her offspring and a host of others down the flyways safely and without mishap for many seasons. Warily, she hung back, attempting to stop her airborne flock from haphazardly spilling down into the crowded mass of white ovoids waiting on the marsh below.

As she suspended herself, surf-boarding the windwaves, waiting and watching the feeding movements of the cottony bodies rummaging below in the reeds, the deep, resonant voice of an ancient gander called up to her, reassuring her that all was well. "This is a fine spot for feeding on such a chilly day," said the friendly goose in the marshgrass. "There is plenty of breakfast, enough for all, and it surely is nice, and cozy, and warm, and comfortable, with all my fine companions, my children and myself, down here picnicking, out of the icy bite of the wind."

Bill Grainger was awestruck! Each note and tone that issued from the High Tider's throat sounded exactly like goose conversation as he coaxed and pleaded with the real snow geese suspended like feathered parachutes against the clouds above. It didn't seem possible for the words of goose speech and dialect to be translated and reproduced by the weak-volumed larynx of an earthbound man. But it was, as testified to by the loud, piercing yelps and soothing feeding gabbles that vibrated the Yankee's earlobe.

The High Tider-turned-greater-snow-goose got the attention of the lead goose with an assertive double-note call "Ar-rongk! Ar-rongk!" which she immediately answered, silencing the rest of the birds in her flock.

That did it! Abandoning all caution, barrel-rolling and gyrating their bodies from side to side like pendulums on pivot points of magnificent snowy wings, the great birds cascaded earthward. Like powdery drifts of snow crystals that slide from the limbs of a blizzard-struck pine, they plummeted toward thc decoys, webbed feet outstretched to break the force of the headwind, ebony wing tips fanned open wide. The whiffling of their wings sang a wind-shearing hiss as the supporting of buoyancy of speed and air slipped away between their primary flight feathers.

199

Too late, the lead goose saw the movement in the myrtle bushes below. Too late, she was startled by the flash of pink man-flesh faces and the glint of sunlight off gunsteel as the hunters rose to shoot!

"Keronk! Keronk! Keronk! Pull-up! Pull-up! Pull-up!" her panicked alarm cries stabbed the arctic air as she warned her disorganized flock away in a boiling, frightened mass of feathered confusion.

"You shoot to the right and I'll take the left!" the High Tider ordered as he leveraged himself from his companion's back and pointed his gun into the port quadrant of the boiling flock.

Relieved of the weight of Styron, the Yankee jerked his gun to shooting position in a spray of crumpled myrtle leaves. Picking a goose on his side of the blind, he fired. It was an easy shot, 30 yards out at a hovering bird rapidly beating its wings in an attempt to overcome the momentum of 60 mile-an-hour descent. Instantly dead, the goose fell, crashing through the ice directly in front of the blind.

Pumping out the smoking empty the Yankee fired again, too quickly, wasting the shot at an impossibly spiralling target of windmilling wings, twisting and turning against the clouds as it clawed against the friction of air to regain the safety of altitude. The shining bead at the end of the Yankee's gun barrel bobbed and wobbled as the goose flared high and away. It followed the desperately departing bird until it leveled off, capturing the white silhouette against the clouds. Stabilized, it tracked straight-line escape flight. As silver bead passed flesh-pink goose bill knifing through the wind, the gun fired, bucking hard against the Yankee's shoulder. A swarm of steel BB's found their mark. The majestic bird folded its wings, and joined its companion floating, belly up, in a hole in the ice.

The Yankee was vaguely aware of shots being fired simultaneously by another gun near his shoulder. Seeing something white fall in his peripheral vision, he knew that his companion had also found his mark.

Struggling to regain the control of conscious thought, his mind disengaged itself from the instinctive overdrive of target fixation. Turning to follow the reorganizing flock, the Yankee noticed that one goose seemed to be losing altitude, unable to keep pace with the departing wedge.

The wounded goose continued to lag behind as the remainder of the flock moved northward. Calling loudly to each other, the members of the flock counted their losses and beseeched their faltering companion to rejoin them. Their plaintive urgings were of no help to the injured goose. He crash-landed ungracefully into the marshgrass two hundred long yards beyond the edge of the ice-filled moat that surrounded blind number 9.

"Blasted steel shot!" The High Tider cursed as he rummaged in his pockets for ammunition with which to reload. "I killed my first two geese outright so close they were, but that last one was out there fifty-five or sixty yards—an easy shot with lead, but obviously too far for a clean kill with this stupid steel!"

Reloading, he turned his attention to the downed birds. "Yank, you pick up the dead 'uns and prop 'em up beside those canvas decoys. Use some of those left over canes. Stick 'em in the mud and slide the geese's bills over them to hold their heads up like they're restin' or feedin'. When you're done with that, feel around the bottom of the blind with your feet and find the bucket or dipper that oughtta be there and start bailing water. I'll go chase my cripple, over yonder!"

The Yankee protested as the High Tider extracted himself from the tightness of the blind. "Let me fetch that cripple for you, Bill. You stay and finish setting out the decoys. I don't know how to set up dead birds to look like live ones!"

The High Tider seemed not to hear what the Yankee said. But, as he started wading across the pond toward the albino, snake-like neck that marked the crippled goose's location in the hollow-stemmed grass, he turned back toward the blind.

"I appreciate your offer, Yank. But that there is my bird, so this here is my walk." He turned and resumed the agony of forcing his way through the ice, the water, the mud, and the marsh.

Halfway to the fallen bird, he almost wished he had taken the Yankee's offer of making the long retrieve. Halfway back, he was certain of it. Winded and panting, he nestled the heavy bird

Miles E. Forbes, Jr. My kill, his cripple—his walk!

in the cordgrass and knelt at the edge of the frozen pond to rest his aching leg. His heartbeat slowed its hammering while he watched the big Yankee dip down, then up, repeatedly dumping water the color of burnt tea over the side of the blind a gallon at a time. He thought about the hard work this giant of a man had done this day, the trek through ice-covered pools, carrying more than his share of the load, the setting of the decoys, and now, the bailing of water from the bottom of the blind. Not one complaining breath had passed this man's lips. Truly, he was a fine gentleman and a good partner, worthy of sharing this day in this marsh.

The High Tider returned to the blind along the trail he had chipped though the ice on his way to the crippled goose. He stopped upwind of the blind to add the bird to the decoy spread. Three others rode the wind-ripples in the small pocket of open water beside two antique canvas and wire hoop decoys. Sloshing the remaining distance to the blind, he looked into its shadows and observed the Yankee bobbing up and down like an oil well pump. On the wooden seat board beside the Yankee lay the fifth goose. Placed carefully on its breast with folded wings, its fat body and outstretched neck spanned two-thirds of the sit-down space in the cramped little box.

The Yankee completed his task, having removed enough water to reveal the floorboards through the inch of accumulated trash of previous occupants—empty shotshell hulls, candy wrappers, crushed bayberry leaves, and cedar twigs. He glanced up at the High Tider, wiping beads of perspiration from his face with the back of his coat sleeve. "That's a good way for a man to warm himself," he joked at his guide-for-the-day.

"Yes it is," agreed the High Tider, "and so is fetching a crippled goose." He chuckled as he daubed his own brow free of sweat with the back of a scratchy wool glove.

The Yankee lifted his goose from the plank and sat in its place. Cradling the bird in his lap, he smoothed the entire length of its ruffled ivory flight feathers and examined their black velvet tips.

A backside of Styron bounced heavily, making the seat board bounce and creak as the High Tider re-entered the blind. He watched the Yankee for a while, admiring the man admiring the bird, his first-ever greater snow goose, reduced from Nature's grand possession to the trembling hand of a humbled man.

"They certainly are beautiful creatures, aren't they?" asked the Yankee. The High Tider didn't respond directly to the rhetorical question. He meerly nodded in silent agreement.

"I wonder if I've ever before seen so clearly the color white—white so brilliant it hurts your eyes. Maybe it's because it is contrasted so sharply by the black," he speculated as he fingered the coal tar end that graced a wingtip. "My wife wishes she could get bedsheets or my tee shirts this white. It's as white as drifts of new snow. Snow! Yes, that's it. I've seen eye-stabbing white like this before. I've shoveled it off porches and sidewalks ever since I was a kid. It's the white of snow, sparkling so brightly under the winter's sun that it forces you to blink against its glare."

"Why do you think we call 'em snow geese?" grinned the High Tider. "Most years those white feathers are the only snow we get to see on these here Outer Banks." He paused for a moment and squirreled the lid of his shooting eye into a mischievously exaggerated wink. In a voice with just the right volume to guarantee the Yankee's undivided attention, he asked slyly, "Kinda makes you want to change the letters on that fancy license plate of yours, doesn't it? You wouldn't want to be a Jonah and jinx our hunting trips, would you?"

The Yankee's eyebrows fluttered as he turned to face the High Tider. Bill Styron's shoulders were shaking with the restrained rumble of laughter. The board beneath him began to shudder in sympathetic vibration. Bill Grainger smiled, a little at first, then cracked a toothy grin as he caught the joke. Soon he was laughing uncontrollably in unison with the High Tider.

The blind erupted an earthquake of boisterous jests and counterjests. The High Tider guffawed. The Yankee let go a belly laugh. The noise of their mirth was loud—loud enough to cover the sound of nearly silent goose wings slicing through the wind overhead.

Possibly, it was the shadow of movement or, more likely, the shadow of instinct that spurred the High Tider's reflexes at the whisper close presence of goose. Instantly jarred from his revelry he catapulted to his feet. In a blur of motion, he jumped erect, his gun barrel arching skyward to cover the dusky form sailing effortlessly above. Craning its neck from side to side as it scanned the vast expanse of white decoys, a lone gray goose searched for a place to land among its own kind. Not spying the dark outline of a potential mate or companion, the Canada hailed a questioning "Har-onk?" hoping to hear a response from a sympathetic soul hidden from his vision by the reeds of the marsh.

Unable to rise, anchored as he was by the heavy lapful of snow goose, the Yankee waited a breathless eternity for the report of the High Tider's Winchester to blot the shadow from the sky. The shot never came. The lonesome goose flew on, unmolested, toward the ocean and marshes east. The Yankee stared in amazement as the High Tider lowered his weapon and slowly melted back down onto the seat. Never once did the hunter divert his attention from the dusky form as it shriveled away, shrinking ever smaller with increasing distance.

Puzzled, the Yankee alternately watched the vanishing Canada, then the High Tider, switching his gaze from one to the other. He couldn't understand why the Canada had not been added to their bag, as close as it had it passed above the master waterfowler beside him.

"Why didn't you shoot, Bill? The Canada goose season is still open, isn't it?" asked the Yankee of his silently staring blindmate.

The High Tider caught a deep breath—once, twice, three times. Rubbing the outside corner of his eye with the collar of his coat, he explained, "Must have got somethin' in my eye. I couldn't see well enough to shoot. Besides, the open season on gray geese is only ten days long now. The limit is a paltry one per hunter per day. Since today, January 31st, is the last legal day, it just didn't seem right to kill him, with as heavy a burden as we already have to carry out of this marsh."

Pausing he watched the nearly-vanished goose dot, then continued, "You know, Yank, when I was a boy, there wasn't no open season for hunting white geese, but the season on grays was months long and bag limits were high. Canada goose season began before Thanksgiving and lasted until January was a memory. The limit was four birds back then. You can believe me when I tell you that I shot my share of gray geese over the years—piles of 'em! If you think about it for a minute, you'll see that things now are just the opposite. Snow goose season started November 3rd and ends today, with a daily limit of five birds. I've even heard rumors that the season may be extended mid-way into February next year in an attempt to increase the kill, to give the farmers on the mainland some relief from the strip-row way of grazing the tremendous, restored flocks that have destroys vast acres of winter wheat."

He paused again. Darting his head around, he attempted to see the departed goose through the dappled shadows of wax myrtle boughs that screened the front of the blind. "Yank," he stated softly, "I'm not gonna shoot any more gray geese until they return to these marshes in numbers too many to count, like those— my daddy's snows." He deferred a glance to the magnificent white bird laying across the Yankee's lap.

A sudden volley of four shots rumbled across the marsh from the vicinity of blind 11, demanding the hunters' attention. Staring into the glare of ten o'clock sun they strained to make out the younger hunters' intended target.

"Those boys must have been firing at your Canada," the Yankee decided. He rose from the plank and carefully laid his feathered prize at the base of the myrtle bushes on the outside edge of the blind. Turning to face the source of gunfire, he slipped and nearly fell when he placed the weight of his foot on a roller-bearing object in the bottom of the blind. Reaching down and probing the ankle deep water with a waterproofed neoprene-gloved hand, he found the object of his search. He shook salty water drops from one of the shells he had dropped while frantically loading his gun at the flock's surprise arrival earlier that morning.

"Skybusters!" spit the High Tider. "That goose had to be at least 80 yards high! The only thing they could have accomplished at that range was to cripple the bird or bruise him badly, especially shootin' steel shot like that in the shell you're holdin' in your hand."

The Yankee rolled the cigar-length shell in his fingers and remembered back to the years of gunning with lead. Size number 2 lead shot had been his preference for shooting Canada geese. Unfortunately, lead shot had been found to be hazardous to waterfowl. Mainly ducks, but also geese and swans ate the spent lead pellets that accumulated on marsh bottoms, mistaking them for seeds or gravel. The powerful grinding action of their gizzards atomized the lead, releasing it into their bodies and causing some to die of lead poisoning. The use of lead shot had been banned, marsh by marsh, state by state, over the last decade and a half. On National Wildlife Refuges, its use had been outlawed from the mid-1970's. Nontoxic steel shot was an inferior ballistic substitute, having a weight one-third lighter than that of lead shot of equal size. A hunter had to use much larger steel pellets to obtain the same energy as lead down range. This translated into fewer pellets in each shell, allowing fewer hits on a goose.

At first, steel loads were undeniably inferior to lead, resulting in many lost cripples. The shell the Yankee held in his hand, however, was created by state-of-the-art modern technology. It was quite an improvement over the archaic loads of the 1970's. The 12 gauge shell was elongated to three and one-half inches. The previous maximum length of a lead shot shell had maxed at 3 inches. This increased the space inside the shell to provide a denser swarm of pellets.

The Yankee's gun, too, was state-of-the-art. Its barrel was created with sophisticated metallurgy and fitted with hardened, screw-in choke tubes that eased the passing of larger steel pellets during the violence of powder ignition.

He studied the High Tider's marsh-scarred Winchester resting comfortably in its place against the side of the blind. In its day, the Winchester, too, had been current technology, designed for use with paper hulled shells wrapped around heavy charges of lead.

The Yankee set the wet, plastic-tubed shell on the wooden shelf that ran the length of the front of the blind. The Yankee attempted to educate his friend.

"The old steel shells weren't very good. I used to cripple a lot of birds with them. These newer shells, however, and these newer guns, specifically designed to shoot steel shot, do a good job—not quite as good as the old lead loads in classic old guns like yours, mind you—but they work well enough if you keep your shots close. Your gun was designed to shoot soft lead shot and is choked too tightly for the hardness of steel. It's like trying to pass ice cubes through a garden hose nozzle. Tight chokes were right for use with lead, but they make steel pellets fight each other and jam together at the muzzle, disrupting the pattern at longer ranges."

The High Tider lovingly stroked the fore arm of his ancient pumpgun, then looked admiringly at the Yankee's new Mossberg. "I did notice that you made quite a long shot on that second goose you killed. He was hiding his head inside a cloud. That sure seems to be a mighty fine fowling piece you have there. Somehow, though, I just wouldn't feel right huntin' geese with a different gun. My daddy gave me this one. It was bought with money he made market gunning. I know that it might not be the very best gun for shootin' steel shot, but it's the only one I'll ever shoot out here in this particular stretch of marsh . . ."

Stopping in mid-sentence, he cocked an ear and raised an index finger to his lips for silence. Poking the finger west at the sky above Pamlico Sound, he informed the Yankee, "Geese! Over there! Don't you hear them?"

The Yankee stared into the section of mid-morning sky approximately identified by the High Tider's finger. Straining his ears, even cupping his hands over them for increased volume, he could not capture the haunting notes of high flying geese. All he could hear was the aggravating trickle of pencil-sized streams of water that cascaded through the side of the blind. They masked the sound of goose talk from his untrained ears.

"Look hard," said the veteran hunter as he tried to help the Yankee. "They're right over there, across the corner of the blind." He stuck his finger directly in front of the Yankee's nose so he could sight along it like the barrel of a gun. "They're right there, about two miles out, twin flocks, I think. Look directly above that cedar bush and below that grayish cloud. Look for two dark lines wavering in the sky."

The Yankee stretched his senses of hearing and vision to their maximum limits, yet still could not determine the flocks' location, far out above Pamlico's silver mirror.

"Look for something that appears to be two short pieces of dark sewing thread being blown about by the wind or a couple of pencil lines that undulate slowly up and down. They're flyin' south to north."

Even with expert assistance from the High Tider, the Yankee's dulled city senses did not enable him to find the goose lines in the sky. Undetected by him, they flew onward to farmfields and the promise of breakfast.

The High Tider watched the bare sky for a few seconds after the dual lines of geese had vanished from his sight. It was incomprehensible to him that The Yankee had neither seen nor heard the snow geese as they traveled the high flyway.

"I suppose years of factory work can knock the edge off a man's eyesight and hearing," he said gently to the Yankee to avoid hurting his feelings.

"That may be so," the big man agreed, "but I believe that if these branches and leaves were pruned a little thinner and this water wasn't dribbling so loudly into the blind, I could have spotted them."

The High Tider reached forward to unnecessarily adjust some dry-crisp foliage along the edge of the plywood, explaining to his friend, "The brush of a blind has got to be thick, because the better you can see out, the better the geese can see in. With their telescopic eyesight and their suspicious nature from having their tail feathers shot off all the way from their stopover on the St. Lawrence River to Hatteras Island, snow geese will be long gone at the smallest gleam of a pair of beady little hunter's eyes staring up at them from a blind.

The water that drips in or pours in, depending on which blind you draw, is something that you learn to cope with. The Park Service has other things to spend its money on, refurbishing old lighthouse keeper's homes, for example. It never seems to have the cash it takes to repair a few worn duck and goose hunting blinds. There was a movement by some hunters to rebuild the blinds a few years ago. They put a shoe box on the counter at the Whalebone Junction Hunter Check-in Station and taped a sign on it that asked for a couple of dollar's donation from each hunter toward upkeep of these rotten old blinds. As I remember it, the fellows volunteered to come down from Virginia on summer vacations and actually rebuilt some of the worst ones—18, 19, 20, maybe some others. But the lack of support from others eventually forced them to quit. Or, it may be that they just got too old, or too tired, or felt they had done more than their fair share."

The High Tider snapped off several pieces of dried wax myrtle twigs from the leading edge of the blind, releasing the spicy aroma that once scented bayberry candles. Handing them to the Yankee he instructed, "Take these and plug 'em into those holes to stop the leaks as best you can. Scoot that dipper floatin' in the bottom of the blind over to me with your foot before you get started. It's my turn to bail water."

The main concentration of snow geese had long since left the haven of Pea Island Refuge. The sun climbed higher in its day's arc from ocean to sound. One degree south of straight overhead, it warmed the damp, cool interior of blind number 9. Its occupants had lunch and a laugh, then alternated turns napping and standing guard against the possibility of an errant ribbon of geese dropping in unexpectedly to pay their compliments to the decoys. In this manner each hunter dozed, resting eyelids made heavy from squinting into the platinum haze that burned beneath the noon-south sun.

The air temperature climbed. The ice mantle covering the marsh began to melt. Receding glacier-like, it retreated from the black, heat-absorbing water in the center of the pool, creeping slowly toward cooler edge waters that were shaded by rushes and canes that nodded from the bank.

By two-thirty, the hunters were refreshed and rested. They roused and stood, yawning and stretching, trying to iron the wrinkles from their muscles that had been brought on by the heated exertions of their morning ice-capades and the too-long period of confinement in the clamminess of the claustrophobic blind.

The Yankee watched as the High Tider massaged his right thigh and knee in an attempt to restore the circulation and dull the ache that must be there. Sliding his wrist free from his coat sleeve, he took note of the time.

"What time do we start back in?" he asked.

The High Tider winked his reply, "Sunset. I believe I heard you mention this morning that you had all day."

"Yes, I did say that. I meant it, too. Right now, at this moment, I can't think of anything else I would rather do or anywhere else I would rather be than hunting out here in this leaky little box in the marsh. It's such a pretty sight, watching those trash bag decoys, lazily rocking from side to side. I'm amazed at how you've made them look so alive. They look exactly like one of the flocks of snow geese I've seen at Pea Island Refuge."

He looked around the pool and surrounding sea of wheat-colored grass and noticed that several of the decoys had been shifted or knocked over by receding ice or deflated by the icepick spikes of needlerush tips. He sneaked a glance sideways at the High Tider's knee. "I was just thinking that now might be a good time to pack up the decoys and start back in. That would give us plenty of time . . ."

". . . and ease the strain on my leg!" The High Tider completed the Yankee's thought. "Don't worry none about me, Yank. I'll make it back with time to spare. The ice is almost gone. I won't have to fight it again. Besides, I've got you to pull me out if I get stuck in a sucking mud hole again!"

"Well, I might pull you out! But then again, you still need a bath," the Yankee chuckled. He swished his booted foot back and forth, releasing the thick methane odor of decaying particles of organic matter suspended in the water that had once again accumulated in the bottom of the blind.

To the sound of his own laughter echoing across the marsh, the Yankee hopped from the pit. At the High Tider's direction he repositioned the damaged and deflated decoys. The High Tider stayed inside and bailed the blind.

The Yankee soon rejoined his friend in the pit. He repositioned bayberry limbs that had been dislodged by his departure and return, making certain that the foliage was thick enough he could see out but geese could not see in. Waxy gray-blue pellets of bayberries the size of number four shot rattled off the blind boards and showered onto his boots.

The High Tider stood in a half-crouch, his good knee resting on the seat board, facing north. He motioned that the Yankee do the same.

"Any snow geese returning to the refuge will come from the north. If we're lucky, they'll fill their bellies early and come home to roost before sunset brings the end of shooting hours."

The two men scanned the northern flyways, stretching their combined vision to its limit in anticipation of returning geese. They continued their vigil for hours, enjoying the peaceful solitude as the tired sun drooped toward the western horizon.

The High Tider was first to hear goose sounds above the hypnotic trickling of water that found its way back into the blind.

"Listen! I hear geese!" he said, clutching at the Yankee's elbow. "Watch over there, above that patch of tall reeds. You can't see them with your eyes yet, so look with your ears. Try to imagine them appearing in that spot."

The Yankee strained to see the advancing flock above the reeds. He saw nothing, heard nothing—nothing but the incessant sound of dribbling water, the sighing of marshgrass, and, maybe, the barking of a distant house dog.

"I can't hear a thing above the noise of that waterfall," he said to his companion. "All I can hear is a dog."

The High Tider jerked at his elbow excitedly, "You can't hear no dogs from blind number 9! It's too far away from the nearest house! That's snow geese you're hearin'! Get your head down!"

Shifting his grip from the Yankee's elbow to his shoulder, he pressed him down, forcing his eyes to look through tiny gaps in crinkled leaves. The Yankee shifted his head about, trying to find a hole in the thick foliage through which to see the flock's approach.

The dog barks became louder, magically changing into the honks and yodels of snow goose speech as the velocity of their flight narrowed the distance from miles to yards. The High Tider spoke to them in his most formal goose-ese attempting to turn their attention to the decoy spread.

"Keronk-keronk! Keronk-keronk! How are you folks doing on this fine afternoon?" asked the High Tider of the winged cottonballs flying formation against the Carolina blue sky. "Keronk! Keronk! Keronk! Keronk! Ongkh-ongkh-ongkh? Ongkh-ongkh-ongkh? Why tire yourselves flying ten more miles to Pea Island when you can rest yourselves down here with us. Stay the night here. It's comfortable and safe, with lots of tender green shoots to munch on throughout the evening to tide you over through the long coming night."

The Yankee's body began shaking as his system inflamed itself with hot gushes of adrenaline, preparing to override the mechanisms of conscious thought with the involuntary reactions of predatory instinct. He stared, heart pounding at the sight of a lancepoint of sixty-five geese closing the gap to four hundred yards. The noise of their gabbling grew louder as they answered the gander named Styron. Suspiciously, they argued his invitation among themselves.

"It doesn't look like they're gonna do it," whispered the High Tider to his wide-eyed friend, "but I'll see if I can swing them over this way. If I can get 'em to come over the blind for a look, we may have a shot."

The High Tider pleaded with the geese. The speed of their flight slowed. One leg of the perfect "V" wavered. Dipping toward the decoys, it sought to pull the balance of the flock with it. The lead goose, however, was having none of it.

"Gerunk-gerunk! Gerunk-gerunk!" She admonished her rebellious flock. "Continue onward to the next island! I know it is safe there. Sometimes these marshes are full of hunters!"

She continued to scold her charges, commanding them to repair their formation. All of the birds complied with her order as the flock slowly reshaped itself into the perfect wedge. That is, all but two yearling birds whose feathers were still gray and dusky with youth. Seduced by the reassuring tones of the High Tider's calling, they broke ranks and descended, gliding on cupped wings toward the great congregation of nearly two hundred imitation geese feeding and resting in the sparkling pool and rustling reeds below.

"Keronk! Keronk! Mutiny!" shrilled the lead goose after the impetuous youngsters. The rest of the flock grew silent as she tried to coax the strays back into line.

"Get ready, Yank! They're a bit high but we might have a chance!" hissed the High Tider.

He continued giving reassuring feeding grunts as the two errant geese drifted closer. Larger, and more distinct they grew as they were drawn down, inch by inch, like a pair of child's kites being spooled slowly to the ground, tethered tightly on a string.

The Yankee clenched a composite plastic pistol grip and forearm in a white-knuckled grip and thumbed off the safety with a metallic click.

At sixty yards, the pair held back, hovering cautiously checking over the decoy spread. Perhaps it was the sound of the Yankee's safety snapping or perhaps it was a heed to the calls of their departing comrades that made them hesitate.

"They're turning away. It's now or never," the High Tider whispered frantically to his friend. "Let's get 'em!"

The blind spat thunder, smoke, and flame! Both men emptied their guns the maximum-allowed-by-law three shots at the targets of white-feathered wings pumping desperately for escape.

The goose on the right, the Yankee's side of the blind, crashed dead from the air. The goose on the left faltered, then regained his wings and flew shakily on. Wing-tipped and body shot, the crippled goose wheeled low and half-glided, half-flew toward the safety of Pamlico Sound. The wounded young gander lost altitude, erratically flapping his broken wing. Eventually, he stuttered in flight, folded, and crashed, lung shot, into the thick grass and sucking black muck of Bodie Island a long three hundred yards from blind number 9.

"My bird! My walk!" hollered the Yankee, clearing the blind in a single leap. He wrestled his way out, crunching through the dried bushes and jumped-churned into the pond. The High Tider tried to extract himself from the blind, profanely protesting to the Yankee that the cripple was his, but his stiffened leg slipped from beneath him and he slumped back inside.

The Yankee slogged on, turning his back to the High Tider's sputtering protestations. He shouted over his shoulder, "I can't hear what you are saying, Bill. This water is splashing too loudly around my waders."

It took the Yankee considerable time and effort to reach the sea of grass and reeds into which the broken body of the goose had fallen. Semi-solid marsh bottom oozed away underfoot, making each step especially difficult for a man whose legs were accustomed to walking on concrete pavement and polished hardwood floors. Salty perspiration stung his eyes, drooling from his forehead in spite of the fifty degree air temperature. His persistence was gloriously rewarded when he found a trail of starkly visible bone-white fluff clinging to the bronze tips of Phragmites reeds. Following the feather trail to its end scant yards from the edge of Pamlico Sound, he found the crumpled pillow heap that had been a greater snow goose.

Hefting the dead bird by its neck, he marvelled at the weight of it and was justifiably proud that he had not given up the search and let the High Tider down, losing the magnificent bird to become the nocturnal meal of a mink or raccoon. Admiring the bird, he rotated it proudly right then left, noticing how brightly its feathers reflected the slanting rays of the setting sun. He rested as long as he dared against the imminent loss of daylight, then slung the great body over his shoulder by the handle of its neck and began the long trudge back through the marsh, backtracking his trail to blind number 9.

The High Tider had not been idle in the Yankee's absence. Moving methodically through the water and mush with a limping but practiced grace, he reverted the decoys, one by one, from living greater snow geese into inanimate white plastic garbage bags. As he came to each bag, he unknotted its neck from around the knuckles of its switch cane support, then collapsed the air out of it and stuffed it into another white plastic bag to join as many others as could be compressed to fit.

He had nearly completed gathering in the decoys when the Yankee arrived at the edge of the pond from his oddessey through the marsh.

"I thought maybe you got lost out there," the High Tider joked. "I see you found 'your' bird though, so I take it the trip was worth the effort."

"Well worth it," answered the Yankee. He smiled broadly between panting breaths and presented the trophy to its rightful owner.

"Just put him over there in that pile of geese beside the blind. Here, take this with you and use it to tie the geese together by their necks." Reaching into his coat pocket, the High Tider produced a hunk of the versatile tarred nylon hand line and handed it to the Yankee.

After gathering up the remaining goose balloons, the High Tider joined the Yankee on the tiny island blind set in the middle of the glistening pool. Gently, he laid the two ancient covered-wagon-style canvas and hoop snow goose decoys on the ground, then turned his attention to the last of four bulging white garbage bags full of other white garbage bags. Stuffing the foot of his good leg inside, he stomped down hard to deflate as much air from the wadded up plastic as he could. Stabbing the compressed package with the sharp, machete-cut point of a switch cane, he punctured it to release as much air as possible before stomping it again.

"It's amazing how they can get one hundred and eighty snow geese into two itty bitty cardboard boxes, ain't it?" He chuckled at the Yankee.

"It surely is," replied the Yankee as he straightened his back and hefted the heavy bouquet of seven tied-together snow geese, grunting under its weight.

"I see why you said this was the best blind this morning, except for the long walk, of course. What a bunch of geese!"

The High Tider knotted the mouth of the fourth plastic bag full of plastic bags tightly closed and knelt to examine the damage done to half of the pair of antique decoys in its fall to the ice that morning. He thought deeply as he inspected the decoy, then looked down the length of Bodie Island. Wiping a coiled lock of salt and pepper graying hair from his brow, then removing his hand from his forehead, he swept it around, open-palmed, in a tremendous sweeping arc that sought to encompass the entire vastness of the sunset marsh.

"Look out there, across the marsh. Search its depths with your soul. If you're lucky, you'll discover the reason I call blind number 9 the best of the blinds. Look long. Think hard. The quality of this blind doesn't have anything to do with the number of fowl you are holding in your hand. With luck, good calling, and a large enough decoy spread on any given day, one of the other blinds could have produced as many birds for a good pair of hunters as this one has today."

The High Tider returned his attention to the lop-sided decoy he held in his left hand and contemplated options for its repair while rubbing his chin with his right. He reckoned that he would have to remove its canvas covering, replace its broken wire hoops, and tack the canvas back in place. He rummaged the tool shed behind his home in Rodanthe with his memories of long ago, hoping it still stored a coil of copper communication wire that had once been used to link the Pea Island and Chicamacomico Life Saving Service Stations with one another. Torn from the beach sand by a hurricane who's name had been forgotten, those tarnished green copper strands were the only possible replacements for the broken originals of the decoy's battered ribs.

The Yankee bent low, letting the string of geese slip from his hand. Straightening himself erect, he balled his fists into his lower back to ease the strain of old age. He probed the deepening recesses of shadows that were creeping across the marsh. Thinking, looking, observing, he circled slowly in a complete, three hundred and sixty degree turn, taking in the splendor of the grand view in its entirety.

There was nothing to see out here but nature at her best—nothing but golden marsh and shimmering water, highlighted by the rays of a setting sun that winked its tired last glow before drifting off to sleep under the blanket of the western depths of Pamlico Sound. The Yankee stopped in his pivot, staring in silence at the scrubby tree line to the east through which they had passed that morning and through which they would soon be passing again on their return trip out of the marsh. The tree line created a screen that completely hid from sight all the buildings along the oceanfront a mile and a quarter away. This, he now knew was what the High Tider meant when he referred to number 9 as the "very best blind." The illusion of solitude was perfect. A man such as the High Tider could find peace, in this secluded pocket of marsh, with its vista unbroken by the scars of man's handiwork.

The Yankee was momentarily surprised when a civilized sound reached his ears across the evening stillness—surprised for an instant, but scarcely more. Initially mistaking the vibrations stroking his ears for the barking of a distant dog, his newly reconditioned mind quickly reinterpreted the sound to be the contented conversation of a flight of snow geese returning to Pea Island along the invisible flyways above Bodie Island.

"Listen, Bill," the Yankee whispered hoarsely. "Can you hear them?"

The High Tider, preoccupied as he was with his examination of the injury done to his most precious possession, had not heard the flock knifing south above the marsh. Without looking up, he instructed his friend.

"That's right Yank. Look with your ears first. Try to imagine where they are in the sky by the location of their calls and they will soon become visible to your eyes. Look for a wavy, ragged line that appears to be the bottom edge of a cloud or some sort of scratchy writing or doodling or black ink pen scribbling across the sky."

The High Tider kept his attention riveted to the decoy in his hand while the Yankee searched intently above the horizon for a tiny, wavering line that read "geese." Straining his vision to its maximum limit, the Yankee concentrated on the precise point in the sky from which the broken clarinet-reed gabble seemed to emanate. The row of snow geese miraculously appeared, popping into surprisingly easy view.

The Yankee was amazed at the stark blackness of their silhouettes, so brilliantly white were greater snow geese in the full light of day. He watched them fly onward toward the refuge of Pea Island, above swaying bronze reeds and golden grasses. They winged their way home against a backdrop of blazing oranges, pastel pinks, and muted blues interrupted only by patches of scattered clouds that reflected the silver beams of the sun's final rays.

It was a picture no camera's film could ever capture, no mortal artist's brush could ever paint. Moved from awed speechlessness by the beauty of the marsh at the whisper of twilight, the Yankee parted his lips and breathed in a reverent hush. "I can see the line of geese, Bill. It does look like writing but it's not doodling or scribbling. It's a signature. I'm certain that it's God, signing his name."

🦢 🦢 🦢

If you happen to visit North Carolina's Outer Banks on your next summer vacation and you just happen to be driving south

*Erosion threatens Pea Island. Sand washed onto
N.C. Highway 12 by a nor'easter was bulldozed back
to re-form fragile dunes, temporarily protecting
the island's tenuous link with the mainland*

along the gray ribbon of Highway N. C. 12, slow down a couple
of miles above the Herbert C. Bonner Bridge—assuming of course
that the bridge is still there and has not been called to its final rest
by the surging of the tides through Oregon Inlet. Steal a glance,
if you will, out your passenger side window toward the eastern
marshes of Bodie Island. If by chance, you see two figures moving about in the marsh, beyond a weathered wooden plaque announcing "PARKING AREA—BLINDS 15, 16, 17, 18," stop
for a minute and get out of your car. You might catch the rot-
ten-egg aroma of nitrogen-rich vegetation decaying in black marsh
waters or the spicy scent of crushed bayberries if the wind is blowing lazily west to east.

You may hear the sharply clipped consonants and staccato
syllables of a Yankee's accent mimicking the metallic chatter of
machinery of mass production. It will be sharply contrasted by the

mellow, rounded tones of a Hoy Toyder's Elizabethan brogue echoing the gentle roll of the breakers against the beach. If the conversation blends harmoniously together in the mutual chorus of robust laughter at some small joke you couldn't quite make out because of the distance separating you from blind 16, you will know that the "Two Bills" are out there, replacing the rotten plywood in the bottom of the blind. Please drop in at the newly renovated lighthouse keeper's house or at the Whalebone Junction Hunter Check-in Station as you continue your travels. Find a Cape Hatteras National Seashore Park Ranger. If you happen to have a small amount of spare cash, let's say two bills—one dollar bills that is, or about the same price as a brace of High Tide Pheasant during the height of the Great Depression—ask if you can make a donation to help two close friends in their sweaty task of renovating the decades-old hunting blinds of Bodie Island.

Hyperborea atlantica is the poetic name given the greater snow goose by ornithologists. It means, translated quite literally, "From Beyond the North Wind to the Atlantic." When once again the greater snow goose migration reaches its peak numbers on a shivering winter's day, pairs of hunters drawn together from different niches in the world through the lure of the marsh, the goose, and the gun will have comfortable blinds from which to wait and to watch—to watch the sky fill with January Snow.

Mark! A dove in trouble!

Chapter 5

Quest For The Limit

Alongside Williams Dairy Road, in the southeast corner of Guilford County, stretches a field that flows with green fluid waves of fescue grass. What sprouts from the sticky clay clods of red piedmont soil today is nitrogen-rich pasture on which dairy cattle graze. Years ago, this same acreage was covered with a mixed forest of tall hardwoods and gigantic pines. Massive hulks of granite boulders lay above, below, or half buried in the ground, surrounded by white and pink specklings of quartz stones and cobbles. The exterior skins of the gray granite rocks were stained the same shade of brick red as the surrounding clay soil through the weathering processes of daylight and dark, freeze and thaw, dryness and rain.

Alterations of heat and cold would have reduced them, over millenia, into the same soil from which they had grown.

Down the road apiece, at what is today is considered the distance of a short drive, sits a tiny garage apartment. This was once the home of William Frank Jobe and his wife Annie Kennett Jobe. Many yesterdays ago, the distance separating this small dwelling from the pasture was a long, arduous walk behind a harnessed mule team. It was Frank who painstakingly cleared the land, converting it from forest to field, day by day, tree by tree, stump by stump, red-stained rock by red-stained rock.

The Jobes were parenting a rapidly growing family. A newborn graced their home with regularity, every year or two. Frank needed access to the abundant game that thrived in the surrounding forests and farm fields for supplying his children's growing bodies with the necessary protein to help them grow tall and strong.

Somehow, he had to find a way to purchase himself a gun. But guns for sale were scarce in those days. The only thing that was more scarce than a gun for sale was the money with which to buy it. His wages from operating machinery in the textile mill were a mere pittance in comparison to the cost of a new firearm. Money was tighter than twisted hemp twine around a swollen bale of green hay negligently left afield and soaked by an Indian Summer thunderstorm.

All Frank had to offer of any material value were the strength in his back and gallons of sweat. That was adequate legal tender for Mr. Williams who needed new pasture in which to graze his expanding herds of black and white milk cows more than he needed an extra scattergun. And so, the bargain was struck. Five acres were cleared by the hard labors of one man in exchange for the possession of a brand-new gun, a hammerless, double barrel shotgun in 12 gauge, Remington model of the year, 1894.

Many were the squirrels and rabbits that the classic fowling piece brought to bag under the guidance of Frank's skilled hands. The left hand barrel was choked "full" and could tumble squirrels from the top of the tallest red oak. Their delicate flesh simmered in the family's stewpot or steamed under great lumps of dumplings to stretch the savory taste of frest meat all around the table. Quail in brown gravy were an occasional treat. In his search for game, Frank sometimes lucked into the midst of an exploding covey that massed together tightly enough on the rise to allow certain multiple hits with a single load of shot launched from the more open barrel marked "modified," on the right. He never fired at the small brown birds unless several could be killed for the enormous expense of a single shell.

The swirling swarms of doves that roosted in cedar trees surrounding the pasture were usually allowed safe flight as they darted between hayfield and waterhole throughout the day. Too many shells were required to bring a limit of doves to bag, even in the hands of an expert wingshot like Frank Jobe.

The Jobe family continued to grow. Soon the walls of the tiny frame house were reduced to approximately the size of a number 10 shoe box during waking hours with playfully giggling little boys and girls ricocheting off the furniture and floors in games of human pinball. Frank and Annie toiled to exhaustion as the team of husband and wife, Frank at the mill, and at clearing fields, Annie inside the home. They scrimped and saved every possible penny against their someday hopes and dreams.

A large acreage eventually came up for sale across the county on Thacker Dairy Road. Knowing instinctively that their large family would be better nurtured on land of their own, Frank and Annie dug down deep and scraped together enough cash money to start a dairy operation.

Frank toiled hard, from the waking of daybreak to the blanket of dark. He wore himself to a frazzle clearing pasture land, planting green fodder, stretching fences, milking cows, and the million other things it takes to scratch a family's livelihood from a raw stretch of red piedmont clay.

There was precious little time for him to venture afield for table meat between the labors of herdsman and the responsibilities of fathering. At the very early age of twelve, a double barrel gun, and the role of hunter, came heavily to rest on his oldest son's shoulders. After all his day's chores were completed to the best of his ability, it was now James Lewis who took to the surrounding forests and fields, hunting rabbits and squirrels—and occasional quail.

Lewis became an expert shot in a very short time as measured against the sportsmen of today. It was imperative for him to do so. Bringing home empty shell casings along with an empty game bag put his backside in jeopardy of a whipping. Wasting shotgun shells, and money, was simply not to be tolerated.

On one golden fall afternoon, nearly to the hour of dusk, Lewis kicked his wary legs into the final honeysuckle and blackberry briar tangle to no avail. No fleeting rabbit was nudged by his toe to become a bounding brown streak with a cotton ball after burner. Peeking over the last hill that rolled away toward home, he caught a flutter of movement in the sky with the corner of his eye.

The pink-breasted, gray-winged blur of a mourning dove's silhouette rocketed across his zone of fire from left to right. Fluidly, the fowling piece slid comfortably into its place against his cheek and shoulder. Instantly aligned ahead of the streaking bird, the barrel touched, then passed three, four, five feet in front of the dove's pointed beak. The gun fired as if it had made its own decision. The cloud of number six shot unleashed from the right hand barrel tore a four foot hole in the sky, but the dove was not caught inside it. Doubling his escape speed to the vanishing point, the startled dove turned on his jets and dodged toward the ground to gain momentum in the style of the best fighter pilot. Thrusting himself upward, he plotted his escape in a spiraling curve. Rapid, musical peeps whistled from his nostrils, forcefully ejected by his tiny diaphram under the strain of powerful breast muscles fanning his wings against the friction of air.

Adjusting his forward allowance more rapidly than conscious thought, Lewis swung the gun barrels further ahead of the sixty-mile-an-hour, too-small target. When his antiaircraft mental computer judged that the lead most assuredly must be enough, he consciously added four more feet to his aiming point, far out in front of the avian blur. A tap of a finger against the rear trigger ejected a tightly packed cloud of shot from the full choke barrel. At a point far out in front across the crest of a rolling hill, at what would be considered beyond the normal range for a shotgunner to hit a target so fast and so small, a single tiny ball of lead pierced the body of the dove. Folding his wings he plummeted from the sky, dead as the stone on which he fell.

Lewis raced to retrieve his fallen prey. Picking the dove up from the center of a circle of rose-tipped white breast feathers that had scattered around by the force of the dove's high speed crash, he held it gently. He felt the dove's strength ebb away as the last of the warmth of its life fluttered into the palm of his hand. Turning the dove over on its back, he examined its graceful beauty—the sleek gray wings, the long, pointed rudder of the black-banded tail. The bird was much more beautiful when examined in hand than the overall gray and brown color impressions seen through the veil of great distance. Delicate shades of tan and pink colored its body. Its buff colored head reflected the dazzling close-up surprise of coppery iridescence from the slanting rays of the setting sun.

There was no doubt in the young farmboy's mind that this creature was built for speed. Speed was a desirable quality in game fit for a sportsman—but not for game taken by a meathunter. He had done his best to fill his gamebag, but had only one small dove to show in exchange for the price of two shells. It wasn't much of a trade. Never the less, his freckled face carried a triumphant grin as he congratulated himself for a shot well-taken and pointed his feet toward home.

"I heard you shoot. What did you bring us for supper?" Frank asked of his eldest boy as he opened the back door. Scrapping his boots on the mat on the porch, he cleaned them of barnyard soil before stepping inside.

His six other children were gathered around Lewis and Annie, overwhelming the farmhouse kitchen with their numbers as they giggled and jostled one another in an attempt to gain a better look. The youngest daughter was held above the rest in Annie's arms, her legs saddled securely on her outthrust hip. Toddlers stood on counter tops and chairs for an elevated view above the largest children as all clustered together to see the small bird they had never observed this closely before. Lewis displayed his prize to them with wings fanned wide between outstretched hands.

The giggling throng murmured to silence as Frank strode through them. Slipping his hand around Annie's shoulder, he pecked a kiss on her cheek. "Whatcha got there?" he asked as he took the dead dove Lewis so proudly displayed. He dangled it between his thumb and index finger by a tiny pink foot, lifting it in front of his face for inspection.

His frowning comment of, "It ain't much to show for two shells!" was followed quickly by, "But, that sure is some mighty fine shootin' to down a streaking dove bird using only two!" as he received a pointed nudge from Annie's sharp elbow in his ribs.

Frank made no further comment in front of the family until he had lead Lewis safely out of earshot on the back steps to help him clean the dove while Annie warmed the stove. Two brothers and four sisters scurried off into various rooms to play or finish schoolwork, according to their ages, while supper was being prepared.

Frank plucked the mourning dove clean of its feathers all the way to its wingtips in total silence while Lewis looked on. The billowing pile of feathers that collected in a wooden bucket below occupied at least ten times the volume as they had when compressed on the body of the bird.

"It's a shame that these feathers aren't meat, eh?" The elder Jobe winked at his son. Removing the dove's innards, he recovered the liver, heart, and gizzard giblets, placing them around the bucket rim. Balancing the dressed carcass beside them on the inch-thick red oak staves, he stood and placed the back of his knuckles against his hips, taking care to turn the blood and feather covered palms away from his pants.

"I want you to look at what's left for this entire family to eat, Lewis," he gently told his son, nodding toward the bucket. "I'm proud of the fact that you can hit a streaking dove with just two shells. But, right now, we just don't have that kind of money to waste. I need you to set a good example for your brothers and sisters and show some restraint, some frugality."

Lewis wanted to explain that, in his judgement, two shells in exchange for a small mourning dove was a better proposition than the feel of an empty gamebag at the end of an exhausting day's walk. But he dared not talk back to his father while he was being given a lecture.

"Someday, we'll have enough money to have a 'real' dove shoot, right here on this farm—a real sportsman's shoot where everybody can get his limit, no matter how many shells it takes. For right now, though, it's best you refrain from takin' chancey shots at such low-return targets."

Lewis said nothing. He merely shrugged his shoulders and nodded his head in agreement.

Frank smiled at his son, then scooted him back into the house, carrying the morsels of dove in his hand.

There may not have been much meat, but Annie stewed it with potatoes, onions, and garden grown carrots, then clabbered it all together with bits of beef tallow. The soup was stretched to the final drop to feed everyone fortunate enough to be seated around that table that evening.

The Jobe dairy prospered through the hard labor of nine pairs of loving hands. The hands were variously shaped and sized, and possessed or were learning the varying degrees of skill necessary in the work of farm life. Heavily calloused, muscular male hands dug, milked, ploughed, chopped, hammered, planted, harvested, repaired, roofed, and countless other chores that demanded strength.

Slender, dexterous female hands cooked, sewed, egged, gardened, cleaned, washed, decorated, picked, pickled, healed, and performed the endless other tasks that required a less heavy-handed touch.

All hands, large and small, young and old, powerful and weak, rested and folded together in peaceful prayer at Alamance Church on Sunday mornings. The church was the core of the community, where family and friends renewed their ties and shared their news each week.

The day eventually came when Frank's promise to his son was fulfilled. After one especially soothing sermon thanking the Great Provider for the bounty of his forests and fields, sea and sky, the minister announced that a dove hunt would be hosted on the Jobe Dairy, come Monday a week.

Corn had already been harvested, providing the cooing hoards of doves ample time to find the fields and gluttonously gorge themselves on main courses of spilled golden kernels and the hors d'oeuvre seeds of ragweed and pokeberry interspersed between the broken cornstalks.

Enough guns were borrowed, begged, or bought to fill the hands of all who dared to try their skill against nature's finest avian aerial acrobats. Cases upon cases of red shotgun shells with paper hulls loaded with number eight birdshot were purchased, twenty-five shells to the box, twenty boxes to the case. Hopefully, there would be enough shells available for every hunter to down his twelve bird limit.

The day appointed for the hunt was Labor Day or "Opening Day" as the holiday is known to anyone who has ever hunted in Carolina. The first of September is Independence Day to a hunter, his first chance to point his gun gameward since the end of February, last. What Fourth of July fireworks are to a child, the shots of a dove shoot are to a hunter. That same starry-eyed, breathless anticipation is there, that longing to see streaking objects in the sky, the loud report of exploding starbursts, the satisfying aroma of clouds of gunpowder scorched against paper tubes hovering thickly in the air.

The height of noon marked showtime, the precise instant that first legal volley could be fired at a speeding target. Friends and family making the long journey were extended by law the courtesy of the morning hours to travel by horse or wagon to the appointed hunting fields so they could be there for the opening moment. Since most participants were also farmers and dairymen, this provided just enough time for daily tasks to dutifully be performed in the cool hours brushing either side of dawn. While cows were relieved of distended udders by the calloused hands of their husbandmen into frothing white buckets of cream laden liquid, covered dish picnic meals were being boiled, baked, fried, and packed into travel baskets by farmwives in glowing kitchens.

Frail and strong, man and woman, adult and child, all members of the close knit community called Alamance were on the move to the Jobe dairy that day for the hunt. These people were nearly all related to one another by the blood of birth, or the mixture of marriage. There were Holts and Sizemores, Cobles and Garretts, Causeys and Starrs, and all the other families that, extended into modern times through the intertwining of their kinship, make the telephone books of the Greater Greensboro Area thick and heavy with long lists of their names.

The hunters gathered themselves together in a laughing, joking group near the back steps of the Jobe farmhouse. Their numbers swelled with the handshook, backslapped, shoulder bumped greeting of each new arrival. The women collected inside, filling the house with the sounds of happy gossip and goodwill. Children chased each other in and out, incessantly banging through the screen door to their mother's cries of, "Ya'll will let all the flies in!" Giggling, the children shouted back over their running shoulders to their mothers, "No, we're tryin' to let 'em all out!"

The ladies shuttled back and forth between the outside and the kitchen, spreading a feast of fried chicken, potato salad, and newly canned pole beans on the shady side of the house. Great bubbling pots of pork tenderloin were set on top of red-and-white-checkered table cloths, along with enough freshly baked bread and salty, fist-sized biscuits to sop up every last drop of brown, onion-looped gravy. For those whose appetite had not wilted away in the late summer heat, there was peach pie for dessert, with a sprinkling of sugar crystals sifted on the crust that sparkled in the sunlight like a dusting of uncut diamonds. Pails of milk, fresh from the cow and not yet separated of butterfat, were kept cool under the shade of picnic tables until ladled into glasses thrust forward, begging to be filled by the thirsty.

Annie lazily wafted a dish towel above the feast to ward off the constant presence of buzzing flies, Frank began discussing the hunters' positioning around the field designated for the hunt. After each hunter was given his spot, he grabbed his gear and made his way down the road to the field through the deep green shade of overhanging red oak trees, stopping first to get some shells from the wooden cases set on the back of a hay wagon.

Each hunter carried with him what he thought would be enough shells to knock down his allotted limit. Most took two, three, or even four boxes, tucking them into the pockets of bib overalls or inside wooden "settin' buckets" or carpenter's nail aprons.

Lewis picked up a single box of shells from the wagon bed and hefted its weight in one hand. In the other hand was balanced the double barrel Remington, its action levered safely open. Frank walked beside him with his hand on his shoulder. Cousin John was behind.

"You're gonna need more shells than that, young fella, if you wanta get 'cher limit today," he chuckled.

Lewis was too excited to return an answer. He just looked up at Frank, and Frank looked down at him. Their faces mirrored the same knowing grin.

Lewis approached his appointed position at the top of the hill. From there, he could watch all the other hunters as they took their places. The sour mash smell of dew-dampened, then sun-parched silage was strong in his flaring nostrils as they caught the faintest puff of hot, humid breeze. The sneezy odors of crushed ragweed and dog fennel spiced his senses. His eyes began to water at the mere suggestion of their allergenic presence.

It was hot. Goditwashot! The relatively short journey around the edge of the field had forced sweat to boil from his every pore. He was humbly thankful for the scant relief of the dappled shade offered by the arching limbs of a gnarled peach tree. The tree had sprouted and prospered in an unmowable tangle of blackberry briars and honeysuckle vines that had taken over as their own domain the cornerpost of the barbed wire pasture fence. The fence corner was set at the apex of the hill. It was situated in just the perfect place for a hunter of doves to wait for a chance at a shot.

Although the presence of the shade of the peach tree was certainly a blessing, it was merely a comfortable bonus. It was the convergence of two pasture fences that made this the ultimate shooter's station. The doves habitually used these fences as ground to air coordinates to guide them in their daily flights from roost to field, field to waterhole, and waterhole back to roost. The air above the green pasture was cooler than the thermal waves that shimmered above the harvested field. The fencerow marked the edge of an invisible wall that separated the blast-furnace air above the field from the less-scorching air above the pasture. Along this invisible wall, doves would dart and glide, bringing them to a point directly above a waiting hunter's gun.

The searing sun rolled over the hump of noon as overheated gunners waited for the vast flocks of mourning doves to return to the field from cool refuges of the surrounding forests and feed-lots. Having gorged themselves in the temperate forenoon, the doves were off duty, lounging around mud puddle oasis, gathering grit from sandy places along shaded wagon trails, or dozing comfortably on perches among branches of protective greenery.

The sharpened edge of anticipation dulled away to boredom. Lethargic hunters sitting unscreened from the sun's unmerciless heat shifted position, gathering together beneath the shelter of tree limbs overhanging the edge of the field to converse with their companions. Lewis watched them as they shuffled about. He could name off all the hunters, even through the distortions of heat mirage that shimmered across the span of a hundred acres of corn stubble. Recognition came to him from the style of their clothing, the cadence of their gait, the manner in which they carried themselves, and the vestiges of laughter and speech that barely reached his ears across the great expanse.

Kneeling, daydreaming, his right knee against parched red clay, his elbow digging into his left knee, his chin resting on his hand Lewis was caught completely off guard and out of position by the buzzing gray silhouette cutting above the peach leaves above him from behind. His eyes followed the fluttering shadow as it danced across the corn stubble for a microsecond before his brain could compute the point in the sky from which the shadow was cast. In a flurry of motion, Lewis staggered erect on unbalanced feet and jerked the double gun to its home in the hollow between his cheek and shoulder. The thumb safety clicked off. His index finger brushed past the front trigger. The straight- away dove was at the far edge of range when the silver bead sight touched the tip of his tail. Full-choked persuasion was released in a roar at the feel of the rear trigger's crisp break. Out there—'way out yonder —a cloud of lead shot collided with feathers and coaxed a streak in the sky to the earth.

Lewis kicked a beeline through the broken cornstalks, never daring to take his eyes from the twitching white morning glory flower that marked the dove's point of entry. Hoisting the first dove of the year triumphantly above his head for all to see, his feat was praised with shouted goodwill from neighbors, friends, and family seated along the perimeter of the field.

"Good shot!"

"Mighty fine shootin'!"

"Pure luck!" came the comments from the shadowed tree line. The more humorous comment brought rumbles of laughter from the hunter's ranks.

Their laughter soon gave way, however, to shouts of "Bird! . . . Mark! Right!" and, "Comin' in high, over the trees!" as the beginning of the afternoon flight was announced. It began slowly. But, with the fall of that first dove, other feathered buzzbombs that had been watching from shaded perches became jealous when they observed their scout "landing" in the field to feed.

They trickled into the field sporadically in the beginning, in groups of one to five, although you couldn't tell it by the number of shots that were fired to greet their arrival. Entering one end of the field, a singleton dove would usually evoke a tremendous volley of antiaircraft fire from the battery below, only to reach the safety of the trees on the opposite end with his feathers unruffled by shot.

As the sun's golden disc paled to yellow, burning lower against the reflective furnace of September sky, the action in the field heated up. At mid-afternoon, the sounds of pure ground-to-air warfare issued from every corner of the field. Vast, frenzied flocks, containing upwards of a hundred birds at a time, were strafing the field, looking for a safe place to land. Hunter's adjusted their shooting stations to take advantage of the doves' travel lanes, cutting them off from escape and turning them back into the open field to cross other hunter's zones of fire. The kill was high. The shotshell consumption was magnitudes of order higher.

Lewis guarded his position at the top of the hill well, making fast snap shots at singles streaking over from behind. He even dropped a double to the report of barrels, right and left, on only his third attempt. No one applauded his effort as he smiled to himself and collected that brace of birds. Everyone else was much too busy, frantically reloading and shooting at his own section of a sky that was filled to overflowing with rocketing silver and grey whistling wings.

The acrid smell of powder smoke spiralled from the open action of the boxlock Remington as Lewis extracted his last two empties. Reaching his nose, the rich aroma made him involuntarily draw his head back, to better draw in its satisfying flavor. Limit filled, he wedged a bouquet of half a dozen birds between the fingers of each hand. The gun's open receiver was cradled in one palm. The remnants of a box of shells was cupped in the other as he stood in the shade of the peach tree and surveyed the panorama of the ongoing hunt from his place on top of the hill.

Striking quite a picturesque pose, he stood there, smiling, against the backdrop of the overgrown fenceline and the blue of the early fall sky. He watched the hunters, studying them for a long while. All hunted as individuals, but still, somehow, they worked together in a unified symphony of effort at filling each man's limit. Each hunter was sharing equally in the thrill of the year's first hunt, no matter his degree of skill with a gun.

Nodding his head knowingly at the collective goodness of his friends, his family, his neighbors—his community, Lewis turned and walked back around the edge of the field. Traveling along the shaded lane, he made his way to the farmhouse. First to leave the field with his limit, he was startled at the tailgate of the wagon holding the hunt's ammunition by his cousin, John, who came up behind.

"I told you that one box of shells you carried with you to the field would never be enough! I had to come back for more shells, myself." He chuckled good naturedly to Lewis as he consoled him with a pat on the back.

Returning John's smile, Lewis handed him the remainder of his box of shells, shaking it back and forth until it rattled just loudly enough to make its half-empty volume known. Then he pointed to twelve doves he had laid out gently in the wagon bed, their black-banded gray tails lined up in neat little rows. They had been hidden by wagon sideboards from John's sight until Lewis pointed them out.

"Well, I swan!" John blinked in amazement. "I saw someone knockin' birds down, right regular, under that peach tree on top of the hill. Who'd ever have thought that just a young fella' like you could have shot like that!"

He winked at Lewis, then jabbed at his ribs with a mocking fist. Taking the partially filled box of shells from the young man, he thanked him, then picked up another from one of the wooden crates that weighed down the wagon's tailgate. Turning away, he eased back up the shaded wagon road toward the sound of incessant gunfire, his head shaking from side to side and his shoulders shuddering with the unrestrained laughter of disbelief.

The Jobe dairy hunt became a tradition from that day forward. Times changed. Fashions changed. Automobiles and asphalt paved roads changed concepts of the time and distance of travel. People didn't change. Country folks never do.

Frank and Annie Jobe passed on. They left Alamance community their most precious gifts, their legacies of flesh and blood, and the sweat of their brows. One brother stayed and worked the farm. Another went off to see the world for a while, then returned. Four sisters made new homes with husbands and raised their families nearby.

Lewis was driven by a larger sense of purpose than that which long hours of farm labor would ever allow him to achieve. Perhaps it was being the oldest sibling of such a large family that inspired him to become an officer of the law—a deputy sheriff. This was the stepping stone of his transition to adult life that provided him with the means to shepherd safe watch over his brothers and sisters, their children, and marital kin.

Police radio channel scanners crackled constantly in Lewis' home, keeping him in close contact with community events during all the hours of day and night. Lewis would rush to every call that duty and loyalty directed his way. He would have made a great sheriff for the County of Guilford. It's possible that the incumbent sheriff sensed a challenge to his position when he politically weeded Lewis from the force one bitter day.

Unshaken, Lewis remained emersed to the elbows in the service of his community as a volunteer fireman. Rushing from the security of a warm bed and peaceful home at every conceivable hour, he was always available to help the distressed. Those in need were folks he recongnized instantly by address, name, and face. Giving yourself to your community is a calling which few men are honored to heed. It can be said that his vocation was "Alamance Volunteer Fireman." He found a paid avocation to support his unpaid trade. After a hitch in the service of his country, of Carolina, during the second World War, Lewis had learned the jeweler's art. He loved working with his hands, creating beautiful bands of gold and silver metal set with the jeweler's spectrum of sparkling gems. Jewels cut and set by his hands in shining rings were called precious for reasons other than their dazzling brilliance by those who bonded themselves together through their exchange. Many were the Christmas Eve's he returned home late to his patiently waiting wife and three daughters, explaining to them his tireless work on some consigned piece of jewelry that "just had to be" under the tree of someone they all knew the morning of Christmas Day.

On his pinky finger of his left hand he wore a ring he called his own. The gilded band blazed with the red sparkling fire of multi-faceted rubies. They reflected the color of the waves of red hair that flowed from his head, passed on to him by his Scotch-Irish forebears. It was from these stones and his red hair that he claimed for himself the handle, "Red Rock."

Throughout his life, any dispatcher or fellow fireman wishing to contact him over emergency channels could gain his instant response by uttering his call sign. The lives he touched, the property and homes he helped to save from the terror of gulping flames, were too numerous to count. Many were the times that panicked souls were soothed to calmness when Red Rock arrived to salvage a scene of near disaster. The determined look on the face beneath the fireman's helmet fringed with those tired red locks of sweat drenched hair let them know that their fortunes were in the care of a pair of the world's most capable hands.

His familiar smile of reassurance always set the most frantic or despairing personality at ease. Early in his career as a helper of others, he had been the leader of seven children. This gave him the experience and qualities he needed to become a leader and caretaker of his entire community, a referee in the give and take game of life.

The dove shoots on the Jobe dairy continued on. They were held every Labor Day. Lewis was always in attendance. Some said it was a shame he didn't have sons to teach them the ways of the hunt.

"I haven't any sons but I have three fine daughters to bring me sons-in-law," was his half-joking reply. "You can't pick your sons who might bring you grief, but you do have some say-so about who your daughters bring home."

The oldest daughter married, then the second daughter, too. Their husbands joined the Jobe family hunt in their time. His youngest daughter brought several prospects home for Red Rock's review. All were eventually nudged away by subtle outward signs of his disapproval.

Eventually, she brought home a young man who passed the test of "the stare." There was nowhere to hide from the look of those ice blue eyes above the dark frames of Red Rock's reading glasses. Those eyes pierced through a man's shell to read his soul, searching out the tiniest flaw in his character. The quality of each prospective son-in-law was measured in hang time—the number of seconds he could hang in there in locked eye contact. The sooner a young man blinked or turned away, the worse the bad intentions he tried to mask from Red Rock's discovery. This prospect never glanced away, but squared himself to face him. Smiling, Red Rock reached out and firmly shook his hand in welcome.

Over a hot summer's waning months the prospective son-in-law courted Red Rock's youngest daughter. While he performed the obligatory waiting period rituals as she primped her hair to put on her finest appearance for impressing her new found beau on summertime dates, the prospect boasted to Red Rock of his wingshooting skills. Joining the prospect with twinkling eyes on the conversive common ground of the dove hunt, Red Rock nodded and added a few modest stories of his own.

It turned out that the young man considered himself to be quite a hotshot, possessed of considerable skill in the scattergunner's craft. Never had he endured times when a nickle for a pair of shells was best exchanged for meat for dinner for nine. He had always hunted for sport and a gourmet's dinner of tiny, plucked dove breasts. For him, hunting had always been a matter of pure enjoyment, never the serious business of survival. Red Rock had known in advance of the Hotshot's prowess, for whispered references to his reputation had preceded him to Red Rock's home. Very few important such tidbits of information vibrated through the community of Alamance which did not eventually filter down to Lewis' inquisitive ear. In due course, after his bravado had died down to an appropriate number of subtle, humble hints, an invitation to the annual hunt on the Jobe place was extended to the Hotshot by Red Rock.

The hunt was scheduled, as always, for Labor Day. The Hotshot hardly slept the night before, so full was his imagination with visions of huge flocks of doves flying above a harvested cornfield. Red-eyed but brimming with pent-up anticipation, he showed up at Red Rock's home well before the appointed hour of ten a.m.

Red Rock fairly unnerved the Hotshot, unhurriedly rummaging through closet junkpiles for gun and shells, boots, tan work-shirt, folding camp stool, and camouflaged cap. Lewis eyes sparkled at the Hotshot's impatience. He turned his back to hide a grin as he intentionally moved about, slightly slower than was necessary, thereby teasing the Hotshot and fanning the ember of his excitement at being invited to participate in the family dove shoot into a burning flame.

After an hour that seemed like eternity, Red Rock checked the time on a grandfather clock and announced it was, "time to go!" The Hotshot tossed his gear into the trunk of Red Rock's car and slammed the lid closed. As they backed out of the driveway the pair waved goodbye to Red Rock's daughter, the Hotshot's fiance. She waved back cheerfully from the brick front steps, then slipped, smiling, back inside. At ten miles per hour under the speed limit, Lewis drove casually along Alamance Church Road. A very few minutes later, he negotiated the gravel drive that lead to the Jobe clan's homestead. His car seemed to know its way, the way a cow can find its way to the barn after making the journey so many times before.

Red Rock was greeted with shouted hellos, boisterous jokes, and rich belly laughs. He introduced his guest around to each man in the group of hunters who had gathered themselves in the circular dirt drive. They loafed against their cars or sat on the tailgates of pickup trucks. Most were dressed in leaf-imitating camouflage colors from the tops of their caps to the toes of their boots. Each in turn took the Hotshot's hand in greeting, clamping down with varying degrees of firmness. Some crushed his fingers in the warm clasp of welcome, others applied less pressure than a dead fish, signifying indifference, or the general unimportance of making his acquaintance.

But Red Rock was drawn instantly into the warm conversation that had been interrupted by his arrival. It seemed as though he had always been there, so locked in common were his life and the inflections of his speech with the company of the circle of family and friends that enveloped him into their midst.

The Hotshot stood off to one side, alone and aloof, beneath the canopy of a huge pecan tree. In its shade stood a folding picnic table spread with lukewarm fried chicken and trimmings that were scattered haphazardly about in cardboard cartons printed with the name of a fast food restaurant located just down the road. Catching the end of a drumstick between his thumb and trigger finger, the Hotshot nibbled on it while evesdropping in on snatches of discussions of the weather and crops, children and grandchildren, and jobs in town.

As the sun rose higher, nearing its apex, the conversation shifted more and more to discussions of guns and shooting—dove shooting! This was the big buildup that preceded each year's hunt. A rhetorical bet was offered by one of the hunters.

"I'll bet a dollar that Danny will limit out first today," bragged his Uncle Merle.

Someone else bellowed back, "No way! It's certain that George will finish his limit first!"

Gary gained everyone's attention, "You may all be wrong! I don't think there are many birds this year. It may well be, that no one will get his limit, today!"

"It's seems like there's plenty of doves to me . . . " Cousin Andy offered.

Red Rock stole a sideways glance at the long lean chicken-muncher shouldered against the pecan's rough bark. Lowering his voice so the Hotshot could not overhear what he was about to say, he gave his two-cents wager, "I'll bet anyone here, that skinny boy leaning against yonder pecan tree, stuffing his face with chicken and 'tater salad, will get his limit before any one else in the field today."

Everyone fell silent as Red Rock spoke, so that even the Hotshot could hear portions of what he had said.

"Well, of course, we weren't even counting him!" growled a coarse voice in the crowd.

The Hotshot pretended he hadn't overheard the remark. It temporarily troubled him that he wasn't certain how to interpret the fact that his name wasn't to be included in the group's friendly betting. Far removed from his extended family who had prospered in the farmfields of a midwestern state, he had come late to Carolina. Without the supporting arms of a family tree, he had become independent by nature—a loner. He didn't need anybody or expect anything to be given to him by anyone. Hunting for him had always been a solitary pursuit, a chance to achieve a greatness of skill on his own, for his own, by his own. Almost automatically, he assumed that Red Rock's offered bet on his behalf had blown away in the hot breeze, untaken, because he was not considered a member of this tight circle of neighbors, friends, and family. He shrugged off the fact that others in the group might be better wingshots than himself. It didn't matter much to him what they thought, one way or the other. He just shrugged it off and finished eating his chicken.

The sun was tracking the zenith of noon as the hunters began their sweaty parade around the edges of the field. For the Hotshot, the uncomfortable staring eyeball scrutiny of Red Rock's fellow hunters was over. Relieved to be walking out in the open sanctuary of harvested corn, he found that the keen edge of his built-up anticipation dulled quickly in the midday heat.

Red Rock walked slowly at his side, taking the path of least resistance between the rows of cornstubble. Both faces were red and streaked with rivulets of sweat long before they reached the top of the hill.

"This will be your shootin' station," Red Rock announced. "The birds use these barbed wire fences as travel lanes to come to the field to feed. Doves will tend to fly in on your blind side, from behind. You won't see them coming, screened as they'll be by that tangle of briars and honeysuckle at the fence corner. You won't be able to see me, either. But I'll be back there, behind you, under that tall red oak growin' in the middle of the pasture. Gary moved his cows to another pasture to keep them away from the sound of my shootin'—puts the cows off their milk—just so I could sit under the shade of that tree and pick my birds up from the grass instead of this tangle-foot stubble. I'll try to warn you when birds are comin' your way, so you'll have time to get ready to shoot." He lightly kicked a puff of dust from a naked cornstalk with his toe, slightly unbalancing himself with the effort.

"I always enjoyed setting in this very spot. There was shade here, until the last couple of years." He paused and looked longingly at the broken skeleton of a dead peach tree. Rising above the jungle of corner tangle, its naked decaying branches offered no more shade than an umbrella defabriced by a thunderstorm's headwind.

Turning toward the hundred acres of sileage stubble, Red Rock watched the hunters while they took their places. He had trouble picking them out unless they were in motion. Camouflaged clothing concealed the hunters well against the backdrops of trees and overgrown fencerows. Modern hunting clothes had displaced blue demin farmer's overhauls, wooden sitting buckets had been replaced by plastic buckets, and wide-brimmed straw hats by nylon-webbed baseball caps with embroidered advertisements above their bills on the crown.

Sighing at the stark changes in the hunter's appearances over what seemed like such a short span of time, he checked his watch and loaded his gun. At the instant the second hand touched twelve, he fired both barrels into the air. The report of left and right played tag with each other as they echoed across the field, ringing off the timber that lined the far side. All hunters were duly notified. The hunt had begun.

Red Rock found an opening in the honeysuckle and pressed down a strand of barbed wire. The rusty wire chaffed against rusty steel staples making high pitched squeals as the fence stretched open, then shut, behind him. Loading two plastic-hulled shells into the magazine of his pumpgun, the Hotshot racked the action back and forth to chamber a round, then thumbed in one more. He was ready.

"Bring 'em on!" he grinned to himself, glad to finally have the waiting game of a long summer over.

Sitting there, on the padded lid of a plastic store bought "dove bucket," he slowly turned his head in the 270 compass degrees of view that was not obscured by the brier tangle in the pasture corner. His eyes rested briefly on each hunter in turn, as they scattered themselves methodically about the landscape every hundred yards or so. He could identify some of them from among those who had been gathered in the circular driveway. Recognition came to him from the style of their clothing, the cadence of their gait, the manner in which they carried themselves, and the vestiges of their speech and laughter that barely reached his ears across the great expanse. The recognition of a pair of hunters, who were obviously close friends, came slowly as the muffled sounds of their conversation strained to reach his ear through the heat waves that shimmered above the field. It seemed strange to him that he could be in a farmfield, surrounded by thirty, forty, perhaps fifty other people, and still be feeling the hollow twinge of emptiness that told him he was alone.

For thirty minutes nothing flew above the harvested field, except for a single mockingbird that perched in the peach tree behind him and sang a teasing serenade to one so crazy as to be out in the heat of midday, unprotected from the scorching sun. The mocker stayed briefly, then disappeared, hiding from the heat in the shadows cast by a row of shortleaf growing pines at the end of the fence.

Cicadas and grasshoppers buzzed. Wispy clouds drifted. Sun burned. Men stared into the sky above the tree line surrounding the stubble field. Panting for breath, they waited.

A large globule of sweat slithered down the side of the Hotshot's face and fell from the corner of his jawbone. As he momentarily stopped his vigil to wipe the corrosive splatter from the receiver of the gun laying across his lap, a familiar voice shouted at him from the pasture, behind. The voice struggled to gain his attention through the wilting veil of boredom.

Too late, he recognized Lewis' warning. Jerking the pumpgun to port arms, he searched frantically overhead for an incoming target. Too late, he caught the speeding blur as it raced above the dead fingers of the peach, then rocketed straight away, across the field!

Too late for anyone, that is, except a young hotshot, possessed of remarkably keen shooting reflexes and a full-choked duckgun stuffed with shells handloaded full of max dram-equivalent powder charges and an ounce-and-a-quarter of hard chilled shot sized seven-and-a-half.

The dove folded, dead in the air, to the booming report of the Hotshot's gun. For a moment afterward there was silence, until the other lazing and dozing hunters realized what had happened. Following the sound of gunfire with their ears to the top of the hill, they saw the dove plummet, like a stone, to the ground. Con-

245

gratulations were yelled to the Hotshot as he retrieved the season's first dove from the cornstalk stubble. Responding to their cheers, he held it triumphantly overhead. Someone applauded. Everyone watching laughed as the Hotshot tipped his hat to the applause and gave a theatrical bow.

Seating himself again on his bucket, he smiled at a compliment that came from the concealed voice by the fencerow behind him, the same voice that had warned him of the streaking bird's backdoor approach.

"Nice shot!" grinned Red Rock. "I couldn't have done better myself."

"One down," the Hotshot counted to himself as he laid the dove on the ground beside his seat. "Only eleven more to go!"

Two birds entered the field from the opposite side. They were greeted by a tremendous fusillade of gunfire from all along the treeline. One fell outright. The other dodged and swooped low, then contined on, closely hugging the ground. The elevation of his flight path was much too low to allow safe fire as he skimmed across the stubble in front of the Hotshot. Broken stalks nearly brushed his breast.

The Hotshot restrained his trigger finger, to avoid endangering a fellow hunter by taking the low-angled shot. With conscious effort, he held his fire. The frantic bird reached the apparent haven of the fence row separating him from the pasture, behind.

"Comin' to ya!" the Hotshot yelled.

Seconds after the doves disappeared behind a waving screen of dog fennel that sprouted among the briars, the sound of twin shots came from the vicinity of the red oak tree.

"Mark that one down for Lewis," the Hotshot smiled to himself.

The hunters were treated to an aerial display unrivaled by any other shooting sport. Doves cut in their afterburners as they blistered across the field, their tails honed to ice pick sharpness by the velocity of their flight. They billowed in blurring clouds of upwards of seventy birds, shorting out the circuitry of the shaken gunners thought processes as they tried in vain to pick out a single target from among the great flocks that were "here" then "gone."

Singles and pairs strafed low, darting along the treeline. Greeted by ounce loads of number eight shot that soon totalled up to pounds, they wove in and out of windows in the treetops. Doves crashed down to the forest floor in a shower of leaves and twigs. Each hit was searched for by the hunter who dared to call the feathered prize his own that had been shot at by so many others. Everywhere, there were shouts of, "Mark left! Mark right! Bird! Comin' over the trees!"

Nondirectional shouts of, "Heads up!" were met by confused heads swivelling incoherently from side to side, up and down, expectantly focusing squinting eyes into all coordinates of sky. Clumsy fingers clawed at shells, poking them, too late, into smoking, empty chambers. Most of the birds sped on their way, reaching the security of the treeline, with nary a feather out of place.

But busy at his trade, the Hotshot lived up to his well-known reputation. A zipping pair fell to the sound of three quick shots and the metallic "snick-snack" of the pumpgun's action. Three consecutive singles fell to only four shots fired. Half-done, the Hotshot paused to take a long pull of tepid water from the canteen at his belt. Everywhere, hunters scurried about, searching the field-edge tangles and stubble-rows for poorly marked down and, sometimes, lost game. Others fired away, obscuring themselves briefly from sight in grayblue clouds of powder smoke. The dissipating smoke revealed their faces again in about the same amount of time it took for the sound of the shot to reach the Hotshot's ears across the rolling clay hills.

Red Rock's double barrel spoke often, behind, in its two-toned twelve gauge bark. The Hotshot reckoned they were close to even in score. Certainly, they both seemed to be well ahead of everyone else.

Two rapid shots from Lewis' vicinity, followed closely by a shout, warned the Hotshot of, "Incoming bird! Behind!"

The bird topped the fencerow, then spiralled high and away. Up there—way up yonder—she appeared as a tiny cream and gray puff though the broken branches of the dry-rotted peach. She hovered overhead, towering for an instant, assessing the situation before leaving the cooler air above the pasture to enter the heated gauntlet of the field.

Most hunters, except the inexperienced, would have let her go and save himself a wasted shell. By the time she reached the field, her altitude might have decreased enough to allow the higher-percentage shot to be taken by another gunner. Most hunters would have passed up the shot, but not so, the Hotshot.

The barrel of the Hotshot's gun wavered. Vapors of built-up heat miraged the target above the barrel's ventilated rib. The dove hesitated. The sight picture stabilized. The gun barrel levelled in deliberate aim.

The trigger tripped, the gun bucked hard against the Hotshot's shoulder. Seventy yards up, a crippled dove flipped frantically end over end. Faltering, she caught herself, then half glided, half flapped across the harvested cornfield. Nearly reaching the opposite side, she dropped, ploughing a groove in a furrow. A puff of red dust marked the location where she fell.

Pleased with himself, the Hotshot carefully took a line on the fallen bird's position, and made straight-away for his prey. A man and a boy seated together, forty yards beyond where the bird had fallen, helped direct the Hotshot to her location. He thanked them profusely, for he might never have found his game without their help. As he turned to make the return trip to his assigned position, he blinked into the slanting rays of the afternoon sun and noticed someone standing beside his bucket seat at the corner of the pasture fence.

A wildlife enforcement officer was waiting to greet the Hotshot as he kicked his way back through the last row of stubble returning to his place.

"I need to see your license," said the strongly-built man uniformed in taylored tan.

"Sure, Rick." the Hotshot responded and extended the required paper. The name on the badge had prompted his remembrance of the officer's name. They had met each other with some regularity in the scattered gamefields of Guilford County over the past several seasons.

The officer checked the name on the license and handed it back. He took the gun the Hotshot extended to him, port arms, action open. Holding the gun in his left hand he extended his right to receive three shells from the Hotshot and attempted to stuff them into the magazine tube. The Hotshot knew the drill. The officer thumbed in two shells against the tension of the magazine spring, but not the third.

"Plug's in. Gun checks out okay," said the officer. He succumbed to an urge and poked the long-barreled pumpgun skyward. Checking the stock, he sighted along the ventilated rib.

"I'm not real good at remembering names," he smiled as he handed it back. "But I remember individual hunters by the honesty in their faces and style of their guns. I recognized that familiar gun with the long, black snout all the way across the field by its signature—that skyscraper dove it tumbled down. By the way, how many have you bagged so far?"

"Seven."

"You'll be done soon, judging by the way they're flying in the field and the way you shoot. Good luck with your hunt." Officer Rick turned away to continue his duties. Checking the legality of all the hunters strung along the borders of the field, he eventually disappeared from the Hotshot's sight, rounding the tip of a peninsula of trees. Two quick shots, a pause to reload, then the report of a quick followup shot from Red Rock's position returned the Hotshot's attention back to the hunt.

The dove that Lewis had missed streaked overhead, making high pitched peeping noises in synchronization to the rapid pumping of its breast muscles. It fell to three quick shots from the Hotshot's gun fired so closely together that the echoes rumbling back through the pasture blended together and made them sound like one.

Stomping through the jungle of ragweed patch in the middle of the field, he searched long minutes for the downed bird as others buzzed by overhead. Just as he found the dove and was extracting it from a clinging tangle of morning glory vines under which it had slid with the force and trajectory of a feathered bullet, three shots from a nearby hunter's Browning automatic warned him of, "Incoming! Birds! Hard Left!"

A tremendous flock of doves was boiling through the air in three-diminsional helter-skelter panic, bearing down through the center of the field at unbelievable speed. Dodging each other and wishful shots fired by hunters too far away at the field edges to have deadly effect, the hurtling, twisting, diving swarm ate up the distance quicker than conscious thought. Most hunters would have come unglued at the sight

A flock of mourning doves zips overhead at sixty miles an hour. Even the best wingshots come unglued.
It sure is hard to pick one target
250

of a hundred doves massed together like a swarm of mad bees, rocketing by at seventy miles per hour ground speed. Not the Hotshot!

Coolly, he rose from his crouch in the weed patch. Acting solely on reflexive instinct, learned from pounds of powder burned at the games of skeet and trap, and from shooting a thousand doves before, he selected a single target at the head of the swarm. So tight was the pattern on the bird at a twenty yard distance, that the smack of lead against feathers was as audible as the explosion of the shell.

A second bird fell from the flock as it passed directly overhead. The luckless dove had slowed in confusion for the tiniest nanosecond at the sound of the first shot fired. Hard hit in his instant of hesitation, he tumbled down toward the ragweed patch together with the first.

Dove wings windmilled the air as fast as the Hotshot's hand shucked the checkered forearm. The casing of the second shot ejected from the action before the first bird hit the ground. Selecting a straggler at the tail end of the flock, the silver bead at the end of the ventilated rib did a dance all its own and swung far out in front of the bird's shifting flight pattern. The trigger broke cleanly, like the fractured stem of a dropped wine glass. Three doves were suspended together in deadfall at a single moment in time. A debris trail of their feathers, thirty yards long, sifted slowly down in the overheated, nearly non-existent wind.

Few hunters can brag of scoring a triple on passing doves. But here was the evidence, plainly visible for all to see. Standing out there, alone, in the center of a dove field, the Hotshot paused and reloaded his gun. Moving methodically from mark to mark, he looked for his game in the homogenity of the weed patch puzzle, at points his ears had heard the sound of their impact or his eyes had seen the swishing of grass blades that closed in behind the birds as they fell.

The search was long—much longer than he would have liked. The Hotshot muttered abuse to himself for not shooting the doves above the openness of the cornstalk rows. Eventually, though, he found them all, with enthusiastically shouted and arm waved triangulation assistance from the surrounding gunners who had all witnessed his feat from their grandstand seats along the treeline's border.

Returning to his bucket seat, the Hotshot added the four doves to his pile. "That makes eleven," he counted to himself. "Only one more to go!"

The baby "pop" of a .410 bore signaled a bird's approach from the direction of the pair of man and boy seated straight across the field. The Hotshot shouldered his gun. Its bead touched the tip of the incoming dove's beak as it flew, head on. Tapping the trigger, the Hotshot easily made the shot.

"Make that twelve," he grinned, giving himself a mental pat on the back.

The squealing of barb wire being pulled through the rusty eye of a fence staple announced Red Rock's re-entry through the fence to the field from the pasture before the Hotshot could rise to fetch the dove that completed his limit.

Squatting between the strands of barbed wire, Red Rock's legs quivered from the strain and the heat. A barb caught his trouser cuff as he slithered through, causing him to stumble and fall. Dusting himself off, he rose and gathered his fallen gear, glancing around to see if anyone had seen.

The Hotshot saw, but pretended not, to avoid embarrassment to the old gentleman's dignity. Lewis crept to the Hotshot's blind side. Stooping, he counted under his breath the mound of doves at the Hotshot's feet, chin nodding in unison to the numbers clicked off.

"Eleven!" he announced triumphantly. "I beat you, Hotshot! I'm first in the field to get my limit, today!"

The Hotshot had listened to Red Rock's gun fire throughout the afternoon, matching his, shot for shot. He was, therefore, not surprised, at Red Rock's statement of victory. What did surprise him, however, was the single, bedraggled, carcass of a broken-winged dove, dangling by its leg from between the thumb and forefinger of Red Rock's hand. His face wore a quizzical expression as he watched Red Rock unfold a cloth-covered camp stool from beneath his arm. Planting it at the Hotshot's side, Red Rock gave his shaking legs a rest and seated himself upon it. Teeth sparkling brightly through an ear to ear grin, Red Rock laughed an easy chuckle. "This one bird represents a limit of doves for me, these days!" he said. Laying the sleek tan and slate puff of crumpled feathers on his knee, he flicked at its pink toes with an index finger, as he admired its streamlined grace. The grin receded from his face as he reflected back to times long past. The index finger went to the bridge of his nose, pushing up the frames of his glasses. He looked away in the distance, toward a farm pond that mirrored the black and white patchwork of a surrounding herd of Holstein dairy cows.

"There was a time...," he almost whispered, "...when I was as good a wingshot, or maybe even better, than you. There was a time, too, when I wasn't allowed to waste my family's expensive shotgun shells firing away at itty-bitty doves. So I bought me a three dollar .22 rifle and shot them as they coasted in to the edge of yonder waterhole for an evening drink. I got six doves with six shots one day. Most of them had their heads shot off. The .22 cartridges cost less than a quarter for a box of fifty, you see."

The Hotshot stared skeptically at the side of Red Rock's face, then at the single dove resting on his knee. His doubt at Red Rock's former ability was fleeting, however, as he caught the humility and matter-of-fact tone that trembled in Red Rock's voice. Red Rock had never learned in his long life how to tell a lie.

Turning to face the Hotshot, he looked into his eyes over the frame of his glasses. "I realize, right now, that you really think you're something special, shooting a limit of birds faster, better, and with fewer shells that anyone else in this field. Well, I think you're something special, too! That's why I let you sit in this particular spot today."

Red Rock rotated on his stool, sweeping the 270 degree vista of cornstalk stubble with his arm. The field was alive with the sound of gunfire, the movements of hunters searching for lost game, and the speeding, erratic flight of doves passing overhead.

"Those hunters are all my friends, my family, my neighbors. I wanted to see how you would fit in among them. Think for a minute, about what you took from all of them to make possible that little pile of birds beside your feet." He touched the mound of eleven doves with a shaky boot toe for emphasis. "My brother cut this corn two weeks early, before it was completely dried for harvest. That cost him something in lost dollars, I'm sure. It's impossible to calculate precisely how much profit he lost, but it did take money from his pocket, nonetheless."

Shifting his attention across the field, Red Rock pointed to a figure moving beneath a tall tree.

"Isn't that Dr. Julian Grant, your former physics teacher, sittin' under the shade of that big sycamore tree? Don't you know how proud he must feel, after watchin' you shoot today? If you don't think that your act of shooting that triple from that flock that flew over you in the middle of the field can be broken down, simply, into every theory of physics you ever learned from him, then you must have missed something as you slept in the back of his class. Action, reaction, velocities, vectors, mass, energy, momentum—the practical application of everything he ever taught you was on display out in that field, by your example, for all to see.

The pecan tree you were standing in the shade of, eating half a fried chicken, was planted by my brother, John. It grew from a nut he brought home in his pocket as an uneaten treat from Sunday school when he was just a little guy. By the way, it was one of my sisters who bought the chicken."

Palming a handful of red dirt, Red Rock let it sift, hour glass slow, through the bottom of his fist. Then he brushed his palms together to clean them of the remaining clay dust. A puff of red hovered in the hot air. "My daddy cleared this land," he said.

Three quick shots in rapid sequence diverted the pair's attention to the left. A frightened dove hovered, then reversed direction, turning back into the field from its intended escape.

"That'll be Bernie over there. Bernie Blast-a-lot, I call him!" Lewis laughed as he identified the man who had fired the shot.

"We always make sure Bernie sits in that spot, because he couldn't hit a bull in a barn. But blast away he will — at every dove that tries to escape through that gap in the trees above him. That sends them back to the field so someone else can get a shot.

You'll notice, if you can see that far, that Bernie has a few birds hangin' on his belt. They aren't his. Well, they are and— then again—they aren't. Bill Coble always sits just a little ways off from Bernie. Bill is an excellent shot, you see, and also happens to be one of Bernie's closest friends. Whenever they shoot at the same dove at the same time, Bernie claims it. Nobody knows for sure which of those two hunters shot it, do they? No harm's done because Bill normally shoots enough for his limit and Bernie gets his limit too.

Last of all, I want you to look straight across at that little boy, Joey Causey, seated beside his dad. He's hardly fired his gun today. It seems that most of the birds that go his way are shot out of the sky by some hotshot sitting straight across from him before they ever get into range of his little .410."

Red Rock gathered up his gun and gear. The aluminum frame of the camp stool made a metallic clank against the receiver of the Remington double barrel cradled against it in the palm of his hand. Turning to leave, he pointed the barrels of his gun at the pile of doves on the red clay ground. Sunlight glinted off bare silver steel. The barrels had long since been worn clean of any vestige of original factory blue.

"If you want, I'll take those eleven birds with me. Added to mine, I'll call them my twelve. I'll have my limit and you can shoot twelve more. The choice is yours. It's up to you. Chances are, the game warden is long gone and will never know what you did. But look at all those folks around the field. While you are watching them, they are watching you up here on top of the hill. Some will not look down on you in the least for continuing to shoot. Many of them would do the same. They all know who you are by or will by the end of the day. Very few hunters have ever witnessed such an inspirational shooting demonstration as has been put on for them by you today."

The Hotshot could find nothing to say. Lewis took his lack of response as a signal to move on. Shrugging his shoulders, he slowly made his way along the pasture fence on his way to the bottom of the hill.

The Hotshot watched Red Rock for a time as he turned a corner of the fence and travelled along the tree line. A miniature heated whirlwind, a "dust devil," swirled its way across the scorching field, sucking in cornshucks and ejecting them up to the sky.

Red Rock paused at each hunter's side and spoke for a few seconds or minutes, depending on the terms of their conversation. The reassuring sound of his laughter spanned across the distance, reaching the Hotshot's ears each time the story of taking his one bird limit was retold. The tale always concluded with the bird being hoisted, shoulder high, to be respectfully admired by the listener.

Intent on watching Red Rock's movements along the field border, the Hotshot made no more attempts to shoot. There were still plenty of targets in the air. A flock of seven doves rustled overhead on shearing wings from behind the limbs of the dead peach. Unchallenged by the Hotshot's gun, they achieved the safety of the oaks on the opposite side, except for one that was pursuaded to stay behind. With a whoop and a jump a nine-year old boy pounced to retrieve his first dove. Scrambling back to his seat on a plastic bucket, he showed it off to his proud dad.

The Hotshot watched Red Rock as he chewed out an overly-excited hunter for taking an unsafe shot at a bird that was flying too low to the ground. Soon after, he observed him policing a belligerent trio of young men who had sneaked into the field carrying a cooler full of the contraband cargo of yellow alcoholic brew. The three young men lost a heated argument, in spite of their impressive physiques and puffed-up chests. They left the field dumping their cooler and leaving their guns — stared down by an old man with ice blue eyes.

Everywhere else, hunters were hunting. They signalled to each other of incoming doves. Those with cold water or soft drinks shared with others. One hunter with a retriever found lost doves downed behind cathedral walls of trees draped with the impenetrable webbing of honeysuckle vines. Hunters with shells remaining shared those with other hunters who were operating on empty. Each hunter, in his own way, contributed to all the rest, so that all of them, collectively, could strive for the maximum enjoyment of a day afield and the final success of taking home a limit.

Figuring it was time to go, the Hotshot pumped the remaining two shells from his gun. Walking out into the stubble, he collected his twelfth bird from where it had fallen. He placed his limit inside his bucket and replaced the padded lid. Shielding his eyes with his hand against the lowering sun's glare, he tracked Red Rock's position. Gathering his gear, he headed across the field to join him in his journey.

Hidden behind a screen of brush at the edge of a peninsula of trees, a wildlife protector named Rick watched through binoculars and smiled as what he had been certain was going to be his first over-the-limit ticket of the season walk away with a bag of twelve doves.

A few short weeks following the end of that hunt, Red Rock found out what had slowed his gun and created havoc with his muscular coordination. The disease had a name that was not "old age." Amyotropic Lateral Schlerosis in medical terms, ALS in brevity, or Lou Gerig's Disease as it is called by the common man in honor of the famous athlete that it stole from us in the prime of his career, had attacked the body of James Lewis Jobe. In Alamance Community it will always be known as Lewis Jobe's disease.

The doctors gave him three to five years to live. He gave two more, and made it seven. That was his way. Always, in all things, he gave back more that he had ever taken. He kept himself involved in the affairs of his community, right up to the end.

As his limbs withered, he became wheelchair bound, but kept himself busy making and fixing things for others, keeping as much dexterity of use as possible in those shaking, artistic hands. The Hotshot was there, fortunate enough to be seated front and center, at the funeral service held for Red Rock in the sanctuary of Alamance Church. With his back to the congregation, he was relieved that no one's eyes but those of the minister could see the pain on his face. He wasn't sure whether it was the vibrant tones of "Amazing Grace" from the choir loft or the preacher's soul-soothing baritone speech that made the church rumble as though a granite cornerstone had cracked in its foundation. The rumble he felt may have been caused by the breaking of a thousand hearts.

Glancing back through misted eyes, the Hotshot saw through the open church doors a writhing trail of mourners extending well beyond. Inside was standing room only, giving air to more flowers than all the acres of Guilford Battlefield bloom in twenty springs. The preacher ended his eulogy with words of comfort that did little to ease the sense of loss the Hotshot felt at Red Rock's passing. Six pall bearers - a deputy sheriff, a volunteer fireman, a jeweler, a neighbor, a relative, and a friend - carried Red Rock's flag and flower-draped casket outside the church to the cemetery. The casket was lowered into an opening in the red clay soil. After the minister's final words had been spoken and the moment for silence had come, a gentle song drifted down from somewhere in the shade of the oak leaves overhead like a velvet cloak to embrace those who were gathered around the grave. Soothing the emptiness of the Hotshot's heavy heart was the coo of a mourning dove.

Justin Marsh with his twelfth dove on Labor Day, 1994.

Conclusion

Red Rock left me with a sense of obligation, of responsibility to carry on his legacy. For I was once a hotshot dove hunter. I was the one who held his hand and felt the last of his strength ebbing away like the final flutter of a dying dove's wing. I was the one who placed a wedding ring made by his artistry around the finger of his youngest daughter's hand.

In my son's bedroom there is an antique maplewood dresser painstakingly refinished to shining newness under the final strokes of Red Rock's trembling touch. Against it leans an old gun, a hammerless double barrel shotgun in 12 gauge, Remington model of the year 1894. The left hand barrel is choked so tightly at the muzzle, a dime won't drop through it to this day. I hope it will be a fitting tribute to the man who once owned the gun when his grandson grows large enough to thrust the weight of its heavy barrels toward the heavens to capture the darting wings of a streaking dove's flight. That should take place around the first Monday of September, 1994, when all the hunters of Carolina, whether city bred or country raised, take a rest from their life's occupations to celebrate this nation's one hundredth Labor Day.

Each year, I give freely to police organizations. I give to my local volunteer fire department during their fund-raising efforts. I give to the funds for disabled veterans and to the ALS Foundation. These are things I feel compelled to do. But opening my wallet to give mere money is a relatively simple act. My sense of obligation goes much deeper now, because of the challenge issued to me upon Red Rock's passing. From him I learned that no one can take or possess a limit of anything by himself. He taught me that only by giving to one another of that special talent, that special gift, that special individual of composite, complex being which each of us calls "myself," can each and every one of the rest of us hope to achieve our limit of whatever it is we are searching for in that greatest hunt of all called "Life."

A red rock lies at rest beside the back porch of the brick house where Lewis once lived on Alamance Church Road. It was moved there at his request long after he was physically unable to move its heavy weight by himself. I can't call the names of the strong men who transported it there in the bed of a pickup from the back yard of a garage apartment on Williams Dairy Road, but I'm certain that they were among Lewis' closest family members and dearest friends.

The rock is strongest granite, and was removed by the hard labor of one man from a field to create a pasture in exchange for a gun. Lewis always referred to it as the "story-tellin' rock." Its surface was stained brick red, long ago, by the weathering processes of daylight and dark, freeze and thaw, dryness and rain - also, he told me, from the crinkled red clay cutouts left by the treads of hunter's boots. The mark of each bootprint identified the individual hunter who left its track as surely and uniquely as the mark of his fingerprints. The hunters always rested there as they told others of their hunts, foot on rock, elbow on knee, gun and game laid carefully on the ground, close by.

From this rock come the stories of *Carolina Hunting Adventures*. As I sit and write, I can look beneath the rock's red stain and see inside to the very depths of its solid, gray granite core. For me, it is like peering into a story teller's crystal ball. The rock holds many more.

"The rock is strongest granite, and was removed by the hard labor of one man from a field to create a pasture in exchange for a gun."

262